ANGEL FLIGHT 44

The True Story of Two Dedicated Pilots, a 60-Year-Old Airplane, and the Amazing Hurricane Katrina Mission That Birthed a New Aviation Ministry

Glen Hyde
Rich Vermillion

Paradigm
Seed Publishers
www.pspublishers.com

D0424738

Habakkuk 2:2-3

"And the LORD answered me, and said, 'Write the vision, and make it plain upon tables, that he may run that readeth it. For the vision is yet for an appointed time, but at the end it shall speak, and not lie: though it tarry, wait for it; because it will surely come, it will not tarry.'"

King James Version

"And the Lord answered me and said, 'Write the vision and engrave it so plainly upon tablets that everyone who passes may [be able to] read [it easily and quickly] as he hastens by. For the vision is yet for an appointed time and it hastens to the end [fulfillment]; it will not deceive or disappoint. Though it tarry, wait [earnestly] for it, because it will surely come; it will not be behindhand on its appointed day.'"

Amplified Version

ANGEL FLIGHT 44

Copyright © 2007 by

Glen Hyde
and
Rich Vermillion

Paradigm
Seed Publishers ™
www.pspublishers.com

This book contains actual accounts and personal narratives within the story; and is derived from interviews of the people involved, and author research. However, some names may have been changed or omitted, and some details excluded or altered, either intentionally or unintentionally. Any similarities of events herein described to the stories or testimonies of others not personally known to the authors are purely coincidental. The authors and publisher specifically deny and disclaim any liability, loss, or risk that is incurred as a consequence, directly or indirectly, of the application and use of the contents of this book, or from any omissions or errors that might be reflected within this book.

International Standard Book Numbers (ISBN13):

978-1-933141-00-8   (hardback edition)

978-1-933141-02-2   (paperback edition)

Published by Paradigm Seed Publishers, an imprint of
Joseph Books International, Inc.

Visit us at www.pspublishers.com for more information, and news regarding upcoming new title releases. Join our online newsletter list for advanced updates on new releases and special events.

The spine leaf logo and Paradigm Seed Publishers imprint logo are both trademarks of Joseph Books International, Inc.

The Angel Flight 44 logo is the trademark of Angel Flight 44 Ministries.

Book cover design by Kelgraphix (www.kelgraphix.com)

Differentiating Angel Flight 44 from Angel Flight® America

There is a significant difference between the pre-existing "Angel Flight" medical air transportation organizations and the new "Angel Flight 44" ministry highlighted in this book. Therefore, it would probably be appropriate to take just a moment to examine the distinction before you delve further into the remainder of *Angel Flight 44*.

In 1983, Angel Flight of Georgia was founded in Atlanta while almost simultaneously Angel Flight West was founded in Los Angeles, California. These non-profit organizations were formed for the purpose of transporting medical patients who could not afford commercial air transportation to and from treatment centers. Several additional similar non-profit medical flight groups formed thereafter. These medical flight entities still operate regionally today connecting volunteer general aviation pilots with patients who need their services.*

More recently, **Angel Flight® America** was formed in 2000* to provide a national network blanket, with seven member organizations, to cover all 50 states. According to their website, this umbrella organization and their member groups have developed a network of over 7,200 pilots and volunteers. Primarily focused on non-emergency human patient and organ air transportation, this marvelous group arranged over 18,000 flights for adults and children in 2005 alone. In partnership with their donors, this non-profit organization certainly fulfills a critical medical mission for those people in need. To learn more about Angel Flight® America and their wonderful medical aviation mission, the authors of this book encourage you to please visit their website at www.angelflightamerica.org.

On the other hand, **Angel Flight 44** (AF-44) is the name of a *new* aviation ministry dedicated to supplying air support to *Christian humanitarian relief operations* and *Gospel ministries*. Birthed in the year 2005, this new ministry is **not** affiliated with Angel Flight® America, nor is Angel Flight 44 engaged in non-emergency human medical patient or organ air transportation in any way. Rather, AF-44 has its own unique mission and a most miraculous beginning—the story of which is detailed throughout the pages of this book. Additional current information about Angel Flight 44 can be obtained by visiting us at:

Spirit Born • Spirit Fed • Spirit Driven • Spirit Led

www.angelflight44.com

Dedication

This book is dedicated to all the victims of Katrina and Rita, and to all those who went into the disaster areas to rescue them, render aid, and help restore their lives.

Moreover, this book is especially dedicated to the Body of Christ, who through their cooperative efforts, working in harmony through the loving spirit, are overcoming the devastation of the largest natural disaster in American history.

Angel Flight 44 is a living testimony that the Church can overcome all things in the natural through the strength that Jesus Christ gives them (Philippians 4:13). In fact, the efforts within the Body of Christ to minister faith, hope, and love to those who still suffer the aftermath of Hurricanes Katrina and Rita continue yet today.

-The Authors

Book Acknowledgments

Glen:

I cannot thank God enough for the opportunity to serve His people and tell the numerous Spirit-filled stories in this book: about how His Hand of divine intervention kept Angel Flight 44 on its mission to deliver faith, hope, and love to the victims and rescuers of Katrina. Flying these missions has proved to me that when love becomes the deciding factor in all choices we make and the motivating power of all that we think, say, and do—then we really and truly come as one who serves [Luke 22:27; Matthew 20:28]. Everything else in life is simply "chasing the wind." Nothing can fill the God-shaped void in man's life except God Himself. I now see life from God's perspective, and I have received a new meaning and purpose in establishing His covenant on earth. When we have learned to love and give, we have learned to love and *live*.

Kenneth Copeland's continued loving counsel and support of Angel Flight 44 through Katrina and to this day, in the birthing of this new ministry, will never be forgotten. Thank you for your encouragement to record these loving, Spirit-filled stories which are the making of this book. Kenneth, you are a true prophet and a loving servant of the Lord, for whom I will be forever grateful.

I also thank God for my loving wife, Candy, who supported my call to duty in preparing the DC-3S for service. Living on faith, not knowing how or why I was preparing it for flight, she was—and always has been—there for me. I am truly blessed with a loving partner in life.

Rich Vermillion, I cannot express in words the thanks and appreciation for all your blessed efforts and prayers that went into this book. The hundreds of hours of transcribing and editing that you and your lovely wife, Donna, have devoted in the production of *Angel Flight 44* has given me a new appreciation for authors' professional writing challenges—and the devotion you and Donna had to invest in the writing of this book. You not only told the story of *Angel Flight 44* accurately, but it was written from a Christian heart. Candy and I love you and your family: Donna, J.R., Hannah, and we already love the 'baby Vermillion,' who is still to come into this world. Thank you for putting your loving hearts into writing this Spirit-filled book.

Rich:

Without question, *Angel Flight 44* is the result of God's love for and through people. From the first day that this miraculous adventure began and throughout the research and writing of this book, His Sovereign Hand has been orchestrating events, both minor and major. Thus, first of all I must acknowledge the One Who truly made it all possible—Jesus Christ.

Secondly, I have to brag on my wife, Donna, and our two kids. Donna not only supported me in all my efforts regarding this project, but she also transcribed the interviews, edited the text repeatedly, and was a source of tremendous inspiration throughout it all. She is the best wife I could have ever hoped for, and an awesome writing partner. (I love you, my sweet.) Our two children have been very patient and kind as they often wondered when I would emerge from my office. Thank you, J.R. and Hannah, for loaning me to 'Uncle Glen' so that we could bless so many people through this book. You both are blessings from God to your mother and me, indeed.

Third, I must acknowledge the man with whom I authored this text, Glen Hyde. He is a man with a big heart, and almost unimaginable aviation knowledge. Moreover, I am thrilled that through this project he and his sweet wife Candace have become two of our closest friends…or rather, part of our family. Glen and Candy, you are very special people indeed, and we love you tremendously.

Fourth, I should certainly acknowledge all the wonderful, loving, and kind people who were involved in the original Angel Flight 44 missions, and were subsequently willing to share their time to help us tell the story. Though there were many who participated, the primary persons were: Kenneth Copeland, Denny Ghiringhelli, Pastors Larry and Leslie Roques (in Slidell, Louisiana), Chris Clem, Dennis O'Brien, and Mike Ripple. Thank you all for your kindness and participation in this remarkable book.

Additionally, Bill Horan (President) and Jody Herrington (Director, U.S. Disaster Relief) of Operation Blessing International have also been very helpful. Bill spent considerable time on the telephone with Glen and me, and corresponded several times by email during this book project. Both he and Jody also gave us a wonderful tour and interview on site at Operation Blessing's Slidell facility. Thank you both not only for taking the time to help with this book project, but for also being the blessings you both are to so many people in the United States and around the world.

In addition to their wonderful assistance with the *Angel Flight 44* book project, these above (with the help of many others) were key people during the Angel Flight 44 relief operations in 2005. Consequently, you will learn more about all of them throughout this book, and will readily see why Glen and I esteem them all so much.

Thank you, Linda Richardson, for your outstanding editorial work.

Lastly, both Glen and I would like to thank wholeheartedly and acknowledge those who contributed directly to the text of this book. Above and beyond the interviews themselves, the following people actually wrote text which was included in *Angel Flight 44*. In order of contribution, these people are:

Denny Ghiringhelli, Mike Ripple, Chris Clem, and Dennis O'Brien

Thanks guys. You all are blessed men of God.

About the Authors

Glen Hyde

Glen Hyde is a veteran aviator of more than forty years. He began his aviation career as an agricultural (AG) pilot at the tender age of 18, and later served his country as a United States Marine Corps fighter pilot. He flew as a Boeing 727 and 737 captain for Braniff International Airlines and as an international 747 captain for Polar Air Cargo. Glen has logged more than 20,000 flight hours in his 40+ years in aviation in more than 100 different types of civilian, corporate, and military type aircraft. He is also a certified flight instructor and licensed A&P, I-A mechanic; has built, restored, and flown vintage military aircraft; and owns a successful airport in North Texas, which is home to over 500 general aviation aircraft.

However, Glen's most rewarding accomplishment to date is the miraculous aviation relief missions he flew with his copilot, Denny Ghiringhelli, in Glen's Douglas Super DC-3. The story of that adventure, the new aviation ministry it birthed, and the numerous examples of divine intervention, are all the subjects of this book.

Rich Vermillion

Rich Vermillion is an ordained Gospel minister, public speaker, businessman, and author. In addition to gathering the accounts contained in *Angel Flight 44,* he has also penned other inspiring Christian books. Moreover, Rich also has several other unique books in process that will be forthcoming in 2007 and beyond.

Rich has appeared on local, national, and international television programs, and has been interviewed on dozens of radio broadcasts around the United States and Canada, including Billy Graham's *Decision Today* radio broadcast. A dynamic speaker, Rich Vermillion has also addressed groups ranging upwards to thousands in number.

About the Book

Background:

History is filled with stories of adventure. This account, however, also includes the unmistakable presence of the Hand of God. *Angel Flight 44: The True Story of Two Dedicated Pilots, a 60-Year-Old Airplane, and the Amazing Hurricane Katrina Mission That Birthed a New Aviation Ministry* is a book born out of supernatural flight missions that saved countless lives by the grace of God.

Numerous people were interviewed in both Texas and Louisiana to gather background information and personal testimonies. Additional research was then conducted by the writer, Rich Vermillion, in order to present the story to you as factually and accurately as possible—even going so far as to begin flight training as a student pilot in order to correctly describe the various flight events recorded herein.

Disclaimer:

Great care was taken to synchronize sometimes conflicting information in the authors' efforts to present this story to the general public accurately. Nevertheless, neither the authors nor the publisher claim that this book is perfect or without errors or omissions. Furthermore, neither the authors nor the publisher claim that *Angel Flight 44* is complete with regard to the entirety of information available regarding Hurricanes Katrina and Rita. No book could possibly tell the entire tale of those catastrophic events. Finally, any similarities to persons not personally known to the authors or stories not directly related to the authors are purely coincidental.

Organization:

To help stimulate the imagination of our younger readers, the sections of this book are organized similarly to that of a typical movie DVD. Beginning with *The Narrative* in Part I, you will experience the *Angel Flight 44* adventure as if you were watching a movie. The drama unfolds as you relive the adventure from its beginning, and up to the third day of flight operations.

The text then flows into a *Special Feature* in Part II to learn interesting facts about the airplane that made this miraculous relief effort possible. *Extra Scenes* that could not be inserted easily into the final edited version of *The Narrative*, along with those stories which occurred subsequent to day three of relief flight operations, are included for your enjoyment in Part III. Parts IV and V will provide you with special *Behind the Scenes* glimpses of two of the phenomenal Christian organizations involved in providing relief to those affected by Hurricanes Katrina and Rita. A special *Spiritual Commentary* by Kenneth Copeland is then provided about the storm and its aftermath in Part VI, followed directly in Part VII by the *Vision for the Future of Angel Flight 44* by Glen Hyde.

In conclusion, you will learn about *The Most Important Decision* you will ever make, and enjoy *Angel Flight 44 Special Recognitions* in the light of the tale of *Angel Flight 44*.

May God bless you as you read the pages of this book. Enjoy.

- The Publisher

Table of Contents

PART I

The Narrative

"You can't ground God. This airplane is going to march on. Once we determine where we are needed most, we are going to go."

–Glen Hyde

Pictured above (from left to right): Denny Ghiringhelli and Glen Hyde standing aside Glen's Douglas Super DC-3. Photo by Rich Vermillion

Prologue

Tuesday, September 6th, 2005: *Early Morning*

It has been another hot night for the Roques family (pronounced, "Rock") and the remnants of their congregation. Sleeping on the floor in the office of their storm-damaged church has not exactly been a fun camping experience for Pastors Larry and Leslie Roques, and four of their six children: Joshua, Rachel, Lawrence, and Abigail. Neither is it enjoyable for the dozen other church members sharing the floorboard space. It is close quarters…with no power…no lights…and certainly no air conditioning.

Hurricane Katrina had blown the screens off the windows somewhere into the next county. Nevertheless, the windows must remain open in order to have enough air to breathe, in such thick humidity. The occasional breeze makes the interior temperature somewhat tolerable. However, the free-flowing air also creates very easy entry for the swarms of mosquitoes now plaguing the little town of Slidell, Louisiana.

Swat! Scratch. Slap! Rest is all-too elusive.

Nevertheless, they are grateful. After all, the Roques family could have been inside their house while the trees were smashing down into their roof. Thankfully, they had heeded the warnings and escaped the disaster area to a hotel in Laurel, Mississippi, just two hours north of New Orleans. Even so, they still had to weather the Category 3 hurricane—not realizing how much damage it had already done when its storm surge slammed into Slidell, Louisiana in full force just hours before it arrived at their hotel.

Yes, it could be much worse…and the daily presence of unrecovered corpses in the Louisiana streets is a constant reminder of that fact. The bodies are too numerous for the overwhelmed civil governments to collect and identify.

It took the family a few days to journey back through the aftermath of the storm to discover the catastrophe's impact. Larry had made his way into the area on a fact-finding expedition that following Wednesday, August 31st—just two

3

days after the hurricane. The next day they all returned to Slidell. After finding their home crushed by fallen trees, the Roques family sought refuge in the office of the somewhat-less-damaged Joy Fellowship Church building—along with other church members similarly displaced.

Thus, the family awakes this morning thankful—but also concerned. Food and supplies are exhausted. Furthermore, the few relief groups that had managed to get some food and water into the area have not been there again in days. It has been nearly a week since the Roques' return to storm-torn Slidell—and over a week since the hurricane hit—and yet, humanitarian and government aid are shockingly meager.

A Little Help, Please?

Shortly after the Roques' had returned to Slidell, an organization called *Thirst No More* began bringing in small single-engine Cessna and twin-engine Beech aircraft with all their little cargo areas stuffed full of jars of peanut butter and canned Vienna sausages. Larry and his two sons would show up at the airport whenever they first heard the planes coming in, to see if there was anything they could do to help.

The group was always delighted to have them assist, and they would offer Larry and his sons a share of the food in exchange for their kindness. The Roques family, of course, was elated at this unexpected blessing. This new arrangement worked out well at first. Larry's son Joshua was twenty-seven, and young Lawrence, a strapping fourteen. Together with their dad, they would help the relief group and then take their share of the food back to the church.

Beyond the eighteen housed there at the church, however, other members and neighbors had also come to obtain some badly needed sustenance. Therefore, with these shipments being so sporadic, the small portions they received would not last long.

Thankfully, they also received help from World Vision, who had managed to get into the area a 53-foot trailer of initial relief supplies. The driver deposited the trailer at Joy Fellowship Church for Larry and his congregation to distribute. The excitement over having such a large supply arrive caused the Roques family and their remaining church members to reach out more to their community.

They made signs on cardboard and put them up around the neighborhood. As a result, dazed, disaster-stricken people wandered in from all quarters to get at least enough to survive. The church even delivered boxes of food out into the neighborhoods to any elderly or disabled survivors they could find. Consequently, this one trailer-load quickly ran down. Their initial euphoria waned as the supply rapidly dwindled. It lasted a few days, and now they were again without food. In fact, it has been two days now since Larry and Leslie have eaten a substantial meal—and a day since their kids have eaten one.

Anybody Up There?

After assessing the miserable situation this Tuesday morning, Pastor Larry walks back into his office alone to pray. Closing the door behind him, he steps over a few of the sleeping mats to his desk, and sits down in his office chair. With a deep sigh, he looks up and says, "Lord, I don't know how we're going to continue doing this, because we have no more resources. There's nobody I can call for help…I don't have a telephone because there are no reliable phone lines anymore. I don't have a computer…I don't have a fax machine…I don't have anything! Nothing here works."

Hanging his head, he becomes quiet. Fatigue has taken its toll on both his mind and body. The task seems too enormous. The need is so overwhelming. Nonetheless, his spirit still reaches out in faith—beyond his wearied mind and body—to the Mighty One he loves and serves.

In that moment of quiet, he hears the familiar voice of the Holy Spirit rising up from within him as the Lord speaks to this exhausted pastor's heart. "Look up, because that's where your help comes from."

Perplexed, he pauses a moment and then replies, "Okay…you know, I would have never thought of that myself. 'Look up'?" He ponders that for a moment.

After a few minutes he concludes, "Well, I guess that means look to You, Lord."

Wednesday, September 7th, 2005

After another sweltering night, the next day reveals a glimmer of hope. Pastor Larry receives a text message on his cell phone that says, "We need any trucks and trailers you can get out to the airport."

He shows the message to Leslie, "Thirst No More is sending another small airplane or two into the Slidell airport with supplies, and the message indicates they are coming in today sometime. However, the message could be a few days old…"

They both know that the cell phone towers are mostly damaged or without power. Occasionally a signal comes through long enough to deliver a text message. This limited communication has some benefit, but also lacks timeliness. Nevertheless, it is something to go on. By now, it has been three days since Larry and his wife have eaten a real meal—and two days for their kids. They are also down to their last bottle of water, so any opportunity is worth following up on.

"Well," Leslie begins, "I guess you need to check it out."

With a nod of affirmation, he turns to go and locate his two sons. Growing hope and expectancy rise in their hearts as Larry and his two sons once again load up into the minivan and, with a small utility trailer in tow, head to the airport.

As they drive into the facility they notice that the military is beginning to move in. "Well," he says to Joshua and Lawrence, "at least the government is finally starting to arrive. Better late than never," he grins.

As he pulls up to the flight line, he discovers that the two Thirst No More airplanes have already arrived. As Larry and his sons greet the pilots, they realize that they are again prepping their aircraft for takeoff soon. As they talk with the men, they learn further that the relief group has made other arrangements for the precious cargo—and that the assistance of Larry and his sons is no longer needed.

Since Thirst No More did not receive a reply to the text message they sent Larry, they apparently made other logistical arrangements. Consequently, someone else has already picked up the bottled water, peanut butter, and Vienna sausages. The pastor's services are no longer required…nor is there any food or water left to be given to them.

Larry's heart sinks quickly as the somber news begins to register on his mind. Forcing a smile onto his face, he squeaks out a "thank you," as he tries to hide the fact that tears are welling up in his eyes. Turning away from the men, he walks back to his boys as he looks around at the military personnel. Larry begins to realize that they are starting to take over the Slidell airport completely.

Looking at his sons, he says, "There seems to be nothing else for us to do here right now. We might as well head back."

The disappointment is nearly impossible for Larry to hide, as he tells them what has just transpired. The news upsets his sons likewise. Miserable, they head back toward the minivan to leave. As they walk, they hear an engine noise growing progressively louder in the air above them. It starts to drown out the noise of their growling stomachs.

The Sound of Hope

Suddenly, a large white and gray aircraft bursts into view from the treetops. "Wow!" Larry's oldest son exclaims. "Look at that!"

Yet despite his exuberant announcement, nobody really has to broadcast the arrival of a Douglas Super DC-3. Everyone within a few miles of the airport can likely hear its two 1475-horsepower Wright 1820-80 engines as the huge plane circles the airport.

Following the facility's standard air-traffic pattern, its pilots are circling to investigate the runway's status before attempting to land.

"Let's go check that out!" Joshua adds. Hope floods all of their hearts once again.

"These guys obviously aren't here on a pleasure trip," his dad replies. "They're certainly here for something. Maybe we can help them!"

"Yeah!" young Lawrence interjects. "And if we help them, maybe they'll give us some food and water, too."

Smiling, his dad turns toward him and replies, "Well, that thought did cross my mind."

The three watch as the big "bird" comes in on final approach. Landing on that short 4,000-ft runway, the pilot-in-command rides the brakes skillfully as he manages to bring the 60-year old aircraft to a complete stop—with the nose of the plane hanging just short of the landing strip's end.

"Whew! That was a close one!" Larry comments to his sons.

The three head over to investigate as the Super DC-3 begins to taxi off the runway. Little do they know what a marvel awaits them behind those large cargo doors. They also have no clue at that moment what great miracles have occurred to bring this "Super Gooney" there in the first place…

CHAPTER 1

Early Morning Brief

Monday, July 11ᵗʰ, 2005: *Early Morning*

Glen Hyde has a history of being an "early bird." This former U.S. Marine Corps captain generally finds the rising sun a familiar sight to behold. Actually, his early rising predates his Vietnam-era experience as a Phantom F-4 fighter pilot along the California coast.

His time as an agricultural pilot—at the tender age of 18, no less—had him rising early in the morning as he spent long days spraying crops for a living. Now, after nearly forty years in aviation, his habit of early rising had evolved to become something much greater…quality time with his Maker.

"I do my best prayer and meditation between three and four o'clock in the morning," he often says. Most of us are still staring at the backside of our eyelids at that early hour—but not Glen.

This particular morning he is praying about his Douglas DC3-S (or Super DC-3), and contemplating what to do with the vintage aircraft.

Idle No More

Glen's Super DC-3 has been sitting on the tarmac of the Denton, Texas airport for twenty-six months—a proverbial "eternity" where aircraft maintenance is concerned. Generally, any airplane needs regular upkeep coupled with ten to twenty hours of flight time per month to keep it from rotting right where it sits. The active operation of an airplane actually prevents problems from developing and its avionic systems from deteriorating, thus reducing repair costs. For a classic aircraft to sit for so long is to guarantee a lofty bill to get it airborne again—something about which Glen is fully aware.

He sits there this Monday morning praying and asking the Lord what He wants him to do with his "Super Gooney Bird." In fact, this is not the first time he has presented the issue heavenward. The Lord had been strangely silent in the preceding months about this, saying only, "You'll know when it's time."

Nonetheless, with the issue weighing heavily upon his heart, Glen once again opens up the familiar dialog with Jesus and begins to press Him further for a concrete answer. "Lord, should I sell it?" he starts. "It will take a boatload of money and plenty of man-hours to get it operational again...and I'm thinking that it is not doing it any more good to just leave it sitting there in Denton...so, should I look for a buyer? I would rather have some money for it than to see it rot over there."

At 3:44 in the morning, he hears from Heaven once again—but this time, the response has modified considerably: "Get it ready!"

The change of direction catches Glen off guard completely. "What did you say?" he asks.

"Get it ready!" the Spirit of God repeats gently, but firmly.

Somewhat bewildered, Glen pauses, then replies, "Get it ready. Okay. What are we going to do with it?"

The Holy Spirit does not elaborate, but simply repeats a third time, "Get it ready."

Glen does not question Him further. After pondering His Lord's directive a short while, he finally commits to the immense task. "Okay. We'll get it ready." The rest of that day he formulates his plan, makes a few phone calls, and prepares his strategy to accomplish his new mission. However, there is one very key person he purposefully neglects to mention the task to until the following day...

Breakfast with Candace

The next morning Glen gets out of bed and has his usual "morning brief" from the Lord. He then leaves his office to go have breakfast with his wife, Candace. She runs the office at the airport they own, Northwest Regional Airport, in Roanoke, Texas—just north of Fort Worth. Since he is often out the door so much earlier than she is in the morning, they usually meet at a restaurant for breakfast to coordinate their day together. This morning, she asks the familiar question, "What are you going to do today?"

Glen answers, "Well, we're going to start working on the Super DC-3."

Her fork detours from its intended destination as she looks up. This is quite a departure from the direction Glen had seemed to be leaning before, concerning this aircraft. She has been wondering for a while what he was going to do with it, and this plan comes as a complete surprise to her. She asks him, "Now, why are you going to do that?"

"Orders from Headquarters," he replies matter-of-factly.

"Really?" Her sweet hazel eyes grow even wider as her astonishment becomes more evident.

Pointing to the ceiling, he shares, "Yeah, He said to get it ready."

"Really?" (For a short while, it seems that this is the only query she can utter.)

He simply answers again, "Yep."

After a short pause, the reality of what all of this entails begins to set in. Candace has spent most of her adult life with this aviator, and she is quite "up-to-speed" regarding the logistical realities of such an operation. Under normal circumstances, a Super DC-3 requires about 600 man-hours per year to keep its maintenance and inspections current. In dollar amounts, that equates to about $30,000 per year just to *maintain* the aircraft in an operational capacity. Add to that another $30,000 per year in minimal fuel costs, hangar expenses, replacement parts, unscheduled repair expenses, etc., and it is easy to see why Glen's big bird has been sitting idle on the Denton tarmac for so long.

However, a twenty-six month long hiatus from the air also means extensive upgrades and repairs would be needed—above and beyond the "normal" expenses associated with maintaining such an aircraft. Candace is fully aware that this is not going to be a cheap weekend project.

Therefore, she now responds with, "Okay, here's the next question. Where are you going to get the money to get it ready?"

Glen knew this was coming. Candace is the one who pays the bills of the airport as they come in. This is a very practical question from a practical lady.

However, he had already settled this issue with his divine Commander-in-Chief when the orders originally came in. In his usual Texas drawl, he replies, "I don't know. It ain't my problem. If He brings you to it, He'll bring you through it. I'm just following orders."

Candace considers that for a moment, and then asks, "Well, who's going to do it?"

"It's just going to be T.W. and me," he replies.

She could almost digest the answer to the first question, but this second answer is not going down so easily. "But normally you use five, six, or seven guys! It takes hundreds of man-hours to get that plane in the air again…and you think that just you and T.W. can get it done?" Glen's plan would probably not seem so preposterous to her if Mr. T.W. Wheelock were somewhat younger— but he is *over* 70 years old!

Nonetheless, her undaunted mate confirms, "That's true. But it's just going to be T.W. and me. The Spirit told me to get it ready, and all I have to work with right now are these two hands and T.W. So we'll get up early while it's still cool out, grab a coffee and biscuit on the way to Denton, and work until the heat gets too high. Then we'll clean up and knock off until the next day…and do it again."

Candace is no less bewildered now than she was when the conversation began. Nonetheless, she knows her man believes he has heard from God on the matter, and there is no changing his mind. At least she knows what his plan is—as ridiculous as it may seem.

Two Hands and a T.W.

Glen and T.W. begin working on the DC3-S the next day. Every morning they meet at 5:00 a.m. and grab breakfast on the way to the plane. Typically, they work until about noon before the Texas summer heat makes the task unbearable. Covered in sweat, engine oil, and dirt, Glen returns home each day for a shower and change of clothes. After lunch, he heads over to the office for a few hours to catch up on some of the administrative responsibilities that come with operating an airport.

Beyond just man-hours, he needs tens of thousands of dollars' worth of parts and consumables to prepare the aircraft for flight. Since Glen does not own a money-tree farm, he gives this issue some serious prayer. Thereby, he utilizes *resourcefulness* to acquire what they need.

As a certified aircraft mechanic and restorer of classic airplanes and helicopters, Glen has collected quite an inventory of aircraft parts through the years. Consequently, nearly every time he needs money for the project, he sells something and uses the proceeds to obtain the parts his Super DC-3 requires. Additionally, he does some good ol' Texas "horse-trading" (bartering) and whatever else he can do (legally and ethically), to procure the parts and materials he needs for the "Super Gooney."

Glen's declaration to Candace, "If He brings you to it, He'll bring you through it" was certainly a sincere affirmation of faith in his Creator's ability to supply every need—especially for a project He had Himself commissioned. Yet, Glen is also an experienced Christian businessman, and has been so for many years.

He knows that the wisdom inscribed by God into the Bible includes admonitions to have a sound work ethic. Heaven, according to the Scriptures, has already provided marvelous provision. However, the Word also indicates that we have to reach out and grasp it with our own hands, for "faith without works is dead, being alone" (James 2:17). Glen knows that his success is guaranteed by God's own promises. Nevertheless, he also realizes that he will have to apply his own efforts because God prospers what we put our hands to (Deuteronomy 28:8, 12).

Throughout history—ancient and modern—there have always been God-honoring men and women who received a word from Jesus (*Yeshua*, in Hebrew), and obeyed it. Such people have changed nations for the better, founded ministries, built corporations, invented wonders, healed the sick, performed miracles—and even raised the dead. In this case, one such man is simply obeying his personal "word" from the Savior…and is repairing an airplane; a seemingly trivial act that will soon spare the lives of thousands.

It seems quite fitting that the *Savior* would direct one of His men to do something that will ultimately *save* a multitude. After all,…is that not what His love is all about?

Gettin' 'er Done!

With some divinely inspired "horse-trading" and sales from his own parts inventory, Glen manages to keep the DC3-S parts supply flowing. He tracks down the expensive components piece-by-piece, and he and T.W. install them as they come in.

The two continue working on the Super DC-3 day after day…week after week. Swinging wrenches, they tear down large parts of each engine, replace the worn and failed parts, change the lubricants, and put the engines back together again. The two men then rework the cockpit instrumentation and replace faulty gauges. They subsequently rework the electrical system and run considerable amounts of new wire from the aircraft's nose to its end. Now, the hydraulic system has to be completely drained, the leaks repaired, and the system refilled.

Crawling around the aircraft inside and out—from the tail to the nosecone—the two examine the plane, make repairs and all necessary upgrades, and then put it all back together again. As Glen later recalls, "The plane needed a lot of work, but we just kept whittling away on it and got it running."

Remarkably, after six greasy, sweaty weeks they have it finished. Now that it is running, it is ready for the FAA-required check-flight for airworthiness.

"Now," thinks Glen. "What do you have in mind, Lord, for this old 'Super'?"

CHAPTER 2

True Allies

Monday, August 29ᵗʰ, 2005: *Hurricane Katrina makes landfall.*

After first striking the Florida east coast as a Category 1 hurricane the previous Thursday, Katrina skirts across the Sunshine State and picks up strength again in the Gulf of Mexico. The warm waters of the Gulf infuse tremendous energy into the storm. The winds and waves intensify significantly. At one point, the storm reaches a sustained wind force of 175mph—making it a healthy Category 5 hurricane—before slowing to a Category 4, just before landfall in Louisiana.

Offshore, Katrina has created storm surge waves in excess of *thirty feet high* while still at Category 5 intensity. Smashing into the Louisiana and Mississippi coastlines in advance of the eye wall, these waves are wiping out entire populated areas. As the hurricane continues to come ashore, Category 4 winds well in excess of 131 mph bombard the coastal areas for hours.

The eyewall makes its second landfall, drenching the coastline with immense rain. It has now slowed down somewhat to a Category 3 hurricane. Yet the preceding Category 5 storm surge and Category 4 winds have already wreaked major havoc on the Gulf Coast. Therefore, this added precipitation and flooding, along with the 120-mph winds, make a terrible situation even worse.

The devastating shape of the hurricane, combined with the hydrology of the location, has created an evil mix of catastrophic conditions. Yet despite the destruction caused by this immense storm, the "God of Comfort"—Jesus—had already been preparing His provision to relieve those affected thereby.

Calling Bill Horan

Tuesday, August 30th, 2005: *Mid-morning*

This first day after Katrina ravaged the Gulf Coast, Kenneth Copeland rises out of bed with a heartfelt desire to call Bill Horan, President of Operation Blessing International (OBI). Because of OBI's role as the humanitarian arm of the Christian Broadcasting Network (CBN), Kenneth knows that they are already in the thick of the action providing disaster relief.

He shares this inner-witness with his wife, Gloria. Subsequently, they decide it might be an appropriate idea to watch CBN's *700 Club* broadcast in a short while to get an update regarding Katrina. They turn on the television at the time of broadcast and sit down together to catch the latest information. Of course, the hurricane is the lead story…and moments later, Bill Horan himself appears on the air to update the viewers regarding the initial relief efforts of Operation Blessing.

After Bill's update, Kenneth jumps to the edge of his chair. "That's it. I've got to call him!" he exclaims. The witness he had felt before in his spirit had now grown into a full-blown burden of the Lord.

Gloria calmly replies, "I know his number."

He turns toward her and declares, "Well, give it here!"

She goes to find her address book while Kenneth heads over to the phone to meet her there. When she joins him, they dial Bill Horan's direct office number on their speakerphone. They expect to get his voicemail, but to their surprise, he actually answers.

Gloria first introduces herself, and then shares that she and Kenneth are sending an immediate financial contribution to the disaster relief effort from their own personal funds; and that one will be coming shortly thereafter from Kenneth Copeland Ministries as well. She then tells the Operation Blessing chief that Kenneth wants to talk to him…

Kenneth speaks up, "Hey Bill, this is Kenneth. What do you need?"

"I need an air force, more than anything!" Bill replies, somewhat proverbially—not really intending it as a definite request. "I have got to move some relief supplies, but the preliminary reports I am getting are that many of the highways are down. Of course, we already had trucks staged and ready before the storm hit; so we've probably already run a hundred trailer loads into the areas where we do have access. We're still evaluating the situation, but one thing I know—I've got to move more of this emergency relief now."

To Bill Horan's surprise, Kenneth responds, "You don't know it yet, but

Operation Blessing already has an air force."

Bill had rarely personally talked with Kenneth Copeland. He knew Kenneth was a friend of CBN and of its founder, Pat Robertson—but he had very little previous personal contact with the Copelands. The two ministries had known each other for quite a long time. Nevertheless, until the tsunami that occurred in December of the previous year, Bill never had any prior contact with the Copelands. The day they came to Virginia Beach to give OBI a considerable donation for the tsunami relief mission was the first time he had met them.

Consequently, he does not initially know how to interpret what Kenneth has just said. However, Kenneth continues, "I have a dear friend by the name of Glen Hyde..."

After explaining a short summary of Glen's aviation background to the Operation Blessing president, Kenneth concludes, "This guy's got a Super DC-3 airplane that he's got all restored and in perfect condition—and he's willing to fly *anywhere* at *any time* as your Operation Blessing air force. He can support your disaster relief efforts down there in this Katrina thing. In other words, if you need an air force—I've got the 'commandant' himself. I'll call him, and he'll call you."

The parties all say their goodbyes, and the Copelands hurry off the phone to allow Bill to get back to the mission at hand. However, immediately after hanging up the phone with Mr. Horan, Kenneth tracks down Glen on his cell phone and summons him to meet him at the KCM airfield later that day. This first day after the hurricane hit, Glen Hyde is to visit with one of the few ministers who knows the true potential of aviation as a *tool* to minister to the hurting and afflicted.

Aviation Ministry

Before becoming a minister in 1967, Kenneth flew as a commercial pilot for several companies—including a couple of his own. Upon his conversion to Christ in 1962, however, he walked away from aviation as his "religious thinking" seemed to dictate to him that flying and Christianity could never mix. In part, he realized that he loved flying so much that it had become a "god" to him—something he knew did not please the Lord Jesus. "If I never fly again," he committed, "Lord, I will serve you all the days of my life." This part of his consecration was certainly necessary at the time for his continued spiritual growth.

Nevertheless, his thinking at the time was similar to those of Christians in the 1950s who thought that *television* and Christianity were incompatible. These sincere—yet, extremely misguided—Christians and ministers turned down the FCC's original offer to sell them licenses for little to nothing. Only later did the American Church wake up and realize that they missed a significant opportunity to bless the population of America. They had essentially given away the airwaves to godless people by failing to recognize the opportunity set before them. The repercussions of that error are evident even today on televisions across the nation.

Thank God, the Body of Christ did eventually wake up and begin to harness the power of television to bless humanity worldwide. Likewise, Kenneth Copeland eventually made the connection between aircraft and Christian service (and he eventually went on to make use of television as well).

Jesus gave aviation back to Kenneth. He indicated thereby that aviation was a vital ministry tool that He wanted employed for divine service. This realization occurred while Kenneth was attending theology school at Oral Roberts University (ORU). The thirty-year-old freshman and minister-to-be was hired to Oral Roberts' flight crew and traveled from city to city with the renowned evangelist. As his copilot, Kenneth Copeland became keenly aware of the ministry potential for aviation as he saw multitudes healed of their infirmities and saved by God's amazing grace. Aviation was a key element that allowed Dr. Roberts the flexibility to accomplish so much, so quickly.

Learning firsthand the impact air transportation could make in affecting people's lives in service to his Lord, Kenneth later adopted aviation as an essential part of his own ministry's outreach capabilities. By the time he and Glen Hyde sat down to discuss Katrina, Brother Copeland had been utilizing aircraft to spread the Gospel for nearly forty years worldwide, "From the top, to the bottom, and all the way around."

"It's Ready!"

A few hours have passed since Kenneth has talked to Glen on his cell phone. Now, the two are sitting down in Kenneth's aviation office to touch base about the storm and its impact—and to determine what to do about it. Since the two generally talk often, Kenneth is aware that Glen has been working on his Super DC-3. However, Glen was hard to get on the phone during the time he was working on the plane. Therefore, Kenneth is not fully aware of how *dramatic* the progress has been in returning the vintage aircraft to a flight-ready condition.

Kenneth asks, "What's the status of your Gooney Bird?"

"It's ready. I finished getting it ready just two days before Katrina hit. It's ready to go."

"Really?!" he exclaims.

Glen replies, "Yeah, I've been working on it for the past six weeks…just me and a 74-year-old friend of mine. Just the two of us did all the labor on that thing."

Kenneth pauses a moment to contemplate God's perfect timing. "Well then

Glen, I think you really need to call this guy…" and he begins to share the details of his earlier phone conversation with Pat Robertson's right-hand man—the President of Operation Blessing. "Glen, you need to call Bill Horan. I already told him we've got some aeronautic capability to help them out. They need your Super DC-3."

The airplane is basically ready for the mission. The purpose Jesus obviously had in mind when He told him, "Get it ready!" is presently staring Glen in the face. Now, one of God's generals has just given him a firm "suggestion" regarding his new marching orders.

Remarking on this moment, Glen later shares, "When Kenneth Copeland asks me to look into something or to do something, I always look at it as an order. He is a vessel the Lord is using to bless the Body of Christ…but also to speak into my life. To *me*—it's an order! When he speaks, I listen. That man spends four to six hours a day in prayer, and then another two hours or so studying the Word of God—*every day*. He is so strong in the spirit that when he speaks…well, you'd better listen to him."

Consequently, when Kenneth "suggests" that Glen give Bill Horan a call, Glen agrees. "Okay…I'll call him. Since it is late in the day, I'll do it tomorrow. However, there are a couple of other issues we really need to pray about concerning this, if we are going to be able to support relief missions with my 'Gooney Bird'."

"What?" Kenneth asks.

"Well, two things: for starters…I'll need a copilot." FAA regulations require two pilots at the control of an aircraft that large when it is airborne.

"Yeah, that's true. I had already wondered about that. What else?"

"Just one more thing…" Glen begins to share. "…I've got to set up a check ride with the FAA, because I'm out of currency."

"Out of currency" in aviation simply means that he had not completed a proficiency check for that aircraft within the Federal Aviation Administration's (FAA) mandated time requirement so that he could be considered "current" as the pilot-in-command (PIC) of the airplane. According to FAA regulations, to operate an aircraft weighing over 12,500 pounds, the PIC must be type-rated for that specific aircraft—and have passed a proficiency check within the preceding twelve months. In other words, since Glen has not operated the DC3-S in over two years, he is not currently "legal" to fly that large twin-engine transport without the required proficiency check ride. An appropriate FAA examiner conducts these.

Normally, the FAA requires a thirty days' notice to schedule a check ride in an aircraft—and *both* Kenneth and Glen know this very well. However, that is about thirty days more than can be spared where humanitarian aid operations are concerned. People need help now.

"Anything else?" Kenneth asks.

"Fuel," he answers. "We're going to need quite a bit of it to keep that Gooney Bird in the air for so long."

Many hurdles have already been surmounted. The aircraft itself is certainly ready for this disaster. However, several serious issues remain to be conquered. "Let's get into agreement in prayer," Kenneth responds.

The two begin to pray…only to discover later that God has *already* been working on their behalves for the completion of *His* work.

CHAPTER

3

Busy Days

Wednesday, August 31ˢᵗ, 2005

One significant prerequisite to the air-relief operation going forward is making the captain of the DC3-S *legal* to fly the relief airplane. As Glen had told Kenneth the day before, "…I've got to set up a check ride with the FAA, because I'm out of currency." He needs to get on the phone first thing today and get a check ride scheduled ASAP. However, Glen is not sure if "ASAP" is actually in the FAA's vocabulary.

He grabs his office phone and calls Jack Calvert—the FAA's Maintenance Chief at the Flight Standard District Office (FSDO) in Fort Worth, located at Alliance Airport. Miraculously, his call reveals that the FAA has already changed its regulations to allow for aircraft associated with the Katrina relief effort to get priority handling when requesting check rides. Thus, when Glen tells him he needs to schedule a check ride in his DC3-S, they give him the *highest* priority handling because of the immediate need.

What normally takes thirty days to occur he now schedules for a date only forty-eight hours later. As anyone familiar with government agencies can easily attest, such a rapid change in Federal policy is nothing less than *the Hand of God* intervening.

"Great!" thinks Glen. "That's taken care of. Thanks Lord! Now…Operation Blessing." The next call Glen makes is to Bill Horan. He pulls the number

21

Kenneth had given him out of his shirt pocket, and dials him up.

The "Commandant" Calls

Like the day before, Bill Horan personally answers the phone. He has been working almost around the clock synchronizing OBI's Katrina relief efforts. Consequently, when the phone rings, Bill is there to pick it up. Once Glen introduces himself, Bill is delighted to meet the man Kenneth Copeland had called, "the commandant."

Glen begins discussing the Katrina relief efforts with Bill. He reiterates that his Super DC-3 is at Operation Blessing's disposal as needed. "I'm going down there to Louisiana. There's no question those people are hurting and needing some help—right now," Glen shares.

Bill replies, "That's great, but where are we going to try to run the air operation down there?"

Glen pauses a moment and says, "Bill, I don't know where we are going to set up shop—the Spirit hasn't revealed that part to me yet. But I'm going to make a few more phone calls and get started with the logistics. I'll get back with you once the plan comes together."

"Sounds good, Glen. We'll be in touch."

Once Glen gets off the phone with Operation Blessing's chief, he sits back in his chair a few moments and prays. An idea "clicks" into his mind.

Picking up the phone, he calls his brother, Ronald, and asks him about whatever contacts he has in Louisiana. Ronald refers him to a good friend of his named Dr. Walter Atkinson, who works out of Baton Rouge.

Ronald explains, "Glen, you could easily operate out of there. He's got an apartment in a hangar at the airport there, and they've also got 100-octane low-lead fuel for your 'Super' at the FBO. Hook up with him and you're good-to-go."

After hanging up the phone, Glen says to himself, "Good. That's what we're going to do. We're going to load up with food and water and head over to Baton Rouge, and see what the Lord would have us do from there. Now, Lord…all I need is a fuel budget, a copilot, and a check ride."

Fuel to Fly

Glen prays again for a few minutes. "Lord, you know this Super DC-3 burns a whole lot of fuel. If we're going to be able to sustain this operation, we're gonna need a whole bunch of 100 low-lead to get this job done."

After praying a while along these lines, he then picks up his phone again to call his fuel distributor, Ken Moline. Northwest Regional Airport has been a long-standing dealer with British Petroleum's aviation fuel division, Air BP. Glen needs them to become partners with this venture. The aircraft has a consumption rate of 120 gallons of aviation fuel per hour of flight at its standard cruising speed. That is *six gallons of fuel per minute*. People's lives depend on whether Air BP or some other fuel vendor would be willing to underwrite the plane's expensive fuel habit.

"Hello, Ken? This is Glen Hyde at Northwest Regional Airport."

"Hey Glen! It's good to hear your voice. What can I do for you today?"

"Well, you're aware of this Katrina disaster..."

"Yeah?" Ken replies.

"Well, as you know, this thing has devastated about 90,000 square miles of our country, and there are people hurting down there. In many places, there is no way to get supplies in to these people but by air. I've got a Douglas Super DC-3 that I own, and I am planning to fly it myself to help these people out—but it burns a whole lot of fuel.

"Now, Kenneth Copeland Ministries, Eagle Mountain International Church, and Pat Robertson's Operation Blessing are all willing to furnish relief supplies and logistical support. What I need now, though, is for Air BP to partner up with me in this thing, and help us get these supplies down there to these people."

"Man, Glen, that's great. But, how much do you think you'll need for such an operation?"

"I'm thinking this will take at least a few weeks to make a dent in helping these people before trucks are rolling again into the disaster areas. So I'm thinking between $30,000 and $40,000 in fuel. If you guys can credit my Air BP account, I can get enough 100 low-lead to keep the bird flyin'. I'll use the Multiserve system to buy fuel everywhere there's no Air BP, and pay it back off with your credit to my account."

"Well, how about $35,000? That's right in the middle. Do you think that will cover it?"

"Yeah, I think it would," Glen replies.

"I'll put a call in to the President of Air BP, Mike Delk. He's the only one who can make a decision like that. I'll give you a call back," Ken concludes.

Glen puts the receiver down and prays. "Lord, work this thing out in Jesus' Name!"

About an hour later, Ken calls back. "I talked with Mike Delk," he reports. "He said, 'If he's doing Katrina relief work, tell him he's got the $35,000 fuel credit he needs.' So, you're covered, Glen. Get that big Super DC-3 in the air as soon as you can."

"Thanks Ken! I'm gonna do just that! Tell Mr. Delk I really appreciate Air BP comin' on board with us in this. There's gonna be a whole lot of people helped because of you guys."

"Glad to do it, Glen. This is a national emergency thing, so we're just happy to help out."

Glen puts down the receiver and again says a prayer, "Thank you, Lord!"

Fuel for the missions is covered. The Spirit of God is at work, and the pieces are coming together. "Just two more pieces left…" he ponders. "And surely, the Spirit has those worked out already too."

A Willing Recruit
Thursday, September 1st, 2005

Captain Denny Ghiringhelli is an experienced aviator of well over thirty years. For more than twenty years, he has been working for American Airlines. He has captained Boeing 767s and even 777s. However, Denny recently decided to change base airports to be home with the family more often. This meant he had to downsize back to captaining Boeing 737s.

At this point in our story, Denny is currently awaiting 737 recurrent training before he can begin his next assignment, and has been tinkering around in his hangar at Northwest Regional Airport for a few days now.

With time on his hands, Captain Ghiringhelli has been restoring his 1942 Stearman biplane. After working on it for most of the day, he gets in his car and begins to drive back across the airport. As he is just beginning the drive, he decides to dial information to obtain the number of a local aircraft parts supplier.

As Denny recalls, "I had dialed in 411 and was about to push the call button when something made me look over as I was driving past Glen's office. There was Glen's truck parked outside. My thumb froze as a thought entered my mind, 'Go in and say hi, and use Glen's phonebook, and save a nickel while I'm at it.'

"So I walked in and saw Candace at her desk. I said 'hi' to her and asked if I could borrow her phonebook. She looked up, kind of stared at me for a second, and said, 'I think Glen is going to want to talk to you.' I could sense by the look on her face something was up.

"I could see Glen through the window between his office and Candace's. He was on the phone and motioned me in. As I entered the room, I overheard Glen say, 'A DC-3 pilot just walked into my office right now. I'll call you back.'

"As he hung up the phone, Glen asked me, 'Are you off? When do you have to go back to work?'

"I nodded my head and said, 'I'm off until the 15th—I start training on the 737.'

"Before I could ask what was going on, Glen said to me, 'Well, you just might make it back by then. I need you to go home, pack a bag, grab some tools, and come back. I just volunteered my Super 3 to Kenneth Copeland and Operation Blessing for a relief effort flying supplies into Louisiana. I need a copilot. You're it! Hurry back. We've got just enough time to run up to Denton for a test flight. I have a check ride set up for tomorrow, and then we head for Louisiana...details to follow.'

"Mostly what I heard was, 'You might just make it back in time, NEED, bag, tools, NEED, volunteered, Super 3, NEED, copilot, you're it, NEED, and hurry back...details to follow.' Glen's hand was still on the phone. I nodded my head, said, 'bye' to Glen and Candace, and turned for the door. I could hear Glen dialing as I walked out of his office."

Checking Out the Super DC-3

That afternoon Denny meets Glen, and they head up to Denton to test the airplane. On the way, Glen fills him in on his involvement with Kenneth Copeland Ministries, explains Operation Blessing, and says it looks like they will be operating out of Baton Rouge. It is only a fifteen-minute drive, so there is not a lot of time to elaborate.

The two pilots arrive at Denton. There she sits—a Douglas Super DC-3. Denny Ghiringhelli's first big airplane job in aviation was as a copilot on a DC-3 hauling skydivers...thirty years ago. Since then Denny has flown other "3's," at one point instructing in them, but they were all standard DC-3's. This airplane is a "Super."

As they walk around the airplane, Glen explains the differences: bigger engines, extended fuselage, a sweep to the trailing edges of the wings, gear doors, a retractable tail wheel, etc. Denny takes note of the changes, and yet cannot help but see the familiar outline of the tried and true DC-3 lying beneath the surface. Glen must have sensed this because as they climb into the cockpit, he turns to him and says, "Just wait 'til you see what this old girl can do."

During the test flight, Glen goes over all the procedures and just what he wants Denny to do the next day on the check ride. It has been almost ten years since Captain Ghiringhelli has flown a DC-3, and he is looking forward to another opportunity.

The test hop goes well. Glen, Denny, and the "Super" do not miss a beat. They land at Denton and taxi to the ramp. They finish the parking checklist, and then Glen turns to Denny and comments, "Not bad for sixty years old."

Denny asks, "Are you talking about *you* or the airplane?" They laugh.

Supplies and Tools

On the drive back to Northwest Regional Airport, Glen tells Denny more about the operation. "Available details are scarce and do not count on having drinking water or other 'necessities.'"

The two review lists of what they think they will need for the operation. Glen then asks Denny to meet him for breakfast first thing in the morning. Denny replies, "I'm all packed, but I still need to put together some tools and pick up a few supplies. I'll take care of that tonight and meet you in the morning."

Denny goes to his hangar and starts packing tools into his bag. In addition to being a pilot, he is also a certified airplane mechanic. Consequently, he picks tools he knows he will need for maintenance and possible repairs, the ones he *thinks* he might need, and some he hopes he will not have to use. (Older airplanes and their radial engines require some specialized tools for certain repairs, and some of those repairs are neither fun nor are they easily performed away from a maintenance base.) He then stops by Wal-Mart for some supplies and heads home for what will be the first of many short nights.

When Denny returns home from his errands, he finds his wife, Pam, waiting for him. She helps him box up his supplies and tells him she has been thinking about the mission and listening to the news concerning the situation. She is quiet, but looks as if she wants to say something to her husband.

Denny is fully aware that his wife has a strong belief in God, yet he is still surprised by what she says: "I believe when something like this happens, God presents the right people with an opportunity to do the right thing," she says, "It's up to them whether or not they do it." Denny stares at her warmly for just a moment, and then finishes packing his supplies for the trip.

CHAPTER 4

Last-Minute Preparations

Friday, September 2nd, 2005

The next morning, Denny gets up early and meets Glen and Candace for breakfast. Candace and Denny eat, while Glen tries to have his meal between phone calls. She then remarks to Denny that Glen has been on the phone most of the night, trying to establish their point-of-contact in Louisiana and to coordinate on-site logistics.

As Captain Hyde hangs up from another call, he turns to Denny. With Glen's phone still in hand, they go over a list of support equipment for the airplane. After breakfast, they head for Northwest Regional Airport, and the two men meet at Glen's hangar. "Put your stuff in my truck," he tells Denny. "We'll load the support equipment and head to Denton."

Glen is on the phone the entire ride. Calls to Louisiana are sporadic at best. "Cell sites are down, and calls aren't getting through," he explains. "We are supposed to have contacts down there, but I can't get through to them."

Whenever the calls do get through, Denny notices the same response coming from the DC3-S captain, each time he hangs up the phone: "Well, okay. I see. We'll just have to take care of that on our end."

Oily Check Ride

They arrive at Denton and meet with John Boatwright of the FAA, who has come from Lubbock, Texas to give Glen the required check ride in his Super DC-3. With Glen in the captain's seat and Denny flying copilot, John hops into the jump seat behind Glen as they begin their preflight checklist.

After they are airborne, Glen and Denny begin working through the after-takeoff checklist. All is going smoothly, as Denny reads the checklist and Glen responds appropriately. Denny gets to the part of the procedure where each pilot is required to look outside and visually inspect his respective engine.

Denny takes note of the right engine and announces to Glen, "Clear, clean and smooth," indicating that the right engine is operating perfectly. ("Clear" means that there is no fire or unusual smoke emanating from the engine. "Clean" indicates that there is no oil coming out of the engine. "Smooth" signifies that there is no shuddering or shaking—that the engine is not out of balance or experiencing mechanical problems.) Now it is Glen's turn.

Glen looks out the left side of the cockpit at the other engine. As he peers through the glass, he discovers engine oil blowing back all over the left engine, the cowling, and back across the wing. One of the three prop seals on the left engine had begun leaking during takeoff…and it is making a real mess.

Glen is an experienced mechanic himself. He is also intimately familiar with this particular Super DC-3. Realizing that the prop seal failure is not detrimental to that day's flight operational safety, he quickly thinks to himself, "It's Friday, and we can't postpone this check ride until Monday—there are too many hurricane victims. They need us now!"

Thinking quickly, Glen turns back toward Denny and with a wink declares, "Clear and smooth"—omitting "clean"—and the DC-3 duo simply face forward, continue their flight procedures, and keep flying the aircraft safely. Glen aces his check ride, and two hours and forty minutes later, they return for a smooth landing back at Denton.

Denny exits the airplane to install the control locks and wheel chocks to secure the aircraft from moving, while Glen mans the controls and holds the brakes until they are in place. Denny can hear John, as he exits the plane, talking to Glen—something about *oil*. As Denny walks around to the left engine, he sees the oil and realizes that a prop seal has let go. Although the leak is not bad enough to stop today's flight, the aircraft certainly cannot fly to Louisiana in its current condition.

John Boatwright is eager to get to Dallas to catch a flight back to Lubbock. Thus, he is intending to get back to the Denton airport terminal quickly in order to process Glen's paperwork. However, as he exits the airplane, he notices the oil all over the left engine, down onto the left wing, and even blown back onto the tail of the aircraft. "Glen, what's up with all this oil all over the place out here?"

Glen is still in the cockpit with the window open. He hollers out, "Awe! You know these old birds need to *mark their territory* whenever you fly them."

John has been around aviation long enough to know that Glen's statement is true and common with vintage aircraft, such as this one. Actually, with the older engine technologies, a completely dry engine could be a sign of something much worse. Therefore, John confidently replies, "Yep. If it ain't leakin', don't fly 'em. See you back at the terminal."

Glen and Denny briefly discuss repairing the prop seal, and Glen goes with John to process the paperwork. In the meantime, Denny stays behind to load their gear into the plane and check the fuel and oil.

A short time later, the paperwork is complete and Glen returns. Glen informs Denny, "I've called Melvin. We can fly her down to Copeland Field. They can pull the prop tonight."

Prop-er Repairs

Glen and Denny then get back into the airplane and fly it to Kenneth Copeland Ministries' airport—known to local air traffic control as "Copeland Field." The mechanics at the ministry pull the old bird into the main hangar and begin to remove the prop that very afternoon. Glen tells Denny to go home and rest, and meet him at his hangar first thing in the morning.

Meanwhile, Melvin Tomlin—one of the mechanics and Glen's close friend for many years—calls Byam Propeller Service, Inc. in Fort Worth at only ten minutes before 5 p.m. and explains the situation. Emphatic about the urgency of the mission, Melvin says, "We need this prop tonight! We need to get this airplane airborne in the morning to fly Katrina relief supplies into the hurricane disaster area." The shop's owner agrees.

As a result, Shawn Young from Byam Propeller Service drives up late that Friday afternoon during rush-hour traffic, and works with the KCM mechanics to pull the prop and take it back to his shop. Melvin returns to his shop with him to assist. Keeping the facility running all night, these dedicated men work to replace all three seals—including the leaky one—and to get the propeller back into operational condition. They return with it to Copeland Field and have it reinstalled on the aircraft by 4:30 the next morning—Saturday, September 3rd.

Glen runs the engine and successfully tests the new seals. Once he powers-down the engine again, he returns home to pack for his flight and grab a quick nap. The aircraft will soon be loaded, and he needs to be fresh for the mission.

CHAPTER 5

Pre-Flight

Saturday, September 3rd, 2005: *Mid-morning*

Denny meets Glen and Candace at their hangar, and they all head to Copeland Field. Glen informs his copilot that the prop seals have been replaced and that the propeller is re-installed and tested. "We are good to go," he says confidently.

The drive takes about thirty minutes. As usual, Glen spends most of it on the phone. However, it is apparent to Candace and Denny that he is not getting the information he is seeking.

As the three arrive at Copeland Field, they see the Super DC-3 parked outside between the hangar and the fuel pit. Positioned with its nose into the wind, it seems to beckon, "Come on guys, let's go! We've got work to do."

The previous evening's flight into Copeland Field was Denny's first visit to Kenneth Copeland Ministries (KCM). Therefore, after parking the truck, Glen greets Kenneth Copeland and introduces Captain Denny Ghiringhelli to him and to the rest of the KCM personnel. The staff then leads them into the open hangar where pallets of water, food and other supplies are waiting to be loaded. They need to determine how much can be loaded and which of the supplies should be highest priority.

Glen's cell phone rings again, and he steps away from the group. What Denny can hear of Glen's side of the conversation sounds familiar, "Well, I see. We'll just have to deal with it. Thank you."

Glen hangs up the phone and says, "Baton Rouge is out. The military has moved in and taken over—nothing but military aircraft in or out. We will need to find a new base of operations." Glen asks Denny to get a Louisiana 'sectional' (aeronautical chart) from the airplane as he, Chris Clem, Dennis O'Brien, and Pastors George and Terri Pearsons follow Kenneth into his office.

Chris and Dennis are managers at KCM. They have put together a list of KCM partners, friends, partner churches, etc., in the Katrina-affected area. However, efforts to make contact have been frustrating due to the damage to phone lines and cell phone towers. Chris informs the group, "We know many of our partners lived in the path of the destruction. What we don't know is if they are still there, or what their status might be."

All eyes turn toward Kenneth Copeland as he sits pondering what Chris had just said. His immediate and deep concern for the ministry's partners becomes evident as everyone can see an obvious transformation taking place in his countenance. Silence follows.

After a very intense pause, Kenneth turns his head gradually toward Glen. Tremendous passion fills his eyes as he then leans forward in his chair. With resolute determination, he slowly declares, "Glen…we are going to fly to Louisiana…and we are going to find our partners."

All Glen can do at this moment is nod his head in affirmation, and answer, "Yes, sir."

The mission is now decided. The objectives are now clear. Find the KCM partners, and help them—and help as many other people that they can while they do. The Super DC-3 captain is overwhelmed by the love and integrity he is now witnessing in his old friend. Moreover, Kenneth's passion to help his partners, and then many others who are suffering, supercharges the veteran aviator for the mission he is about to undertake.

Loading the Super DC-3

There is an undeniable sense among the group in Kenneth's office that the storm-stricken people are in dire straits. There is also an unmistakable frustration of not knowing what the situation is on the ground in the disaster area—or *what* his partners need specifically. It is reasonable to assume survivors of a disaster of such magnitude are going to need everything. The question now confronting the people assembled in Kenneth's office is, "What can we do right now that has the most benefit?"

It is determined that, of the supplies on hand, what would best serve the immediate need is water. Glen then tells Denny to start loading. "Get as many cases as you can in between the seats. If you haven't hit 10,000 lbs. by the last row, then load the light food supplies from there to the tail. Go ahead and top off all the inboard fuel tanks. That will get us anywhere in Louisiana." Denny complies, hands Glen the sectional chart, and heads out to the plane.

A group of KCM staff and volunteers stand in the hangar, eagerly awaiting instructions. Captain Ghiringhelli then steps out of Kenneth's office and begins to direct the loading and fueling operations. Two of the mechanics, Melvin and Jeff, reposition the airplane and begin fueling. A forklift brings the first pallet of water to the aircraft and lifts it up to the cargo door. Then a 'bucket brigade' of Eagle Mountain International Church (EMIC) volunteers and KCM staff begin passing cases of water forward.

The cases are stacked in front of the seats, under the seats, on the seats, and between the seats, until a wall of water bottles seemingly engulfs them. They use a large roll of shrink-wrap to secure the cases. Some quick math reveals that they have a few pounds to spare. Therefore, they load some lighter foodstuffs behind the seats toward the rear of the plane. They lock these in place with shrink-wrap also.

Next, the team employs cargo straps to secure the load further. They place the toolboxes and support equipment in strategic places along the left side of the aircraft to balance the load, and then tie them down as well. They tie down the crew luggage and supplies forward of the cargo. The aircraft is ready. Now all the pilots need is to know where to go...

Where Do We Go From Here?

As Glen looks over the sectional chart to review his options, he pauses a moment to reflect, "Lord...thank you for steering me. Now I know that Baton Rouge was *not* where you wanted me to go."

Kenneth walks over and asks, "What are our options, Glen?"

He smiles, and replies, "Well, we'll just back off and head to Lafayette. That's outside the TFR [Temporary Flight Restriction area, which in this case, has been designated by the military through Martial Law]. We'll just go in there. That gets us close...and there's bound to be relief operations working out of Lafayette. We can probably get more information from those folks, and then we'll figure out where to go from there. Besides, I have an old friend in Lafayette who can probably house Denny and me if we need a place to sleep at night. Let me see if I can get him on the phone now."

Using the number he had recorded in his cell phone, Glen calls his old friend, Dr. Frank Anders. A pilot for many, many years, Dr. Anders—a highly skilled and successful orthopedic surgeon—decided to lay aside his lucrative medical practice to pursue his life-long dream of being an airline pilot. Now flying for Frontier Airlines as the captain of an Airbus A320 passenger jet, he had also been at one time an FAA examiner—which is how Glen met him eighteen years ago.

Glen knows that his doctor friend has a three-bedroom home in Lafayette. He figures that his buddy might have at least a spare bed and a couch for him and Denny to sleep on during the relief operations. Unbeknownst to Glen, Dr. Anders had relocated to a condo in Denver, Colorado due to his airline career—but he still owns the house in Lafayette.

"Absolutely!" his old friend tells him. "I've got a lady that keeps the house for me down there, and I'll give you her number so that she can get you a key. She even cleans up the place and does laundry, so you guys won't have to worry about a thing."

"Oh, no. That's not necessary. Denny and I can do our own laundry. That's no problem," Glen insists.

"Listen, you guys are flying these relief missions and you're going to have enough on your plate. You guys just sleep and shower—whatever you need to do—and she'll take care of the linens and stuff and keep the place clean. Just get some rest while you're there and consider the place your home-away-from-home."

"Thanks Frank," Glen concludes. After signing off, he returns his cell phone back into his shirt pocket and reaffirms to Kenneth, "Well, that settles it. I'm not yet sure where we'll ultimately land and end up unloading all of these relief supplies. But I really believe that Lafayette is where the Lord is leading us to go first…"

With the aircraft loaded and fueled, Denny heads back to the office to find out what has developed. He arrives in time to hear, "…We are going to have to take a leap of faith." Hearing his copilot enter, Glen turns to look at Denny and says, "We're going to Lafayette."

Pastor George then asks, "Glen…is there anything else you need?"

Turning back toward his pastor, he replies, "Prayer. With all the spiritual darkness and voodoo down there, the thing we need more than anything is prayer to keep us safe and this operation flowing smoothly. Keep us covered in prayer and there is *absolutely nothing* the devil can do to stop us from helping these people."

Pastors George and Terri bow their heads and begin to pray earnestly, along with Kenneth, Chris Clem, and Dennis O'Brien, for the mission. As they do, Glen and Denny step out of the office to make ready for their departure.

So they all head out toward the plane. Melvin and Jeff have repositioned her again so she is once again pointing into the wind, beckoning the pilots to go. Candace meets them with a bag of food, "Here. You guys better eat something. It might be a long day."

A few minutes later, the ministry leaders emerge from Kenneth's office and join them at the aircraft. The crowd of EMIC volunteers and KCM staff has also assembled around the airplane. Additional prayer ascends heavenward for the Super DC-3's safety, and for that of her crew, and for their success in finding those in need.

As Glen and Denny climb into the Super DC-3, Glen sees the wall of bottled water cases and says, "Wow! Man, you guys did a great job," turning toward the now-tired loaders peering in through the cargo doors. They return the compliment with smiles.

The plane is prepped and loaded. Angel Flight 44 is about to head for Louisiana…and now the real adventure begins.

CHAPTER

6

The Flights Begin

The pilots seat themselves in the cockpit; Glen then tells Denny he will fill him in on the details of the mission once they get in the air. They run through the checklists, taxi out to the runway, and begin their first takeoff for Louisiana.

"Good job on the weight and balance," remarks Glen, as the trees on the far end of the runway disappear under the aircraft's nose. They are finally airborne for Lafayette.

They level off in cruise, and Glen proceeds to tell Denny some of what transpired in Kenneth's office. "We know people are hurting down there. We also know that Operation Blessing has people on-site already. However, communication is virtually nonexistent so we have no reliable way of coordinating with them. We are just going to have to go down there and find them. Our first priority will be to the partners, members, and friends of KCM.

"As you know, we got knocked out of Baton Rouge. Lafayette is the next biggest airport that puts us close to the disaster area. It's still open and has fuel. That means that it's likely other relief efforts will be using that facility as a base as well. I called our buddy, Dr. Frank. We can stay at his place, so we have that covered. We're going to Lafayette to get our plan together, and then we'll figure out some logistics while we are there.

"Buddy Shipp, a KCM partner, is supposed to be in Hammond, Louisiana with his feeding operation. We haven't been able to contact him so far, but we can try connecting with him over there. I guess we'll probably end up working out of Hammond."

As Denny takes it all in, he nods in affirmation and then asks, "Where are we going to park this big 'Super' in Lafayette?"

Glen replies, "I don't know."

Denny ponders that a moment, then he asks, "And you don't know who we are going to give all this stuff to, right?"

"That's right."

Denny has envisioned for several days that they would be joining a massive, coordinated relief effort. This picture is now beginning to fade...rapidly. What replaces it now is a feeling he would later share with Glen: "It was like taking off thinking you are going to be part of a huge flight formation, and when you get in the air and look around, you discover that you are the only airplane in the sky."

They continue to fly on towards Lafayette for a while, and then Denny quizzes him again. "Okay. We're going to go to Lafayette, find someone either affiliated with KCM or from Operation Blessing, and give them everything on the plane. Is that the plan?"

Glen nods his head, "Yes."

"Good, because for a while there, it was starting to look like you had no plan," Denny says light-heartedly.

They have fuel and lodging lined up; they have confidence in the airplane and in their own flying abilities, and tremendous faith in God. "Worse case scenario: we drop off the water and fly back to KCM. I can work with that," Denny consoles himself.

Heavenly Coordination

For six weeks, Glen is not sure where each step will lead. He is certain, however, that he has received direct "marching orders" from Heaven, and he will not draw back. We who are Bible-believing Christians call that "walking by faith and not by sight" (2 Corinthians 5:7). What seems strange to unbelievers and many professing Christians is *supposed* to be quite normal to the modern Spirit-filled believer:

> "...those who are led by the Spirit of God are sons of God."
> (Romans 8:14, NIV)

> "My sheep hear my voice, and I know them, and they follow me..."
> (John 10:27, KJV)

Glen Hyde has been spending the better part of a decade learning how to be attentive to the voice of his Good Shepherd. This is the key to Glen's walk of faith. As he embarks upon the great adventure that "Headquarters" has assigned to him, he has the assurance of knowing he is simply "following orders." Without two-way communication with God and an uncompromised obedience to the directives he has heard, the mission would never occur—much less be the phenomenal success it would eventually become.

To those of us who are former military, the "walk of faith" should actually seem normal. Every Marine, soldier, airman, seaman, (and husband) has heard something similar to, "Hey, the orders have come down. We're going to such and such a place." Then there begins the process of packing, staging, and embarkation. Meanwhile, people are often thinking, "Why in the world are we going over there?"

Generally, we Marines would not always know the big picture before we went. Nevertheless, we would follow orders and do what we were told. Likewise, the walk of faith is simply obeying God by following *His* orders, given by His Word and His Spirit.

Glen has learned through the Word of God, prayer, and sound biblical teaching, how to hear the voice of God for himself. Once he heard, "Get it ready," he did. When Katrina hit, he also knew his mission by the Spirit—in general, anyway. With forty years of aviation experience, including search and rescue operations, Glen has the knowledge base necessary to coordinate the operation on the fly. He also has an extremely well-qualified copilot assisting him, who also is willing to walk by faith. Therefore, Glen is heading toward Louisiana with the assurance that his every need shall continue to be supplied, and that the Commander-in-Chief of the Universe will guide his steps.

The reality everyone learns through Katrina is that when there is a natural disaster of such a magnitude, there are far more variables than anyone could have ever predicted. The government certainly proved it could not plan comprehensively for such a catastrophic event. Surely, they took some steps beforehand to prepare. However, once Katrina hit, total and utter chaos ensued.

Glen and Denny soon learn that the local, state, and federal governments are overwhelmed. There are people running everywhere with no rhyme or reason, just trying to survive. In many places, there is no law enforcement, and anarchy abounds. Even the hospitals are completely overrun with people. Essentially, it is just total calamity and confusion.

Yet, in the midst of it all, there is one group of people in position above the others to make a positive difference—Spirit-led Christian believers. While government agencies are still determining protocols and agency coordination, and filing forms, the people of God are moving forward with their mission to save and aid those impacted by the storm. God is coordinating their efforts, and miracles are taking place.

"You Can't Ground God"

They land in Lafayette and taxi to the ramp. Off to their left is a mini-fleet of helicopters coming and going, with more parking on the flight line as they taxi in. Denny begins to think that he was too hasty in dismissing his vision of a large relief effort.

The two park the DC3-S on the flight line. After they lock up the aircraft, Glen tells Denny, "Let's go check in and find out who's flying the emergency relief work around here. Let's see if there's anywhere in particular we need to go. Otherwise, I think we're going to probably fly into Hammond and start taking supplies into there."

The pilots start walking over to one of the two Lafayette airport FBOs (Fixed Base Operator—where the airport activities are coordinated, and where one usually buys fuel) to find out who is in charge of emergency relief efforts out of Lafayette, and to secure logistical arrangements. Glen acknowledges the extensive helicopter traffic as they head toward the FBO.

Immediately, a FEMA agent appears, approaches them, and states, "Just so you guys know, there's a FEMA shut-down going on right now. There's no flying authorized."

The Federal Emergency Management Agency (FEMA) became embroiled in the political wrangling that emerged even before the hurricane struck its blow. State and local officials, along with the various federal agencies, are still arguing about command and control issues, jurisdiction—and, of course, paperwork. Meanwhile, people are dying across the Gulf Coast devastation areas. Now, FEMA has every contracted aviator grounded while the government agency figures out the bureaucratic mess.

In reaction to the man's sudden declaration, Glen and Denny both look at each other. Turning back to the man, Glen then asks, "What are you talking about? The federal stuff?"

He says, "Yeah. If you guys fly, you're not going to get paid. You'll be considered in violation of your FEMA contract if you don't obey the grounding order."

Baffled somewhat by the contrast between the man's statement and the helicopters they see coming and going, Glen then asks, "What about *those*?"

The man answers, "Those are privately funded, mostly oil platform and cell site repair. There are also a limited number of controlled FEMA flights in and out of New Orleans. But everyone else is grounded, so you guys better not fly."

Chuckling, Glen informs him, "Well, thanks for the update. But this airplane isn't being paid for by FEMA, so your order doesn't apply to us anyway."

The man's eyes pop open wide. He says, "That DC-3? It's not a FEMA airplane?" He just cannot imagine a large transport aircraft like that operating without federal money. Even the owners of small airplanes are chaining themselves to the government agency as they seek out lucrative contracts for relief operations. Getting paid to fly an airplane is, for most, a pilot's dream. Nevertheless, the moment these unsuspecting pilots sign on, they are "grounded until further notice."

However, with even the operators of small airplanes signing up with FEMA, the agent reasons aloud, "Surely, an airplane so large would be on a FEMA contract!"

Smiling, Glen fills him in…

"No. That Super DC-3 is actually sponsored by the Body of Christ. Kenneth Copeland Ministries and Eagle Mountain International Church are sponsoring it." As the befuddled man's jaw drops open, Denny leaves the two there to finish their little talk. The man blinks a few times as Glen continues, "You can't ground God. This airplane is going to march on. Once we determine where we are needed most, *we are going to go*."

The man replies, "Oh really? Wow, that's going to be expensive!"

"It is. But I furnished the airplane, Air BP has pitched in money for fuel, and EMIC and Kenneth Copeland Ministries invested quite a bit of money for food and water. People need us—and we're going to press on."

Still smiling, Glen leaves the FEMA agent to ponder it all. Denny hears Glen chuckling behind him as they both head toward one of the airport's FBO's.

Glen needs to arrange for a fuel truck to service the DC3-S. He also needs to investigate where the command center is for the Katrina relief effort, and work out some form of logistics. However, the promised Air BP credit has not yet been applied to Glen's account. Consequently, the fuel issue is looking to be an interesting situation to resolve.

CHAPTER 7

Making It Happen

Saturday, September 3rd, 2005: *10:15 a.m.*

There are two things that Denny already knows about Glen; that he truly cares for people and would do anything he could to help them in a time of need. The two pilots have known each other for years—initially by reputation through the aviation community, and most recently since Denny is a hangar owner at Glen's Northwest Regional Airport.

However, Captain Ghiringhelli is now learning a few *new* things about his old buddy. First, he learns that Glen has enough courage to step out by faith into the unknown and "walk on water" to wherever Jesus has indicated he should go. Second, any obstacle that tries to get in his way during this journey of faith is not going to oppose him for long. Glen is either going to go around it, over it, or *through it*—but nonetheless, he will keep moving forward toward his Commander's stated objective.

Amused by the exchange he just witnessed between the FEMA agent and Glen, Denny ponders these things a moment as they continue toward one of the airport's FBOs.

Fuel "On Account"

They then step into Paul Fournet Air Service (PFAS) at Lafayette Airport—a landmark at this airstrip for over fifty years. Its founder, Paul Fournet, had passed

43

away. In his stead, his son, Richard Fournet is now running the company and happens to be working the counter as they walk in.

Glen starts off, "Hello, my name is Glen Hyde," and sticks his hand out to the man.

Richard kindly receives the handshake, "Glad to meet you two. I'm Richard Fournet. What can I do for you today?"

"Well, my buddy and I are here as a part of a private operation to fly in Katrina relief supplies using my plane. We're working with two ministries to help these people: Kenneth Copeland Ministries and Eagle Mountain International Church. We have a Douglas Super DC-3 on the flight line full of water and food, and we are looking to set up logistics here in Lafayette as a stopping point from Fort Worth as we head into Hammond with supplies. Right now I need to find a staging area to park and service my DC-3, and I'm going to need to buy fuel on account."

Richard says to Glen, "Oh, you have an account with us?"

"No..." Glen replies, "...on account of that I don't have any money..."

While Richard bats his eyes in wonderment, Glen quickly adds, "...but, you *will* get paid."

Understandably cautious, Richard replies, "Okay. Who's going to be paying for it?"

"Eventually, Air BP. They're donating $35,000 toward the fuel costs of this operation."

He says, "Well, we're not an Air BP dealer..."

Glen quickly responds, "I know you're not. But if you can work out of Multiserve, or something similar, we will pay you when they finish transferring the money over into my FBO's account. We're an Air BP dealer at my airport, Northwest Regional. We haven't worked out all the logistics yet because this disaster just happened. But I've got a go-ahead from the President of Air BP himself for the $35,000 they are donating to help with this operation. Now I just need to work out something with you, and we'll get you paid whenever we can work out a transfer of those funds."

Richard thinks a moment and asks, "Okay. So, you're going to pay me when you can?"

"Yes."

Richard agrees. The favor of God is working on their behalf, and the man gives them "fuel on account"—on account of they did not have any money. (Of course, later, when the mission flights were all over, Northwest Regional Airport and the KCM flight department were able to use the Multiserve fuel credit card system to pay the bill off with the generous donation Air BP had contributed.)

Glen later reflects, "Here was a guy who let us park on his ramp…he put up with us coming in and out of his terminal building all the time, asking for tools and other things. He gave us all this support and just told us, 'Pay us when you can.' The can-do attitude of all the people who helped us with the mission was phenomenal…and Richard Fournet of Paul Fournet Air Service there in Lafayette was truly a God send. There are people alive today because of that man's willingness to work with us."

Richard Fournet sends a fuel truck over to the Super Gooney to fill its tanks with 100 octane low-lead (100LL). Denny begins fueling for the next flight—wherever that might be.

While working out the other arrangements with PFAS, Glen and Denny are also informed of where the emergency relief efforts are being coordinated at the airport. So, after refueling, they head over there to investigate things.

A Change in Plans

Glen receives a call from Buddy Shipp of American Samaritan on their way over to the emergency briefing area. Buddy's ministry has been working in Hammond, Louisiana to feed relief workers involved in the Katrina effort—mostly military, police, and emergency medical workers who volunteered from around the country. Glen's original plan is to deliver relief supplies to Hammond, given the fact that Buddy Shipp—also a KCM partner and friend to the ministry—is working his barbeque pits and portable kitchens in the area. However, when Glen answers the phone, Buddy informs him, "You're not coming to Hammond. They've just declared Martial Law, and the Army is taking it over."

After thanking him for the update, Glen signs off and hangs up the phone. He quietly prays as he continues toward the emergency briefing area, "First Baton Rouge…and now Hammond. Lord, I guess you didn't want me to go there either. Thank you for steering me…but, now where do you want me to go?"

The two pilots head to the other large FBO on the field, Acadian Air Ambulance (AAA). On the way, Glen comments, "Well, with Baton Rouge out and Hammond out, we're going to have to find another place to go. If the military keeps this up, there won't be any places left we *can* go."

AAA is bustling with activity. Outside, helicopters are landing and departing, and trucks are offloading supplies into a large hangar. Inside, pilots and crewmembers are coming and going. There are tables against the wall laden with food and beverages, and there is even a sign that says, "CLEAN UNDERWEAR AND SOX," with an arrow pointing down the hall. "Wow! These guys thought of everything," Denny comments with a grin.

They notice an office at the other end of the hall. Covering the walls of the hallway leading to the office are maps of the surrounding area, showing the various landing sites.

While Denny examines some of the charts in the hallway, Glen continues into the office to look at an area chart to find a suitable airport that is in the Katrina-affected area. It needs to be large enough to accommodate the DC3-S—but *not* under the control of the military. A few minutes later, Denny also walks in.

"Slidell—Slidell looks to be right in the path of where Katrina made landfall," Glen remarks to Denny as he points to the map. "The runway looks to be long enough and doesn't appear to be controlled by the military. It will certainly be a challenging landing, but we can do it."

To be sure that they have found a viable solution, the two pilots look around the room at the other charts that depict which landing areas are closed. No chart indicates that Slidell has been rendered inoperable by the storm or taken over by the military. People are still coming and going. Consequently, Glen decides to verify their choice once more. "Anybody know the status of Slidell?" he hollers out into the bustling room.

Need a Lift?

Somebody's ears perk up in the briefing area and the person replies, "Who said 'Slidell'? Who's doing airlift to Slidell?"

Curiously, Glen answers, "Well, I said 'Slidell.'"

The man announces, "The four guys standing outside need to go to Slidell right away. They're with a pharmaceutical company, and they've got a few van loads of emergency medical supplies they are trying to get there."

Denny and Glen look at each other, and Denny suggests, "Let's go talk to them and see what they say."

They walk out of the briefing area and find the men standing outside of the building. The four look dejected and defeated. Glen pipes up, "Who needs to go to Slidell?"

Surprised, they turn around, "We do!"

"I hear you guys need to get some medical supplies over to there," Glen announces.

They reply, "Yeah, we're with McKesson Pharmaceutical, and we've been told that they already have about 700 people at that little hospital down there in Slidell, and the numbers just keep going up. So they've already run out of supplies, the roads are closed—and there is no fuel down there."

The two pilots listen intently as another one of the men continues, "Because the situation is so bad, the truck drivers won't drive down there. They've heard about the vandalism, and the closed roads, and the lack of fuel. They've told us that they're going to wait until it all settles down between here and there before they're even willing to go…and all the pilots we talked to have already signed FEMA contracts. They won't fly because they're afraid that they'll lose their FEMA money.

"But the hospital's supplies are down to just plain aspirin. They're out of bandages and antibiotics… they can't even prep the operating room. These doctors are even close to having to do some amputations without anesthesia! It's like they've gone back in time to the Civil War era or something. There are people down there that are going to be in bad shape—and probably won't make it through the night—if they don't get some supplies."

It is no wonder that these guys felt dejected before Glen and Denny first approached them. Nevertheless, hope has arrived…

Glen smiles real big and says, "Well, buddy, if you'll walk right around this big old hangar here, you'll see a Super DC-3 parked on the flight line. How many supplies do you need to ship down there?"

One of them quickly responds, "We've got four vans filled with supplies, but we don't have to ship the entire load. We *will* need to ship about three or four thousand pounds of critical supplies there immediately, though." A glimmer of hope seems to brighten their faces just a little.

Glen announces, "Well, you're in good shape! I've got 10,000 pounds of food and water on there now. We'll download some of that and put some of your supplies on there in their place, and we'll just fly it in!"

Another asks, "When do you want to do that?"

Glen answers, "Now."

Shocked, the man replies, "Now?!"

"Now," Glen insists. He then explains, "When does someone need you? They need you when they need you—and that means *now*. They don't ever say, 'I'll need you in three days for an emergency, can you help me out?' No. They need you when they *need* you—it is never expected. Those people at that hospital need us, and they need us right now. We just came in from Texas to help people like them, and that's exactly what this airplane is for."

The McKesson pharmaceutical men are overwhelmed. One of them comments, "Well, we don't know how we can pay you…"

Glen interrupts him by saying, "Don't worry about that. I've got gas covered. I've got food and water provided by my church, Eagle Mountain International Church, and by Kenneth Copeland Ministries. We've got all that—and *you've* got the pharmaceuticals. We'll figure out how we'll pay for it later. If you could just try to help me cover some of the expenses and fuel, I'll be happy. And if you can't do that, don't worry about it. People are in pain, let's just get them some relief."

The four men are stunned by the extreme generosity. Denny later comments, "Their jaws seemed to hit the floor." After all the excuses and rejection that they have heard from every truck driver and pilot they talked to, these four guys can hardly believe this sudden blessing.

They follow Glen and Denny around the building and their mouths drop open yet again when they see that big plane sitting there waiting. The huge Super DC-3 almost seems to be saying, "I'm the plane you guys have been waiting for—let's get started!" Immediately, the six of them start mapping out logistics.

Speedy Delivery

As one of the McKesson reps is about to leave and have the supplies brought around to the airplane, Glen says to the four, "You call that hospital and let them know we're coming. Let's get some phone conversations going back and forth with them to make sure someone can meet us at the airport to get the supplies. We also need to exchange cell phone numbers with them—and you guys—so that Denny and I can coordinate with everyone. I hear that cell coverage is very marginal down there, and landlines are in a shambles, too. Communications may be horrible overall, but we'll have to do what we can with what we've got."

The pharmaceutical reps all agree. One of the men is John Brannan, the McKesson Health System Account Manager for Louisiana. He picks up his cell phone and calls the head nurse at the hospital. Almost miraculously, the phone begins to ring. What is even more surprising is that she actually answers!

"We've worked out transportation and some of the medical supplies are coming there tonight, but you'll have to send someone to pick them up."

"Oh, that's great! Where and when are you coming?" she asks.

"The Slidell airport. We've found a guy with a big DC-3 airplane who is going to fly them in for us, along with some food and water. He said he'll even be there before dark tonight…"

The nurse does not listen to another word or reply. She immediately drops the phone away from her ear and bellows out, "Prep the operating room! Medical supplies are going to be here within two hours!" John can hear the people in the hospital start clapping and cheering.

Many of them had prayed for a miracle…and the miracle was now on its way.

CHAPTER 8

Medical Relief Arrives

Saturday, September 3rd, 2005: *Approximately 6:00 p.m.*

Glen and Denny head back to the plane. They are both looking at the sun as they walk, calculating just how much daylight they have remaining. John Brannan arrives with a borrowed pickup and the other guys bring over their vans. The medical supplies are more bulky than heavy, so they decide that the removal of the support equipment will be sufficient to compensate for the additional weight. John backs up the pickup to the cargo doors and the equipment is soon offloaded. Next, they bring the vans into position and their contents are stacked into the Gooney Bird. Once the load is secure, Glen and Denny climb into the cockpit and prepare for the flight to Slidell.

With a total time of less than an hour, the plane is reloaded and airborne. In less than forty-five minutes, they will be landing in Slidell, Louisiana at about 7:40 p.m.—just before nightfall. The flight over to Slidell is uneventful. However, as they descend to a lower altitude in advance of their landing, they get their first glimpse of what Katrina has done to the people they have come to help.

Hiroshima

Denny reflects, "Since Glen was the most experienced with his plane and I was working as copilot, he had the job of maneuvering the Super DC-3 and landing it. He simply flew the kind of approach you would make in an airplane of that capability. He was making it do what he knew that it could do. The main thing about coming into Slidell, though, was just the sheer devastation we saw around there.

"Trees were knocked over, snapped in half. You could see a progressive pattern created by the spiraling winds of the hurricane…like a wave. There were trees that were pushed over, trees that were completely uprooted, trees that were snapped off, trees shoved through people's houses. There were houses completely blown apart—you could see the strewn debris from the airplane very well at that altitude. There were cars and boats in people's yards…and even inside what used to be houses.

"There was an area down to the south of Slidell over the water [Lake Pontchartrain] that looked like it was covered with pilings. We kept thinking they had been fishing piers blown away by the storm. About the second or third night when we were staying at Dr. Frank Anders' house in Lafayette, watching the news, there was a woman on there speaking from Slidell. She had been taped earlier that day. She was standing on this bridge…in shock…as she was talking about the area behind her—which was the same area with those pilings sticking up. As we watched, she explained that those were actually footings for houses that had been there before the storm. These houses had been built on stilts over the water along the shoreline—now they were gone. As I listened, it occurred to me that, not only were the houses gone, but the *wreckage* was gone too. There was no debris. Where in the world did all the debris go?"

The bridge the woman had been standing on during the interview Denny described was the I-10 Bridge that connects New Orleans to Slidell. The area of devastation where Denny and Glen saw only "pilings" sticking up is the area called "North Shore." Prior to the storm, this area was where the "high-end" homes (by Slidell's modest standards) were built, on and around the waterfront of the lake. Now, the waterfront homes are all but gone, and the rest of the area's buildings have been severely damaged—many beyond repair.

Slidell was near the epicenter of the hurricane. Katrina's eye traveled directly across Picayune, Mississippi—less than twenty miles east of Slidell, before turning eastward towards Biloxi and Gulfport in Mississippi. The proximity that Slidell had to the storm's eye caused it to bear the full force of the storm's winds. Furthermore, the hurricane did some very unexpected things, none of which had been predicted by either meteorologists or local officials.

Many people know that New Orleans is vulnerable to the sea, being that much of the city is below sea level and protected by levies. However, the residents of Slidell thought themselves safe because of their town's being situated at a higher elevation. Well-above sea level, they appeared "shielded" by New Orleans to the south. One man later commented, "We figured New Orleans might get blown off the map, but we thought we were pretty safe up here on higher ground."

The majority of flooding in New Orleans was originally expected to come from possible breeches in the levies on the Gulf of Mexico. However, it was actually the levies on Lake Pontchartrain that became the source of flooding. It was also unexpected that the storm surge wave would sweep in all the way from the Gulf, crossing the lake, and then *obliterate* Slidell's northeastern shore.

Considering the evidence of the damage and other effects of the wave, some have estimated that it was about thirty-five feet high at its peak when it came ashore. It cleared those waterfront houses right off of their footings, and carried the debris inland. The surge was so massive that it traveled several miles and flooded even downtown Slidell. Four miles or so inland, the downtown government buildings, businesses, and homes are still showing the evidence of waterline marks six to eight feet above the street level.

Reflecting back on what he had seen, Glen later adds, "It was like looking at Hiroshima after it had been hit by the Atomic Bomb. Trees and debris were scattered everywhere, especially the closer you got to the lake. Then we saw a bunch of sailboats in a marina stacked on top of each other. It looked about sixty or more feet in the air! It seemed like there were about twenty of them."

Pastor Larry Roques later shares, "The wave of water that came inland took the cars at several car dealers and shoved them all up against the buildings. It piled them all up there on top of each other. At one place, there were cars stacked up probably forty feet in the air."

Denny then adds, "There were house trailers that were upended. They were on their sides, on their end, or upside down. The devastation we could see from the air as we came in that first time was enormous!

"Thankfully, as we came into the Slidell airport we found that people had cleared the runway. There was still debris on the taxiways, but the runway itself was clear. From the air, and after we landed, we could see that there were airplanes turned upside down and thrown around. There was a hangar with the roof ripped off, and inside there was a small Cessna airplane cut in half—inside the hangar! There was another airplane sticking straight up and down, stuck into the hangar like a dart.

"The lights weren't working on the runway, and that first time we landed we were going in there right at dusk. Glen turned on the powerful landing lights and illuminated the runway. That gave us just enough extra light to see what we were doing as we landed. But if it had been just ten or twenty minutes later, we would have had to fly back to Lafayette. It would have been just too dangerous to try and land in the dark with completely unknown runway conditions, a full load, and no runway lights."

Medical Supply Miracles

Shocked as they are at the immense wreckage they are witnessing from the

51

air, there is certainly no time for sightseeing. These two experienced airmen know that they do not have much time to get the big bird down on the runway before dark. Their professional training immediately takes over and they begin landing procedures. On final approach, Glen gives the command and Denny lowers the flaps. They touch down, and Glen immediately applies the brakes to slow the aircraft. With only inches to spare, they bring the heavy aircraft to a stop just before the 4,000-foot strip runs out of pavement.

They taxi over to what is left of the flight line, shut down the engines, and open the cargo doors. Some very jubilant local volunteers and staff from the hospital greet them. With the help of Glen and Denny, they quickly unload everything onto flatbed trailers and pickup trucks, and then rush off to deliver it all. The hospital is able to begin operating on patients by 8:30 that night. The added food and water also help to strengthen both the patients and staff within that facility.

Concerning the urgency of this "medical supply miracle," Glen later comments, "Without those supplies, there were many people down there who would not have lived through the night. There was even one guy who needed surgery on his leg, but they could not perform it because they did not have any anesthesia.

"They had babies going into insulin shock. I did not know this, but babies can be born insulin dependent. When they start shaking and going into shock, they usually last twelve to thirty-six hours. Two or three of the babies had already been in twenty-four-hour shock—so they were going to die at any time without their insulin. I did not know that could happen. I did not know that insulin was that important...but it is.

"So we landed there at 7:40 p.m. They had an estimated 10:00 p.m. cut-off for getting medical supplies to some of them, or else certain people would be dead by midnight. They rushed the stuff over to the hospitals and they saved them all—including the babies.

"That little hospital, which only had about 172 beds, suddenly found themselves with about 700 people within forty-eight hours. I heard that three days later there were about 2,700 people in there.

"I also found out that one of the reasons the hospital ran out of supplies so quickly was that their inventory was stored in the hospital's basement. During the hurricane, the storage had turned into a swamp. The wave of water that ripped through the area had knocked out the basement windows and filled it with water. Then some alligators, washed inland by the wave, came in—along with snakes. So, the staff couldn't go into the basement. They did not have any light down there because the basement water prevented them from turning on any power. They also had no way of dealing with the alligators and snakes while they picked through the boxes to see what was still usable.

"I quickly realized that if we didn't keep delivering to the people in Slidell the medical supplies they needed, there would be a lot more people that wouldn't make it. Some were injured with compound fractures and such, which is normally not that big of a surgical emergency. But if you're in a remote area and nobody can get to you—and you're bleeding—and the doctors don't have any medicines or tools to help you with…then you're in *serious* trouble.

"I never dreamed that medical supplies would ever be a higher priority than food and water. But think about it: These were people who were dying right then. In a situation like that, you've got to prioritize people based on their condition—and the ones that need blood transfusions need it immediately. People can last a lot longer without food and water in a situation like that, than they can without medical treatment.

"So, over the next two weeks we often flew in medical supplies from Grand Prairie, Texas where McKesson Pharmaceutical would load us from their distribution center in Arlington. We had boxes of syringes stacked up to the ceiling. We must have flown in a 'million' of them—it seemed enough to inoculate the entire southern part of Louisiana. But given that there were ninety thousand square miles of disaster—the largest natural disaster to ever hit the North American continent—they needed a lot down there."

They certainly needed a lot—and the Lord Jesus certainly provided.

Very quickly, the little hospital in Slidell became the *distribution source* for many of the other hospitals in the region, since they were the only ones receiving supply. Consequently, if God had not connected McKesson Pharmaceutical with Glen, Denny, and that Super DC-3 just a few days before—thousands would have died in hospitals all over that area from lack of treatment.

Taking Off

By now, the aircraft has been unloaded, and the Slidell volunteers and hospital staff have rushed off to deliver the precious cargo. Glen and Denny now decide that they are probably not in a good place to camp out for the night. They have heard unconfirmed reports about the lawlessness and lack of police to quell the chaos in various areas of Louisiana—especially in New Orleans. Consequently, the two pilots are now not any more confident in what the conditions might be here in Slidell. Since Glen had already arranged for a safe place for them to stay in Lafayette at Dr. Frank Anders' house, they determine to relocate there.

The only issue is the fact that they *first* have to get safely back to the Lafayette airport. Before that, they have to take off from this airport at night. With no lights on the runway, the only illumination they have for takeoff is coming from the DC-3's powerful floodlights.

At 8:50 p.m., with darkness having overtaken them, the two taxi the aircraft out onto the runway. Despite the serious conditions, both are experienced pilots. Consequently, they think it much safer to take off from an unlit runway at night than to possibly find themselves having to defend the airplane from looters, vandals…or worse.

Powering up the 1475-horsepower twin Wright engines, they light up the airstrip with the headlamps, and embark down the dark runway as they accelerate to takeoff speed. Glen allows Bernoulli's Law to do its wonders as it creates lift over the accelerating Super DC-3's wings. He then gently pulls back on the yoke of the now-empty aircraft and begins his ascent to clear the tree line they now see just beyond the runway.

However, after the floodlight's beams rise above the tree line, the "nothingness" of the dark sky beyond absorbs their brilliance completely. It is now as if the lights are not even on. Thus, the lack of runway lights is not the only danger facing a nighttime departure.

"It reminded me of nighttime takeoffs from aircraft carriers in the Marine Corps," Glen later comments. "You just shoot off into pitch blackness with nothing to see below or above you. There were absolutely no lights visible in Slidell as we took off at night. There were not even any across Lake Pontchartrain in New Orleans. The only things you could see on the horizon were the lights faintly shining from the distant offshore oilrigs. They had their own power systems to keep them going.

"Other than that, it was just sheer 'nothingness' out there. Denny and I had the DC-3's instruments, of course. However, the problem was that if anything went wrong after takeoff, requiring us to put the aircraft down, we would not have seen any lights on the ground to identify an emergency landing site. We would not have known if we were landing in water…or even in the middle of trees!

"Also, there were two large television towers marked on our aeronautical charts, but we had to estimate where they were and hope we flew beyond them. With all the power out in the area, you could only see them in the daylight. Coming in that first time, I had said to Denny, 'Take note of those towers over there. We'll need to make sure we don't find them accidentally in the dark tonight!' So, each time we took off at night we took an educated guess…and made sure we flew a little farther south than we thought we needed to, just to be sure."

Glen and Denny safely return to Lafayette that night and stay at Dr. Frank Anders' house. The warm showers, hot meal at a local restaurant, and air conditioning to sleep in, are a huge contrast to the disaster zone they have just left in Slidell.

"Denny," Glen comments over dinner, "those people have lost nearly everything they have. Many of them lost their lives, or have lost family and friends…they don't have nice clean beds to sleep in. And we've got air conditioning! They're not eating a nice meal right now. Listen, if you ever hear me whine about anything, take a baseball bat to my legs and drop me to my knees. That's where I belong [in prayer]. After seeing what we saw today, I don't have anything in the world to gripe about—ever again."

Sunday, September 4th, 2005

At 7:45 a.m. the next day, Glen and Denny return directly to Copeland Field at KCM with a new game plan of flying cargo directly into Slidell. With the agreement of the entire Angel Flight 44 team, they begin doing so that same morning. This time, the two pilots fly the Super Gooney into Slidell non stop, and land there early that afternoon.

Beyond the intrigue of aeronautical mission itself, however, Glen and Denny wonder whom they will encounter there next…

CHAPTER 9

Servants' Hearts

Sunday, September 4th, 2005: *1:30 p.m.*

On this second trip into Slidell, it is even more evident what Katrina has done to the little town. The high sun allows a clearer view than the one they experienced at dusk the day before.

Loaded from nose to tail with another precious load of food and water, the Super DC-3 once again descends into the little airport to discover appreciative local volunteers ready to assist. In fact, one of the most disarming characteristics of the people affected by the storm is their servant-like attitude. Despite the chaos surrounding them and the upheavals their own lives had sustained, they continuously look for ways to bless their fellow man.

Outrunning Falling Trees

On this second day, the pilots meet a retired gentleman who ventures to the airport to see what he can do to help. When Glen and Denny taxi over and power off the aircraft, he comes up and introduces himself with a big smile and a hearty sense of humor.

"Good to meet you, sir," Glen gladly expresses. "Were you here when Katrina hit? How'd you make out?"

"Yeah, I was here. I had been living by myself before the storm. I was in my house when Katrina hit. I've rode out a bunch of these 'blows' before, but I should have left on this one. I surely regretted staying."

"Really?" Glen replies, interested to hear the man's story.

"Yeah, my house was surrounded by trees that were about 100-feet tall—great big ones. That wind got so darned strong, they started to break. When they broke, they broke about fifteen feet in the air with a loud pop that sounded like a gunshot. Then they would hinge over and come down with a crashing blow into my house.

"The first one came down during the night as the storm was comin' in to shore. It smashed across my garage and took out one of my cars while I was still in bed. Man, you can't sleep with 100 mile-per-hour winds coming through and cracking trees around you! They all explode! Beside the highway, you could hear the explosion of other trees popping all around—which was really making me nervous. But when that first one came crashing down into the garage, I just jumped right out of bed.

"Then, I heard another one popping next to my house, and I looked out the window and saw it was heading for the bedroom. So I ran out into the living room, just in time for it to crush the bedroom. Then I heard another one pop that was headed for the living room. I thought, 'I'd better figure out a way to get under that tree that's already crashed,' and I ran into the kitchen. Right then that last tree I heard came crashing down into the living room. Now three trees were in my house, the roof was exposed, and rain and wind started coming through the place. I couldn't get out of my kitchen through the garage because the wall was crushed. And that's where I spent that whole night and the next day until the storm blew past—under that tree in my kitchen with the rain and wind howlin' through my walls and roof."

Then he holds out his hands with a grin and says, "But look here. I got all my body parts! I'm alive and healthy!"

Then Glen says, "Yeah, that's the important part! I'm glad you made it through! Man, what a story. But I'm sorry to hear you lost your home. I guess, the government will probably come in and give you a loan to help you out with fixing your house or something."

He replies, "Hey, I don't need no stinking loan! I'm 67 years old. I'm retired. My house was paid for. I've got $1400 per month coming in. It's not a big retirement…but I was out of debt and had money in savings. I don't want no stinking thirty year loan—even if it was *interest-free*. Even if the payments were only three to four hundred dollars a month, I can't afford that kind of debt.

"But that's okay. I'll rebuild. I'll go down to Home Depot or wherever down here and get some hammers and nails and put a tarp on the roof, and start working my way through it. In two or three years, it will all be over—*and I ain't gonna owe anybody a dime.*"

Keeping Busy

Glen is impressed with the man's spunk and conviction. Nevertheless, with a house to rebuild and trees to cut off his roof, Glen starts to wonder why the spry fellow is out at the airport when he has a mountain of work to do at home. "Well, what are you doing out here?" he asks.

The man answers, "Well, everything is still closed; there's no power or anything, so there's not much for me to do yet back at my house. So to keep my sanity, I figured I'd come out here and see what I can do for everybody else here at the airport—to help load and unload planes, fix hangar stuff, and just stay busy. So, what can I do for you, Mr. Hyde? How can I help you out?"

Glen is taken aback. "Whoa! Time out!" he blurts out, making a "T" signal with his hands. "You're the one who lost your house and made it through the hurricane with just the clothes on your back…and you're asking what *you* can do to help *me*? Sir, I'm out here to help you!"

The gentleman stares back just a moment, and then frankly states, "Mr. Hyde, there's a whole lot of people who did not come out of this storm as good as I did. So, if you're bringing in supplies to help these folks out, the least I can do is help you to do it."

"I commend you for your attitude. God bless you. We do need some help unloading this 10,000 pounds of cargo," Glen responds, gesturing back towards the airplane.

The man asks, "Who is this food and water for?"

"Whoever you want to give it to that you think needs it," says Glen with a smile. "*You* give it to them. With a heart and attitude like yours, buddy, you just press on." The man helped unload the airplane that day. (Moreover, he would also lend a hand in several more of the relief deliveries thereafter.)

Everything

When the plane is unloaded, Glen asks the man, "What do you all need here? What kind of things do we need to bring when we come back?"

The man answers, "Everything."

Surprised, Glen blinks his eyes a moment and then responds, "Everything?"

The gentleman replies assertively, "*Everything*. We need food, water, medical supplies, toilet paper—anything and everything. Imagine walking out of your house with nothing but the shirt on your back, and you turn around and thirty minutes later you see that your house and all your worldly possessions are gone, just like that!" snapping his fingers.

Glen solemnly responds, "Yeah. That would be hard to imagine. I can see your point."

A few minutes later, as Glen is preparing to leave, the man walks up to him again to make a request. "Just make me one promise."

"What's that?"

"Just don't quit coming. Please keep coming back. That is the biggest airplane that can get into this airport. Nothing else of any size can get in here. This runway is only about 4,000 feet long. So please, just don't quit coming."

The Super DC-3 is the only aircraft ever manufactured in that size-class capable of landing with such a large load on a 4,000-foot airstrip. This man apparently knows it, and he cannot help but ask, "Please don't stop coming!" What's more, he would not be the only one who would make this same request.

"We're coming back," Glen reassures him. "We are hooked up with three of the best ministries in the world—Kenneth Copeland Ministries, Eagle Mountain International Church, and Operation Blessing. They and their partners are supplying us, and Air BP is keeping us fueled. Listen, God is the One Who sent us here to help you all. Since He is the One Who told us, 'Go!' we are not going to stop coming until the roads are open again."

Lafayette Layover

By this time, it is now dark and the pilots begin taxiing out. Because of the Louisiana heat and tremendous humidity, both Glen and Denny are now dripping with sweat. Taking off, they travel across Lake Pontchartrain, and head back to Lafayette. There, they clean up and catch a few hours' sleep. Sore and exhausted, they are "out" almost as soon as their bodies hit their beds.

Suddenly, in what seems like only a few minutes, the alarm goes off. It is the next day, and time to start it all over again. They had been asleep for six hours— but to them, it seems like a thirty-minute nap. (In fact, this same sensation would occur night after night throughout the entire Angel Flight 44 operation.)

Once they are out of bed, dressed, and fed, they head back out to the Lafayette airport this Monday morning. After prepping the plane for flight, they take off for Copeland Field. There, they load up again with much-needed supplies, and take off again for Slidell.

Over the course of Monday and Tuesday, they fly in a few more shipments to Slidell. They transport the last of the medical supplies and relief aid (left under guard in the hangar in Lafayette since Saturday) into the storm-torn community. The two pilots airlift additional medical supplies from McKesson, and distribute more water and foodstuffs.

The Routine

Their usual daily routine is for their first flight of the day from Lafayette to be directly back into Copeland Field. On some trips, however, they fly into Grand

Prairie to pick up pharmaceuticals and other supplies provided by McKesson, instead. Regardless where and what they load, however, the typical practice is to offload a morning shipment in Slidell, then return there again that late afternoon or early evening to drop off another load. They then head over to Lafayette for the night.

This routine continues seven days a week, for several weeks.

There are a couple of times that they perform "hot unloads" (with the engines still running). This occurs when nighttime is falling, or whenever they are in a hurry to get back to pick up some more pharmaceuticals or other urgent relief supplies. As soon as Glen and Denny land, they just drop the flaps and stop the plane at the flight line. Then Denny runs back to open the cargo doors, and starts hurling supplies out. Glen continues to man the controls in the cockpit. Meanwhile Denny, along with the 67-year-old tree-dodger, goes back and forth, up and down the fuselage of the airplane until they have completely unloaded it. Occasionally, another person or two is also there to help. Then Denny closes the cargo doors, and off they go.

"Don't Quit Coming"

Every time Glen and Denny land, grateful volunteers at the Slidell Airport greet them. All of them seem to have the same request, "Please, please, don't quit coming. Whatever you do, don't quit coming! Keep coming back. You're our only connection to the outside world—you and that airplane. We think everybody else has forgotten us!"

Some even ask, "As a matter of fact, would you bring us some newspapers?"

Perplexed, Glen answers, "Some newspapers?"

"Yeah. We want to know if we're in the news. We want to know if people even think anything of us."

"Yeah. You're in the news—not like New Orleans is in the news, but you are in the news," Glen informs them.

Word quickly spreads about the big airplane and its two pilots. Even the city officials come out to visit the Super DC-3…

CHAPTER 10

An Official Visit

After a few days, a Slidell city official comes out to the airport. He wants to meet the men who are providing his town with the only provisions from the outside world. Overwhelmed by the destruction, the loss of life, the apparent isolation—and the compassion of the men and supporters of Angel Flight 44—the gentleman seems to Glen to be on the verge of tears when he walks up to them.

After introducing himself to the two pilots, he thanks them profusely for flying these critical supplies into his broken community. He then asks, "Does the rest of the world know what has happened down here? We haven't seen anybody! Where's FEMA? Where's the National Guard? Where's the Red Cross...or somebody?! Does the rest of the world even know what Katrina did here?"

Glen replies, "Yes, sir. But the sad news is that all the TV coverage is on New Orleans."

The city official is shocked at Glen's answer. He stares at him in bewilderment for a moment and then declares, "There's a lot more to Louisiana besides New Orleans!"

"Yes, sir. There's ninety thousand square miles that is not getting any TV coverage. None."

The man's frustration is now clearly showing in his countenance. Somberly, he replies, "Mr. Hyde, there's dead people everywhere around here."

"Yes, sir. I know. I've seen them." Glen realizes that the gentleman is being overwhelmed with the enormity of the circumstances. He decides to encourage him by steering his focus another direction—to one considerably more constructive and hopeful. Consequently, Glen then adds, "But, what can we do for *you*, sir? We are here to help you in any way we can. What do you need *right now*?"

Like the tree-dodging gentleman and other locals before, the city official pleads, "Bring everything. Mostly food and water and medical supplies." Then he steps closer to say, "And do me a favor, Mr. Hyde; don't quit coming. *Just keep coming.*'

In response to the man's request, Glen solemnly replies, "I assure you, sir, until these roads open up and we can 'handshake' with the trucks, you can consider that your airplane," pointing purposefully to the DC3-S. "It is going to keep coming until the trucks are able to come in. Now, when the trucks start rolling in here, they can bring a lot more loads. That will be a lot more efficient— in both time *and* money."

The Slidell official looks at him slightly perplexed as if thinking, "What do you mean?"

Therefore, Glen continues, "Sir, the fuel prices right now are gouging the heck out of us. The last trip when I left Lafayette to head back to Fort Worth, we paid $5.15 per gallon. I put 400 gallons in, and so I spent well-over $2,000 *just to get home*. Air BP is helping us with the fuel expense, but still—that's a lot of money. Trucks can carry considerably more cargo over the same distance in those fifty-three-foot trailers, while using only about $200 worth of diesel to do it. So once they start coming in, we'll stop this phase of our operation to see if we can be more useful elsewhere."

"I understand," the gentleman responds. "Thank you for coming in here at such great expense to help us out down here. We certainly appreciate it…and we appreciate you…and the companies and ministries that are backing you. By the way, could I request something else from you?"

"Sure!"

"Could you bring us some newspapers? We want to see what the world is saying about us down here."

With all the requests for newspapers—and now even from the local government—Glen makes a call to his logistical support team back at KCM. They later fly in several bundles of newspapers to help satisfy the appetites of the information-starved folks in Slidell.

CHAPTER 11

Friends in High Places

Wednesday, September 7th, 2005: *6:30 a.m.*

After another short night of sleep in Lafayette, Glen and Denny are flying into Copeland Field this morning to fix some minor "squawks" in the DC-3, to connect with the KCM logistics team regarding the operation, and to load an entirely new cargo of relief supplies for transport.

On the way into Copeland Field, Glen starts contemplating all that has happened up to that point, and what it all might mean in the near future. "Denny," he starts. "I've been thinking about how the Army moved into Baton Rouge, and then Hammond right after that. It seems like the Feds are finally starting to get some traction in their game plan, and I'm thinking something like that might happen in Slidell eventually…maybe soon."

"If it does…" Denny remarks, "…it will likely shut *us* down. They've been stopping civilian flights in and out of those other airports."

"Yeah," Glen agrees. "I'm starting to think we might need to get some political support lined up—just in case something like that happens."

"What do you mean?"

"Well, I've got an old friend from my days in the Marine Corps, Bill 'Spider' Nyland. He had the rank of captain back then. He flew in the back seat of my Phantom when I was a first lieutenant fighter pilot out of Yuma [Arizona]. I think he stayed in the Corps, from what I recall. So I'm thinking I should look him up and see if I can get a little support for what we're doing here. He may have enough rank by now to be a blessing to us. He might even have a 'star' on his collar by now. If he does, he'll be a tremendous asset to us in this thing…and I think he will be willing to watch our backs because 'once a Marine, always a Marine.'"

"That sounds good. I think you should do that…just in case," Denny confirms.

Debriefed

After landing at Copeland Field, Glen is debriefed by KCM "chiefs" Chris Clem and Dennis O'Brien regarding the operation to date. Together, they then plan the next steps. They decide that Chris needs to travel with Glen and Denny on this next leg to get a better idea of what is happening in the disaster area.

Glen explains, "Guys, I've been reluctant to carry anybody else on the airplane up until now. Every time we add a passenger, we have to reduce our cargo by four or five hundred pounds—and those people need that stuff. Also, with the dead bodies lying around everywhere and the mess…well, I just thought it would be a good idea to let them clean up a bit before taking anyone else down there.

"But, now that we've flown a few missions and seen what's going on, I'm beginning to realize that this thing is just too big for us alone. We've got to get the word out to the partners of KCM about this thing. They need to see this on the TV and the website—and get involved."

"I agree," Chris responds. "I've wanted to go down there with you. I need to see what's going on there at 'ground zero' to better organize our logistics. This will help us get this operation as streamlined as we can to ensure we're getting everything flown over there that those people need—and as fast as we can get it there.

"I'm also thinking that I should grab one of the cameramen from the television department. Then we both can go with you and Denny on all the flights today. That will help me get a handle on this thing…and he can shoot some footage for us to use on the website and television broadcast. We can then take this operation up to the next level right away."

"Absolutely! Let's do that," Glen concurs. He then turns to Dennis and says to him, "Chris and I are going over to Kenneth's office to update him. Denny is back over at the DC-3 working with the guys to fix some squawks that developed. While all of this is going on, can you do me a favor?"

"Sure! What do you need?"

"I'm thinking that we're going to need some more political support for this operation in case the military moves into Slidell and tries to shut us out of that airport. Everyone I talk to down there keeps saying, 'please don't stop coming.' So I think we need to get some 'backup' in case someone tries to shut this operation down."

"Oh, sure. That sounds good. What can I do?" Dennis inquires.

"There was a man named Bill 'Spider' Nyland flying in the backseat of my F-4 years ago in the Marine Corps. I want you to write his name down and do some checking on the Internet to see what has become of him. He stayed in the Corps, and I'm thinking he might have at least a 'silver bird' on his collar—maybe a 'star' by now. Get some information about him and find me a contact number. Then I'll try to get in touch with him before we take off again today."

Writing down the information as Glen speaks, Dennis responds, "I'm on it!" and then departs.

Meanwhile, Chris and Glen go to meet with Kenneth Copeland. They give him a full account of the operation from the time it began that previous Saturday, until this moment. Chris also updates Kenneth concerning the launch of the new KCM "Partners-Helping-Partners" website; the outbound-phone-calls effort to contact partners in the Katrina disaster; and other undertakings related to the Angel Flight 44 relief operation. He then leaves the office to prepare for the trip to Slidell and secure a cameraman.

Kenneth and Glen then visit with each other a short while. As Glen shares an overview of the many miracles that had occurred to date, both small and great, Kenneth responds, "Glen, in nearly forty years of ministry I have never seen the Hand of God move so fast and so frequently, as we have in this operation. I have seen God do some powerful miracles, and His supernatural provision many times…sure. But to see them happen one after another, day in and day out, like we have been seeing during this relief effort…I have *never* seen anything like it."

Glen agrees. After they visit a few more minutes together, Glen heads back to the hangar to check on the DC-3, then drives home. There, he visits with Candace briefly and gives her an update as he grabs a shower and change of clothes. He then drives back to Copeland Field.

General Who?

Dennis O'Brien returns to the KCM airport just as the "Gooney Bird" is finishing being loaded. "Glen, I've found your friend."

Glen turns toward him and replies, "Good!"

"Only, he's doesn't have just one star—he's got four!" Dennis beams.

"What?! Man, what did he do to get four stars…walk on water?" Glen exclaims as he walks over and snatches the printout from Dennis. "Hey! He's the

Assistant Commandant of the Marine Corps! Man! He's the second guy from the top!" Glen cannot contain his astonishment. After staring in bewilderment at the printout a moment, he asks, "Did you find a contact number?"

"Yes," Dennis announces happily, pointing toward the bottom of the printout to a handwritten number. "And we called his office for you already. They said they asked him about you and he remembered you right away."

"Really? That's great! I'm going to call him right now," Glen says as he reaches for his cell phone.

He dials the number. A staff sergeant answers and tells Glen that the general is now in a meeting. Glen leaves a warm message for his old buddy, and hangs up his cell phone. He folds the paper Dennis had printed for him, and stuffs it into his shirt pocket. "Well, this might come in handy after all. Thanks Dennis!"

"Sure!" Dennis says with a chuckle.

About that time, Denny hollers over that the DC-3 is loaded, fueled, and ready to go. "Chris and a cameraman are already loaded aboard, and all we need for takeoff is the captain," he shouts with a big smile.

"Well, I guess it's time to go. Thanks again, Dennis, for doing this."

CHAPTER 12

An Encounter with the Marines

Wednesday, September 7th, 2005: *1:00 p.m.*

Loaded and fueled, Glen climbs in and finishes the preflight checklist with Denny. They start the engines and taxi out to the runway for takeoff from Copeland Field. Once they are airborne, Glen and Denny expound to Chris more details from the "front lines" of this operation to date. Chris is astounded yet further at the stories they share.

The Porters

From their initial flight a few days before, two volunteers have been tremendous assets to Glen and Denny on the Slidell side of the relief effort: Mr. and Mrs. Porter. The Porters have been helping to coordinate volunteers at the Slidell airport from Day One. They have often been there to help unload the DC-3 when it landed, and Mr. Porter even gathered up some helpers to repair the runway lights. The runway lights were operational by the second night of Angel Flight 44 flight operations into Slidell—a tremendous help for nighttime and dusk landings and takeoffs.

Mrs. Porter has even been manning the UNICOM (the airport radio frequency) to communicate with any incoming flights. This has been providing a primitive air traffic control benefit to incoming flights by giving them advanced notice of what is occurring on and around the runway.

A Change of Command

However, as they come into the Slidell airport today, Mrs. Porter is not manning the radio as before. An unfamiliar male voice comes over the UNICOM as they come in to land. During their approach, they see military helicopters in the aviation pattern and around the airfield. "Somebody's moving in down there," Glen comments.

After circling the airfield in its standard traffic pattern to investigate the runway below, they come in on final approach, touch down, and "smoke" the brakes to a full stop as usual. Upon landing, they taxi over to the awaiting volunteers and get a full view of the military contingent now moving in. The Marines have landed in Slidell and are taking over the airport.

They even spot the guys they heard on the UNICOM—two Marines sitting on top of a truck with a military radio. Glen speaks up, "Hey Denny," pointing his finger towards the truck. "There's air traffic control." They both chuckle.

After powering down the aircraft and opening the cargo doors, Glen sees a Marine Corps lieutenant heading over to talk with him. Climbing down, Glen introduces himself, "Well hello there, Lieutenant! I'm Glen Hyde. Looks like you Marines are moving in here or something."

"Yes, sir, Mr. Hyde. We are the advanced team sent ahead of the main contingent to establish our command center here at the airport as we take over this area under Martial Law. In a short while, we will have over 500 Marines at this location. Therefore, I must inform you that this might be the last time you'll be able to land your aircraft at this field."

"Now, wait a minute, Lieutenant," Glen calmly protests. "I served my country in the Marine Corps myself years ago as a pilot. As a former captain, I realize that you need to secure the field, but these people are dependent on that aircraft right there bringing in medical and relief supplies to this area. There would be many people dead already if I had not been flying these emergency supplies into here the last few days."

The young man is undeterred from his previously stated position. "That may be true, sir..." the lieutenant replies, "...but we're taking over this airfield now, and I simply have to inform you that you might have to move your operations somewhere else."

"Oh really?" Glen responds. Undaunted, he reaches up into his shirt pocket and pulls out the paper Dennis had printed for him just a few hours before. Unfolding it, he holds the page up to the young officer so that he can view the picture as he asks him, "Do you recognize this guy, Lieutenant?"

He asks, "Who's that?"

Glen answers, "The Assistant Commandant of the Marine Corps, Bill

'Spider' Nyland. This guy here in this picture flew back-seat in my F-4 Phantom thirty-one years ago in the United States Marine Corps while I was on active duty. Here's his personal phone number written down right here," pointing to the notes Dennis had handwritten on the paper.

"Now, let me be very clear on this matter: We've got to fly out of *this* airport with our operation. We've got to have emergency supplies flown in *here*. These people need some help *here*. We can't be booted out of this facility—there are *no more* airports to go to. So, if there's a problem with me being *here*…with me bringing in supplies to these hospitals and such, let's call my old friend Bill 'Spider' Nyland…"

Glen reaches out his hand with a grin and pats the young lieutenant on his "butter bars"—his golden second lieutenant collar insignias, and says, "…next in line to be *your* Commandant, lieutenant. Let's get my old buddy, Bill, on the phone right now and get this thing straightened out."

The lights abruptly "turn on" for the second lieutenant. His semi-obstinate demeanor quickly melts into a cooperative tone…and the "rank" of this civilian standing in front of him suddenly becomes apparent. He quickly replies, "Oh no, Captain Hyde, that won't be necessary, sir! You can fly into this facility if you need to, sir! Your DC-3 is welcome on this airfield, Captain Hyde!"

Glen laughs and waves his hands, "Wait a minute, Lieutenant. There's no Captain Hyde here—that was thirty years ago. I'm just a civilian now, but I really appreciate your new cooperative spirit!"

"Yes, sir, Captain…uh…Mr. Hyde. We're in total agreement here. In fact, is there anything I can do to help you, sir?"

Glen smiles and replies, "Well, I could use some of these young-buck Marines to help unload this 10,000 pounds of cargo every time we come in here."

"Not a problem, sir. How many do you need, sir?"

He answers, "I tell you what, I could use six good healthy Marines right now."

Grabbing his walkie-talkie, the lieutenant shouts, "Gunny!"

"Yes, sir?" the gunnery sergeant responds.

"Send me twelve Marines over here, now."

"Twelve Marines, sir?"

"Yes, twelve Marines! Now Gunny! I said, 'NOW!'"

Thinking back on this event, Glen later comments with a chuckle, "I call that meeting with the lieutenant the 'prayer meeting' story because that Marine officer had a 'come-to-Jesus' moment when he realized that I knew that four-star general!"

Within moments, twelve muscular young men show up in a "six-by" military truck and start unloading the airplane.

Denny and Chris start over towards the Marines to "help" unload the aircraft when Glen intercepts them…

"Now, wait a minute! You two just sit off to the side here and relax. It's hot out here! Let these young buck Marines…who don't have a neck, with their heads sitting directly on their shoulders, and their biceps and triceps bulging out…let them young 'bulls' out there run this show here," Glen insists with a big smile.

While the lieutenant is showing his new enthusiasm for the Angel Flight 44 operation, and the Marines are taking a personal role in unloading the Super DC-3, Glen notices two men and a teenager walking over to meet him.

Sticking out his hand to greet them, he says, "Hi! I'm Glen Hyde."

"Good to meet you, Mr. Hyde. I'm Larry Roques, and these are my two sons…"

CHAPTER 13

A Hungry Pastor

Wednesday, September 7th, 2005: *1:30 p.m.*

The arrival of Glen, Denny, Chris, and the KCM cameraman to Slidell, Louisiana that afternoon proves to have more significance than any of them had expected. God has been moving, both *through* and *for* the Angel Flight 44 operation mightily day after day—and He is still moving on their behalf.

Pastor Larry Roques and his sons walk over toward the Super DC-3 to see what they can do to help. As they approach, Larry seems drawn towards a stately man in his fifties—who is patting a young Marine Corps officer on his shoulders.

"…next in line to be *your* Commandant, Lieutenant. Let's get my old buddy, Bill, on the phone right now and get this thing straightened out."

Larry stops a moment to avoid interfering with the conversation. He is not sure what has transpired up until now, but he knows that the man he just identified as the 'colonel' of the DC-3 operation is having some fun putting the young officer in his place. "This man used to be in the military," Larry thinks to himself. "He knows *exactly* what he's doing with that young lieutenant over there!"

The Marine officer turns and begins shouting into his field radio. Almost immediately, Larry sees a military truck in route towards the airplane. He then turns back and notices the 'colonel' talking with two of his companions. Deciding it is an appropriate time, Larry and his two sons then begin to walk over towards the man who is obviously "in charge."

The man notices them approaching. He turns toward them with an extended hand, and warmly introduces himself. "Hi! I'm Glen Hyde."

"Good to meet you, Mr. Hyde. I'm Larry Roques, and these are my two sons: Joshua and Lawrence the third."

"Glad to meet you. How did y'all make out in all of this?"

Larry replies, "Well, basically, what we're wearing is what we own. Our home was damaged in the storm, and water just about ruined everything."

"Oh, I am truly sorry to hear that." Glen has become quite fascinated with the personal survival accounts that people are sharing with him day after day. He then inquires, "When was the last time you guys ate?"

"Well, we have eaten some Vienna sausages and peanut butter here and there. But the last decent meal I ate was three days ago, and the boys had one two days ago. It's just about the same for my wife and our other children."

Glen then asks, "Where are y'all sleeping? Can you use your house at all?"

Larry explains, "No, it's just uninhabitable. Right now, we and about twelve others are living in the back of the church."

His answer got Glen's attention. This is the first time anyone he has spoken to in Slidell mentioned a church. This is a new twist. He responds, "In the church?"

"Yeah," he explains, "The church took a lot of damage, but not as bad as our homes. So, we've set ourselves up in the back office where none of the rainwater came in."

"How are you associated with the church?" Glen asks.

He says, "Well, I'm the pastor...and really, I'm not that worked up about my own situation because we made it through alright—relatively speaking, of course. What I'm really more concerned about is my congregation right now."

"Really? You're the pastor? Hmmm." Glen seems to be taking it all in, and Larry notices this.

So he elaborates, "Yes. It's a small church, but we've got a lot of elderly people who can't get anywhere. There's no food, and there's no water...there's nothing."

"Really?" Glen replies again—still seeming to contemplate something.

The hungry pastor decides to change the subject from his own situation somewhat. Turning the conversation back to the situation at hand, Larry adds, "Really, sir, my boys and I just came out here to see if we could help out with the relief effort. So, what can we do to help you, Mr. Hyde?"

Glen's curious expression snaps into a look of admiration as he suddenly straightens up. "You haven't eaten a decent meal in three days, your sons haven't had one in two days…and you've come out here and want to know what you can do for *me*? Let's clear something up right now. You're the infield general in this operation, and I'm just a colonel. You tell me what *you* need, and we will do what we can to help *you*," he shares with a warm smile.

Larry is blessed by Glen's statement, and hope begins to arise in his heart that maybe this fellow would give him and his boys some of the supplies he sees coming off the aircraft. Looking then at the Marines hastily unloading cargo from the DC-3, Larry inquires, "Who's sponsoring all of this stuff?"

"It's coming from Kenneth Copeland Ministries and Eagle Mountain International Church back in Fort Worth, Texas," Glen replies.

Stunned, Larry responds, "Did you say Kenneth Copeland? Do you know Kenneth Copeland?"

"Oh yeah. I know Kenneth Copeland," Glen answers. "He's a good friend of mine—a very close friend of mine…"

Larry interrupts, "He's one of the reasons why I'm a pastor! I'm a partner with Kenneth Copeland Ministries. I've got a whole bunch of his tapes back at my church office..."

This time Glen interrupts, "Did you say you're a partner with Kenneth Copeland Ministries?"

"Yes, sir."

"Do you know what you just said?" Glen steps forward and lays his hand on Larry's shoulder. "Pastor, you've now got an army of 600,000 people in Fort Worth and worldwide that are trying to help you. Every partner of Kenneth Copeland Ministries is behind you—and they're the main ones who sponsored this airplane and provided everything I carried here on it today."

Encouraged by Glen's words of faith and comfort, Larry says, "Well…does that mean we can have some of this food and water that's coming off your plane?"

Glen smiles real big, but does not reply immediately. Hence, Larry thinks to himself, "Oh, now I've done it! Should have kept my mouth shut!"

Glen squeezes a bit firmer on Larry's shoulder and announces, "Sir, *all* of this food and water is yours."

Pastor Larry's eyes pop open wide and his jaw drops. "What?" he fumbles out weakly. Then Glen's words register. "It's mine?!" he blurts out louder.

"Yes, sir, everything on that aircraft now belongs to you."

Larry is shocked. "W-why?" he stammers…still taken aback at what Glen has just told him.

"Kenneth Copeland personally told me to fly this food, water, and supplies to Louisiana and to make it my primary objective to find a pastor down here to work with us...as a point of distribution for these things to the people who need them. And here you walk up to me—and you're even a partner to the ministry! Guess what...*you're that pastor.*"

While Larry tries to absorb it all and get over the shock of God's abrupt miracle, Glen continues, "It's all yours—every bit of it. In fact, I need to find out from you: how much more do you need? Up until now, we've not yet had any solid plan for logistics, and it's been a day-by-day adventure. We didn't even know who was going to be here to receive the stuff each trip. We didn't know where we were going to stage it. We didn't really even know what kind of stuff you were going to need. All we knew was that the Lord was going to provide us a pastor down here—an infield general—who would work with us to get all these things established. So now, you tell us what you need and start making us a list."

A Call to Kenneth

While Larry finally begins to float back down to earth from "Cloud Nine," Glen introduces him to Chris Clem. "This man is one of the executives at Kenneth Copeland Ministries. He happened to come with us for the first time on *this* flight so that he could help us set up logistics. You two meet for a minute to get things started, and I'm going to head over there under the wing to call Kenneth and give him a report."

Glen walks over to the Gooney Bird and picks up his "OCC" chair from where Denny had left it under the fuselage after opening the cargo doors. This white plastic lawn chair had been nicknamed by Glen and Denny the "OCC" (Operations Command and Control) chair. On their first few missions, Glen tried to help unload the aircraft, in addition to making calls back to KCM, McKesson, and other contacts, to coordinate logistics. Then he would fly the plane. Denny quickly realized this was not a good idea, so he "retired" Glen from helping with the cargo. They then threw this white plastic chair onto the DC-3 to give Glen something to sit in while he was under the wing with his notepad making phone calls.

"For some reason," Glen later explains, "I could get a cell phone signal if I went under the *left* wing of the DC-3 to make a call. You could hardly get *any* cell phone signals down there. But whenever I went under the left wing of the plane, I had a spot about five feet in diameter where I could get through, and they could call me. So I just placed my chair right in the middle of that spot. As long as I stayed under that wing sitting in the OCC chair, I could take care of logistics by phone."

So Glen carries the OCC chair to his shady "spot" under the left wing of the

DC-3, away from the hyperactive cargo-unloading activity, and calls Kenneth Copeland. "Kenneth, I've miscalculated this down here. This is a whole lot worse than what I ever dreamed it would be. I'm really glad I brought Chris Clem with me down here because we really need to rally all the churches to help out with this thing. You need to get on TV, the Internet, whatever you can do. These people are going to need lots of help. They're telling me they need everything—diapers, pediatrics, food, water, chainsaws, generators, you name it. This whole ninety thousand square miles has got to be rebuilt. It's a mess!"

"Is it that bad, Glen?"

"Worse! You cannot even imagine unless you come down here. There are still bodies floating around in the ditches that haven't been picked up yet. The mosquitoes are landing on them, biting the corpses, and then going to live people and biting them!"

"Man, Glen. I'll do whatever I've got to do. Is Chris able to start setting up logistics down there yet?"

"Yes, and here's the really good news...there's a guy here we just met today who's a pastor. Not only that, he's in the ministry today because he studied your teachings. He's even a partner with KCM and EMIC!"

There is a short pause. Then Kenneth's voice becomes even more resolute as he charges him, "Glen! You tell that pastor that *anything* and *everything* he needs—he's now got a *direct supply line* to whatever he requires. I want you to get together with Chris Clem. You two make a shopping list and call it in back here to Dennis O'Brien before you leave there—and when you get back to Copeland Field, it will be staged next to the hangar and waiting for you to load!"

And when they return to Copeland Field later that day...it is.

"General" Roques

Over time, Kenneth Copeland Ministries ships massive quantities of food and bottled water, baby supplies, hygiene products, clothes, hundreds of generators, four to five hundred chainsaws—you name it, they ship it. And not to leave the vast spiritual needs of the devastated community unmet, KCM ships cases upon cases of Bibles and other Christian reading materials for Pastor Larry's church, Joy Fellowship Church, to dispense to the thousands of people they feed.

Having just received his latest orders, Glen concludes his call to Kenneth Copeland and heads back over to meet with Pastor Larry and Chris Clem.

While the three talk, the Marines are just finishing offloading the cargo from the DC-3. In less than twenty-five minutes, these men have unloaded all 10,000 pounds of cargo into the "six-by" (a five-ton military transport truck). Then the Marines come up to Glen—respectfully—and the staff sergeant asks, "Mr. Hyde, where do you want all of this stuff to go, sir?"

Glen steps over next to Pastor Larry and turns back toward the sergeant. Patting Larry on the back, he replies, "Sergeant, this is your new infield general right here. Meet Pastor Larry Roques. Wherever he says take it, y'all take it."

Larry's face gleams bright, as he says, "You can follow us!" He tells his boys to load up into their mini-van, and the Marines are to follow them back to the church and unload the precious cargo there.

Turning to Glen he says, "Glen, I can't thank you enough for what you've done for us today…"

"Don't thank me," says Glen with a big Texas grin. "Thank the Lord. He's the One Who put all of this together here. I just came along for the ride!"

"Okay, Glen." Looking up to Heaven, Larry shouts out, "Thank you, Lord!" Turning back to Glen again, Larry asks, "How can I get in touch with you again. How will I know when you're coming back in?"

"I'll give you my cell phone number…" Glen begins to reply, "…and you can also check with the airport people to find out when I call in with my call sign on the UNICOM. My airplane's call sign is 'Angel Flight 44'."

Larry's mouth drops open again as his complexion seems to grow strangely pale.

"Are you alright?!" Glen asks with sudden concern.

"Yeah…yeah…remind me to tell you about the '44' thing sometime…"

CHAPTER 14

All Fours

The moment Glen says to him, "Angel Flight 44," Larry almost goes into medical shock. His mind quickly flashes back to May of that same year when his then-peaceful city was still intact…and the thought of hurricanes was far from their minds.

The Lord Jesus awakens Larry early in the morning on three separate occasions—at *exactly* 4:44 a.m. His eyes seem to pop wide open on their own, and he looks at the digital clock on the dresser to see the same time registered in each instance.

"What is it, Lord? Only you can wake me up from a deep sleep *that* suddenly." Rising and finding a quiet place to pray, Larry receives from the Lord a different Scripture each morning—each with a seemingly different message.

The first morning, the Lord speaks to him the Bible reference, Numbers 4:44:

> "…those who were numbered by their families were three thousand two hundred."

As he looks up the passage and meditates on it, the Lord strongly impresses him in his spirit, "Prepare. This number of families is coming to your church in need of ministry. You and the other pastors of Joy Fellowship must prepare."

Larry later recounts, "He was telling me to prepare. He stated a number, and then said that we would minister to that many families. To understand how ludicrous this seemed to me at that moment, you have to look at everything from the natural standpoint. Our little church had only about fifty people at the time (although it is bigger now). Yet, with this word from the Lord, there was an urgency to begin to prepare for something huge."

The next morning, Larry's eyes again pop open, and he turns to look at the clock. For a second time, "4:44" stares at him as if to say, "Time to get up. The Lord is waiting for you."

Leaving the bedroom to pray, Larry senses the Lord speaking to him another passage. This time, it is John 4:44:

> "For Jesus Himself testified that a prophet has no honor
> in his own country."

During this same period, his church is in a season of fasting and prayer for a *spiritual awakening*—for a revival in both themselves and within the community. Larry has called this fast because he is hungering for a move of God more than nourishment for his body. Nevertheless, he has noticed that not all of the church members have embraced the call to fasting and prayer, and many of them seem to be annoyed at it.

"This is for those who choose to fast and pray before Me," the Lord speaks to his heart. "Tell them to stand fast and persevere despite what others may think, for their efforts will be rewarded."

The third morning he is already facing the clock in his sleep when the Lord awakes him suddenly once more. The "4:44" on the clock again speaks to him, "Get up!" As he sits down before the Lord in another room, he hears "Psalm 4:4 and 5" in his spirit:

> "Be angry, and do not sin. Meditate within your heart
> on your bed, and be still. Selah. Offer the sacrifices of
> righteousness, and put your trust in the LORD."

As Larry ponders that a moment, the Holy Spirit begins to elaborate, "The people in your congregation have not been coming before Me in the services with clean hearts and pure worship. Even your worship team and musicians have been far from Me in their hearts as they feign worship with their mouths and instruments. Tell the people to get the sin out of their lives and offer up the sacrifices of praise with sincerity."

Strong Word

After that third morning, Larry begins to sleep normally. Nonetheless, the Scriptures the Lord has given him burn within his heart as he reflects on what the Lord has spoken. For many days, he says nothing to anyone about this occurrence.

Several days later, Pastor Roques travels to the church one Sunday morning very early and prays. Unable to contain the message that stirs in his heart, he decides to call in the leaders who are heading up various ministry-areas of the church. He summons the church's evangelism pastor, youth pastor, children's pastor, administrator, and his wife, as they each come into the building that morning. In tears, he begins to tell them about this word from the book of Numbers, in which the Lord gave him this number of 3,200 families.

"We've got to get ready. God is getting ready to send all these people our way. Something is going to happen—whether locally or nationally, whether it's going to be a terrorist attack, or…well, I don't know what it's going to be. But I'm telling you that God is telling me that we need to get ready."

Following this private meeting with the staff, Pastor Roques ministers the next two segments of the Lord's directive to him in the main service.

"All of you who have been participating in this fast, and seeking the Lord with your prayers…God is saying to you that your labor will not be in vain. No matter what others may think, say, or do—you keep pressing on.

"And those of you who have not been participating with eager hearts—you need to get with God's program if you do not want to get out of sync with the Lord and His plans for this church."

Turning to the worship team, he begins to expound upon the message the Lord had given him for them and those in the service, regarding the quality and sincerity of their worship.

"He's not pleased, and this Scripture He gave me to minister to you is saying, 'Get your hearts right, and get the hypocrisy and superficiality out of your praise and worship.'"

The "strong meat" the pastor feeds them that morning surely impacts the entire "flock." However, if any are thinking that things will blow over once the service lets out, they are seriously mistaken.

As Larry later recounts, "So after that, I went on this big thing around the church. I said, 'I want all the closets clean. I want an exterminator. I want to get the building totally pest-free.' I did not know why I was acting this way, and I started to wonder if maybe it was some kind of a freaky Howard Hughes-type of thing I was going through. I was even in the bathroom washing my hands all day.

"I finally asked the Lord, 'Am I having a nervous breakdown? Is it small-church pressure I am dealing with? What is the deal here?' He just told me, 'I gave you a word. Stand by it.'

"So, I just kept having to go back to May when the Lord had woken me up those three mornings at the same time. I would wake up and look at the clock and it would say '4:44.' It was three nights in a row! That is almost biologically impossible for your body to wake up on its own at the same exact time every day. Each morning I would wake up and start seeking the Lord and He would give me another word.

"The biggest words were to prepare the church and to get them spiritually ready to get them to the point where they could deal with whatever was heading our way. Those words were also for me to get *myself* ready, to kind of brace myself for whatever was about to happen.

"But it got to be July and nothing had happened. I was starting to look and feel a little silly because nothing that monumental had happened. I had no idea *this thing* was going to come."

The "thing" was Hurricane Katrina.

Even after the storm has ravaged the area, however, Pastor Larry Roques does not initially see a correlation between the storm and the message the Lord had given him to "prepare" for something big that was to come. That is, until Glen smiles and says, "My airplane's call sign is 'Angel Flight 44.'"

Wow!

Standing there stunned a few moments on the tarmac of Slidell's little airport, this faithful pastor suddenly becomes fully aware of the significance of the messages he had received from the Lord the previous May—at 4:44 three mornings in a row.

"Pastor? Are you alright?!" his aviator benefactor probes him with concern.

"Yeah…yeah…remind me to tell you about the '44' thing sometime. There's a testimony here that I think you'll really enjoy…uh…wow!...That is…whew!... once I can get *my* thoughts straight about it all."

Somewhat comforted that his new friend is not having heat stroke, Glen says, "Great! I would love to hear it. But why don't you save that for later when we have more time. Right now, you've got a dozen Marines over there hanging all over that six-by, with lots of cargo to take back to your church. You just lead them there—and make sure you let *them* do all the work. You look like you need to take the remainder of the afternoon to catch up on some rest and cool off some…"

Epilogue

Honey, I'm Home!

Leslie and two of the three Roques daughters wait expectantly at the church for her husband and sons to return from the airport. "I hope those 'Thirst-No-More' guys came today. Vienna sausages are starting to sound real good to me right now."

The other parishioners living there with them laugh in agreement. However, the vacancy they all feel in their stomachs is beginning to make joking about food a little more difficult as each hour passes.

They then hear what they believe to be a truck coming. Subsequently, they also hear the familiar beeping of the family mini-van's horn as it turns into the church's horseshoe-shaped driveway. Leslie and her daughters, along with the other church office "campers," run out of the building to investigate. To their surprise, they are greeted with the sight of a heavily loaded Marine Corps truck following in behind the pastor's mini-van...as he tows his still-empty trailer behind.

Somewhat confused, she shouts to her husband, "What's going on?"

"A miracle! God has answered our prayers! Glory to Jesus!" he proclaims jubilantly.

The Marines park the six-by, and a dozen young men begin unloading 10,000 pounds of cargo into the church—while Leslie and everyone else stands there, open-mouthed, and speechless.

In just a matter of hours, this pastor, his family, and their church congregation have gone from having not eaten anything significant in two or more days—to suddenly feeding *thousands* beyond themselves. Little did they know that day that by April of 2006, they would have fed an estimated 200,000 people. It is Jesus' miracle of the "loaves and the fishes" all over again—except this time, He does it *21ˢᵗ Century-style.*

Pastor Larry and his church open up a storehouse in their building, and together in partnership with Kenneth Copeland Ministries, Eagle Mountain International Church, Operation Blessing, the Salvation Army, and Angel Flight 44, they start giving away food and supplies to their congregation and the hurting people throughout the community.

As Glen later comments, "This man went from not knowing what or when he and his family would eat again—all the while sleeping in their church every night—to feeding two and three thousand people *per day*.

"We started flying all kinds of supplies into there—food and water, generators, chainsaws, and so on. You name it, we flew it in there. And Pastor Larry Roques and his church became the distribution point for it all.

"Once he opened up the distribution, the line of cars for people waiting for food and supplies was two and a half miles long. Pastor Larry Roques just kept feeding people. We kept buying food, water, and supplies, and flying it in. We also kept sending money down there to help him with his church's bills. Bill Horan and Operation Blessing also gave him money and assisted him tremendously.

"Pastor Larry just kept his food bank going and kept feeding people. And in the middle of doing that, he and his people would witness to them, pray with them, and give them the Bibles and other KCM materials we brought down there.

"Pastor Larry even did a type of 'meals-on-wheels' for elderly people who couldn't leave their homes. He would just load up his mini-van with food and take it to them.

"Yep, Pastor Larry is my hero, I guarantee you."

PART II

Special Feature

"I always wanted to own an airplane that I had flown in the Marine Corps."

–Glen Hyde

Pictured above: Glen Hyde's Douglas Super DC-3 comes in for a low fly by.

CHAPTER 15

About the Super DC-3

Probably no aircraft in aviation history made as significant an impact as the Douglas DC-3. In fact, the contributors to Wikipedia.org put it this way:

> *The Douglas DC-3 is a fixed-wing, propeller-driven aircraft which revolutionized air transport in the 1930s and 1940s, and is generally regarded as one of the most significant transport aircraft ever made…*

Pilots often refer to the aircraft and its variants by nicknames—a "3," "Gooney Bird," "Dakota," or "Skytrain," are the most typical designations. Consequently, we will use these synonyms interchangeably throughout this chapter. Nonetheless, we will still be referring to the same basic DC-3 and its modified forms during this special feature of *Angel Flight 44*.

The first DC-3 made its maiden flight on December 17th, 1935—exactly thirty-two years to the day after the Wright Brothers flew for the first time in Kitty Hawk, North Carolina. The DC-3 was a significant improvement over its predecessor, the DC-2. This newer addition to the Douglas Aircraft Company product line made transcontinental flights across the United States possible, with only one refueling stop being necessary along the way.

This was during the time in our history when air transportation was first emerging as a passenger industry. The early U.S. airline companies quickly took advantage of the longer range of the newer technology, and soon over 400 DC-3s were ordered and put into service by the commercial carriers. Essentially, this aircraft established the foundation of the modern aviation industry.

However, with the outbreak of World War II in 1941, the military "drafted" many civilian DC-3s and put them into use for the war effort. Subsequently, the military itself began ordering the aircraft from Douglas in various configurations. According to Wilkipedia.org again:

> ...thousands of military versions of the DC-3 were built under the designations C-47, C-53, R4D, and Dakota. The armed forces of many countries used the DC-3 and its military variants for the transport of troops, cargo and wounded. Over 10,000 aircraft were produced (some as licensed copies in Japan as Showa L2D, and in the USSR as the Lisunov Li-2).

After the end of WWII, the surplus of used DC-3 variants immediately became a boom for the world's airline industry. Whereas the U.S. companies had been subject to military commandeering of their newest fleet additions at the start of the war, now they were able to procure thousands of aircraft back at surplus equipment prices. Quickly, the DC-3 became "standard equipment" of nearly all the airlines worldwide. Wilkipedia.org again notes:

> Numerous attempts were made to design a "DC-3 replacement" over the next three decades...but no single type could match the versatility, rugged reliability, and economy of the DC-3, and it remained a significant part of air transport systems well into the 1970s. Even today, 70 years after the DC-3 first flew, there are still small operators with DC-3s in revenue service and as cargo planes. The common saying among aviation buffs and pilots is that "The only replacement for a DC-3 is another DC-3." The ability to start and land on grass or dirt runways also makes it popular in developing countries where the runways may not always be tarmac.

With the rich history of this unique aircraft, its versatility in cargo and transport operations, and the comparably large number of vintage aircraft still in service worldwide, it is easy to see how a DC-3 would be a desirable piece of equipment for emergency relief operations like those Glen and Denny flew. However, Glen's aircraft was even more special and useful in such a mission. It was not just a regular DC-3...it was a *Super* DC-3, also known as a DC3-S.

Super Size It!

With the success of the original DC-3 and its military variants, Douglas decided to capitalize on their experience and the new technologies developed during the war. Consequently, they developed an upgraded version of this proven workhorse. They bought back two surplus C-47 Skytrains and retrofitted them with significant upgrades, naming the new aircraft the DC3-S or Super DC-3. They sold the two prototypes to the U.S. Air Force, who evaluated them in comparison with another aircraft made by Convair. Deciding the Convair aircraft was more suitable to their specific needs, they transferred the two Douglas aircraft to the Navy for their consideration.

The Navy was impressed by the prototypes, and they hired Douglas to take back ninety-seven more of their Skytrains (designated by the Navy as RD4-5's, -6's, and -7's—depending on their original configurations) and convert them into the new version—which they designated as the RD4-8. This gave the Navy a total of ninety-nine Super Skytrains.

The conversions took place from 1952 to 1956. Gradually, the Marine Corps started receiving the decommissioned RD4-8s from the Navy, reworked them, and then placed each one back into service under the military designation of C117D.

Therefore, the obvious question here is, "What's the difference between the original DC-3 and the Super?"

There are significant differences. First, the wings of the original Gooney Bird had a ninety-five-foot wingspan, and had a trailing edge that was perpendicular to the fuselage at exactly ninety degrees. The Super Gooney's wings were shortened to ninety feet in length, and were given a backward sweep of 4.5 degrees on the trailing edge. Furthermore, a heavier gauge metal "skin" was applied to the surface using flush-rivets, rather than the round-head or "raised" rivets found on the Standard model. Thus, the Super DC-3 wing has considerably more strength, yet less drag.

The addition of long-range fuel tanks provided an additional 411 gallons of fuel capacity to *each* wing—giving the Super DC-3 a total fuel capacity of 1626 gallons, verses the original 804 gallons in the standard configuration. The original DC-3 required a fuel stop to complete transcontinental flight. However, the added fuel capacity in the Super DC-3 made the new version a transoceanic aircraft (capable of flight across the world's oceans). Douglas had doubled the flight range of the aircraft.

Douglas also reconfigured the tail section (*empennage*) with larger vertical and horizontal stabilizers that were also more "squared off" than those on the Standard Dakotas. This gave the Super DC-3 more in-flight stability. They retrofitted the landing gear with the superior brakes designed for the larger four-engine DC-4 model. They also redesigned the landing gear doors so that they would completely enclose the gear when retracted (reducing drag further). The fixed swivel tail gear of the Standard DC-3 that was visible during all phases of flight operation was replaced with a retractable design on the Super—again, reducing drag.

The two 1200-horsepower Pratt and Whitney R-1830 engines on Standard Dakotas were replaced with two 1475-horsepower Wright 1820-80 engines—that were also fitted with larger propellers. The power plant upgrades, combined with the enlarged props, gave the Super Dakota an overall increase of 550-horsepower and 50 knots (57.5 miles/hour or 92.6 kilometer/hour) faster cruising speed.

There was an increased load demand on the fuselage created by the wings due to the weight of the larger engines, long-range fuel tanks, and heavier gauge wing "skin." Therefore, the fuselage of the Super DC-3 was also significantly strengthened—and *extended*. Douglas installed a thirty-nine-inch "plug" behind the cockpit that pushed it forward in relation to the rest of the aircraft, while also installing a forty-inch "plug" behind the rear cargo door. These two extensions made the tube of the fuselage seventy-nine-inches longer overall, and gave the Super Skytrain its distinguishing mark of having the cockpit and its windows extend out in front of the propeller line (unlike the Standard Skytrains where the pilots looked out their side windows directly into the propellers).

The overall effect on the aircraft was to increase the cargo-carrying capability from the 6,000-pound limitation of the civilian version of the Standard Dakota, to 10,000 pounds on the Super (and the Marine Corps often carried as much as 12,000 pounds). *Therefore, the Super Gooney carries at least 4,000 pounds more, flies fifty knots faster—and travels twice as far without refueling.*

To highlight these improvements even further, Glen Hyde comments that the pilots of the Marine Corps found that a Super DC-3 superseded the capabilities of a Standard "3" even when only *one* of its two engines was functional and its landing gear was in the down position (increasing drag significantly). They discovered that the thus-handicapped Super "3" could still fly with a higher gross weight than a Standard DC-3, even if the Standard "3" had both of its engines operating at full power and its landing gear fully retracted. What a workhorse!

Great Plane! But...

The Navy and Marine Corps were very happy with their ninety-nine new RD4-8 (Super DC-3) aircraft. In fact, these planes remained in military service until the last one was decommissioned from the Marine Corps in 1980—twenty-eight years after they took delivery on the first of the reconfigured aircraft, and forty-five years after the first DC-3's maiden flight.

Despite the success of these few Super Dakotas, however, Douglas could not find any other buyers to begin full production of the improved model. The massive surplus of *thousands* of Standard DC-3s in the world aviation market made the acquisition costs of them mere *pennies* compared with the cost of the newly re-designed Supers. Consequently, no additional military orders were taken, and only four of the new improved aircraft were ever built for civilian purposes—which is an intriguing story to explore.

Super Mystery

The four built for civilian purposes were for Capital Airlines (C.A.). The young airline placed an order for seventeen Super Dakotas without the long-range fuel tanks. Four were actually built, but only three are confirmed as having been delivered and placed into service. The missing fourth aircraft is the bizarre twist to this story.

Capital Airlines went bankrupt. When investigations began later to locate the missing aircraft, they found FAA records to indicate that the fourth aircraft was actually manufactured. Moreover, Douglas' records even show that C.A. took delivery of the aircraft. However, nobody formerly working for the now-defunct Capital Airlines ever saw it.

Throughout aviation chronicles today, nobody is on record as ever having seen the airplane beyond its manufacture. It is completely missing. To understand the significance of this, one must realize that aircraft do not simply "evaporate" from aviation records. The manufacturers, FAA, maintenance records, and various aviation groups track aircraft meticulously. Every Super DC-3 ever manufactured is accounted for—even those that crashed somewhere. Every one, that is, except the mysterious fourth Super Dakota of Capital Airlines.

What happened to it? According to Glen Hyde, the answer to this question has been a long-standing debate. "Either it was never actually built, or it was built and delivered to someone else—but to whom? No one has ever actually laid eyes on it. Nevertheless, the Douglas type certificate shows *four* civilian aircraft on it." This is an intriguing "Super Mystery" indeed.

Mystery aside, however, recorded aviation history says that there were one hundred and three Super DC-3 aircraft ever built. However, at the time of this writing, there are only four Supers still flown in the United States (Glen's being one of them), and only about twelve are flying worldwide. This also means that there are precious few pilots with any flight experience at the controls of a Super DC-3. Thus, Glen, Denny, and the Super Skytrain are all rare breeds indeed.

Have We Met? (Glen's Super-3)

While flying as a 737 captain for Braniff International Airways in 1990, Glen Hyde landed one day in Oklahoma City. As they were taxiing in to the terminal, his copilot pointed toward an aircraft parked along side the taxiway and said, "Hey Glen, look at the DC-3 parked over there."

Glen looked over and replied, "That's not a DC-3, that's a Super-3."

"How do you know?"

"Because I flew them in the Marine Corps. Notice how far the cockpit extends beyond the propeller line, and how the tail is squared off. There were only 103 of them ever made," Glen answered. Reminiscing, Glen then proceeded to detail to his copilot the differences between the Super-3s and the standard DC-3s.

After parking the 737 at the terminal, Glen called flight operations to find out about the Super Gooney. He found out that it had blown an engine, and was left there until its recovery could be arranged. They also gave him the name of the aircraft's owner: Sandy Faulkner of Airpower, Inc. in Lakeport, California. Armed with the contact name and number from flight operations, Glen called Sandy and inquired of the Super-3's status. Discovering that he was willing to sell the vintage aircraft, he asked them for the bureau number (unique I.D.) of the aircraft, and told them he would get back with them.

When he returned home to Roanoke, Texas, Glen checked his old military flight logs. He wanted to see if he had actually flown that Super during his active duty tour in the Marine Corps. Searching through his records, he found that aircraft recorded. "I always wanted to own an airplane that I had flown in the Marine Corps," he later commented. So, he called Sandy Faulkner back and negotiated the purchase. He later moved it to a tie-down location at the Denton, Texas airport, where it was sitting when the *Angel Flight 44* story began.

Once Glen purchased his Super from Airpower, Inc., he also examined the detailed mechanics' logs of the aircraft. The records show that his airplane's DC-3 to Super DC-3 conversion occurred in 1952—right at the beginning of the Navy conversions.

Today, Glen Hyde is flying an aircraft that he had flown while on active duty. Moreover, this piece of aviation nostalgia is now on record as being an aviation miracle.

Rich's Note: Much of the data and history about the Super DC-3 contained within this chapter came directly from Glen Hyde himself. He has researched the history of this aircraft throughout his years of aviation. However, additional notes and history of the original DC-3 came from other Internet-based resources. If you would like to explore these things further, you can find more history of the Douglas DC-3 and Super DC-3, and the military variants, on the Internet at the following web sites:

http://www.microworks.net/pacific/aviation/r4d_gooneybird.htm
http://www.vaq34.com/vxe6/r4d.htm
http://www.wikipedia.org

Glen Hyde's Super-Gooney parked at Denton Airport. Photo by Rich Vermillion

Denny Ghiringhelli performs a pre-flight check of the Super's right engine. Notice the size of the aircraft in relation to Denny. Photo by Rich Vermillion

PART III

Extra Scenes

"I think what I saw was strength—the strength of a hurricane uprooting trees, blowing a house into a million pieces, and discarding those pieces into oblivion... By the same token, I also saw another type of strength: I saw the strength of people who had just lost everything."

–Denny Ghiringhelli

Pictured above: A devestated home across the street from Lake Pontchartrain in Slidell, LA.
Photo by Rich Vermillion

CHAPTER 16

Denny's Stories

by Denny Ghiringhelli

Rich's note: One of the key figures featured within the Angel Flight 44 story is the copilot who helped make it all possible, Captain Denny Ghiringhelli. Without him, there would have been no flights because the FAA mandates two pilots at the controls of a Super DC-3. More than that, he kept the engines oiled and the plane fueled, and performed mechanical repairs. Denny supervised and assisted with the loading of the aircraft in Texas, and then personally unloaded it again in Slidell— sometimes with only one other person to help. (Imagine, for a moment, unloading 10,000lbs of cargo with only one other guy.)

Denny's extensive aeronautical experience also made him the perfect man to sit in the right seat of Glen's Super DC-3. He had extensive Standard DC-3 experience, and had flown aircraft from small single engine planes up to Boeing 777s in transoceanic flight.

*The contribution of Captain Ghiringhelli's experience, hard work, and faithfulness to the relief missions cannot be understated. Consequently, we decided it would be fitting to devote a whole chapter to this man's thoughts on the mission...along with some touching and humorous stories as well. The remainder of this chapter was written by **Denny** **himself**, relaying each story from his own perspective.*

No Time for Questions

Both during Angel Flight 44's relief effort to Louisiana and in subsequent conversations about those flights, I am often asked how I got involved. When I tell the story of going to Glen's office and the somewhat brief conversation, listeners' reactions are generally the same: "You just agreed to it…right then? Without asking specifically where you would be going, what exactly you were going to be doing or where you would be staying?" When I tell them, "Yes," their response is, "Why?"

I have had a lot of time to think about that since the Katrina Relief Effort, and my answer has not changed since the first time I was asked. "Yes" just felt like the right answer. I do not recall a conscious thought process to consider the variables or even question them. Somehow, I just felt those questions were not important at the time. What was running through my mind was that Glen said he needed my help and that I needed to hurry up.

At the time of the Hurricane Katrina relief missions, I had been working as a pilot for American Airlines for more than twenty years. At American, I was used to operating with a set schedule, a known timetable, hundreds of dispatchers, with schedulers and planners behind the scenes setting up every flight and arranging for hotels, vans, fuel, etc. I was used to every detail being pre-planned and arranged. However, prior to and outside of my position with American Airlines, I have been actively involved with an aviation bloc known as the "war-bird community."

The "war-bird community" is the name given to those individuals involved in the operation and preservation of World War II-era piston engine aircraft. The level of involvement varies from individual to individual. They range from owners, operators, restorers, support crew personnel, or simply those who just like to see them fly. Over the years, I have been a pilot, mechanic, and instructor on many of these aircraft; I have even been involved in aircraft recoveries all over the world. Similarly, so has Glen Hyde—as well as being an owner and operator.

The war-bird community is relatively small and most of the players know each other—either personally or by reputation. As a result, when someone from within that aviation bloc says to me, "I need you to go home, pack a bag, grab some tools, and come back," I already know what to expect. I have known Glen, both personally and by reputation, for many years.

Consequently, when Glen said to me, "Denny, go pack a bag. I need your help," all I had to think of at the moment was whether or not I had the time available to assist. The thought of saying "no," or even questioning what we were going to be doing never entered my mind. I had a strong feeling Glen needed my help right away. And the way I saw it, the rest of the details would simply be worked out later.

On the drive back home, I was thinking about the people in need. The devastation left behind in the wake of Katrina was first and foremost in the news. Nightly TV news and newspapers were full of pictures, and stories of damage and destruction poured out over the radio. The estimates of property destroyed and people killed or left homeless seemed to change by the moment.

I had no idea what relief efforts were underway…but this was a national emergency; surely, the response would be proportionate. I was forming a mental picture of what conditions to expect and trying to envision what role the Super DC-3 would play in the massive relief effort. Little did I know what a major role it would play.

Breaking the News to Pam

While pulling into my driveway, a laundry list of items was forming in my mind. As I entered my home, I heard my wife, Pam, in the kitchen.

"What are you doing home?" she asked me. "I thought you were working on your airplane," she continued, as she followed me down the hall.

My response was, "I was, but now I need to pack a bag, grab a few things, and get back out to the airport to meet Glen."

She then stopped walking. I could almost hear her eyebrows rise as she commented, "Well, hello, nice to see you, too! Is there something else you would like to tell me about?"

"She does have a point," I thought to myself. I looked up at her and tried to console her, "Yes, sorry. Glen has volunteered his DC-3 to help in the relief effort in Louisiana, and he needs a copilot." I then began packing my suitcase. Her eyebrows were still raised.

Pam then asked me, "Lord knows those poor people can use the help. Where will you be flying?"

I told her, "I don't know."

"What will you be carrying?"

I repeated, "I don't know."

She asked me a third question. However, she guessed the answer almost as soon as it left her lips, "When will you be back?"

We both spoke the answer together, "I don't know." Now her raised eyebrows were stuck in that position.

Attempting to put her at ease, I explained what I could to her: "Here's what I *do* know: Glen is going to be using his airplane as part of the relief effort to fly supplies into Louisiana in partnership with Operation Blessing and Kenneth

Copeland Ministries. I don't know what we're hauling, but I suppose it would be food and water. I don't know the details of where we will be staging or staying, but it would have to be someplace that has fuel and the supplies we are going to carry. I do know that the DC-3 is perfect for getting into the smaller airstrips that the larger aircraft can't get into."

In my mind, I was assuming C-5s or C-130s would be offloading supplies at larger airports, while DC-3s and smaller aircraft were shuttling to the smaller airfields.

I then assured my loving wife, "We'll be fine. Besides, Glen won't get us into anything we can't handle. We're going to test fly the airplane as soon as I get back out to meet Glen. He'll fill me in on the details, and I can tell you more tonight." Her eyebrows returned to normal, which I took as a sign that she understood.

"Isn't that a coincidence you are off from American until the 15th?" Pam commented as she walked me to the door. "What time will you be back tonight?" she asked as I gave her a kiss goodbye. I looked at her. Her eyebrows popped back up. There was no need to answer.

That moment would be the first of many "goodbye kisses" during the course of the Katrina relief missions. Throughout the course of the operation, I would be frequently reminded of my wife's encouraging words when it all began: "I believe when something like this happens, God presents the right people with an opportunity to do the right thing," she said, "It's up to them whether or not they do it."

> ***Rich's Note:*** *As blessed as Denny was by his wife's wisdom, he would later be equally touched by the good deed of his own teenage son, Zac. As Denny relays in this next story, which takes place several days into the mission, God used people of all ages to perform selfless acts of love to help those affected by the tragedy.*

Teenage Generosity

With help now from the Marines, we had a good routine for offloading the supplies. While Glen was taxiing in to park, I would head back and unstrap the load. By the time the aircraft was stopped and the engines shut down, the load was untied, and the door was open and ready for the Marines. This freed me up to check the fuel and service the engine oil while Glen made contact with the people at Slidell and KCM. This also cut down on our ground time, and made for faster turnarounds in Slidell.

Pastor Larry and his sons were there to help, too; Lawrence, the youngest, asked Glen if there was something he could do to help. We had plenty of help unloading, so Glen suggested he help me with the oil. I was quite happy to have the help. Then Lawrence and I went up onto the left wing to add oil to the engine. While we were up there, I asked him about Katrina: what damage his family had sustained and what had survived.

He told me their home had been destroyed, and they were staying in their church. He then told me that all they owned now was their car and the clothes they were wearing. Moved by their situation, I then told him I would be returning to Dallas after we finished unloading the plane and asked if there was anything he needed—if there was something I could bring him or do for him. His answer stays with me to this day, he said, "Just keep coming back. Keep helping my dad."

I stopped what I was doing and just sat there on the wing of the airplane amazed. Here was a 14-year-old boy who had just been through a hurricane and had lost everything—and yet what he was asking for was not even for himself. I had to just sit there and reflect on what I had witnessed. I regained my composure and we climbed down off the wing.

I thought of that young man all the way back to KCM, and told Chris Clem about the conversation on the flight back. When I got home that night, I told my wife about him as well; I was so impressed with how unselfish he had been. Although it was late, about midnight, my son, Zac, was still awake. He asked about my latest trip, and so I told him of young Larry.

I then shared with him, "Here is a boy, your age, who has just been through a hurricane. He's lost his home, all his possessions, clothes, living out of a car and his church, who probably hasn't had much to eat in the last few days, and when I ask him if I can bring him anything, he says, 'Just keep helping my dad.' Now that's something you need to think about when you're trying to decide if you have enough pairs of tennis shoes or gym shorts. Try to imagine: these people down there have nothing." Zac left the room without saying a word, but I could tell he was profoundly affected by what I said.

A short time later my wife came to me and said, "Zac would like to talk to you. He's in his room."

I walked down the hall towards his room, and there sat four large garbage bags. Before I could ask, Zac said, "I have gone through all my stuff. These are all the clothes that don't fit, my old stuffed animals for the little kids, and since he's my age, some clothes I think he would like. I called Ben [Zac's friend] and he's doing the same. You can stop by his house tomorrow morning and pick up the bags on your way to KCM. Please take these on your next trip." The earnestness in his eyes was quite apparent. He then asked what else he could do to help and even offered to come along on the relief flights.

Twice in one day, I am surprised and impacted by the actions of youths. The bags were on the next flight to Slidell and given to young Larry.

Rich's Note: Despite the solemn situation associated with much of the Katrina relief operation, there were also some very humorous instances as well. Denny Ghiringhelli, in particular, seemed to have a knack for creating amusing circumstances. The Lord used these funny occurrences to provide many light-hearted moments of relief. These kept Glen and Denny's spirits high during the difficult operation.

The next two subsections are a couple of these funny "scenes" in the Angel Flight 44 saga, again from Denny's perspective.

Surf and Turf

At the onset of the Katrina mission, I had gone to the market and bought some things to take to Slidell that first time because I had no idea where we were going to be, where we were going to sleep…or even when we were going to come back. Therefore, I had with me my emergency beef jerky, my sardines, my Spam, and some Gatorade.

The first time Glen saw me with the sardines he said, "Sardines and Spam?! Man, what are you doing with that on the plane?'

I showed him the cans and said, "It's my emergency 'surf and turf' in case I get hungry. It's better than a can of dog food."

He said, "Denny, don't you dare open those sardines on this DC-3! If you spill that stuff, I'll never get the smell out of this cockpit—and you'll be walking home!"

So, later I asked a couple of the guys who were helping us unload in Slidell if they personally needed anything because, I said, "It looks now like we're going back to Dallas, so I can get all new stuff when I get back there."

They asked, "Well, what have you got?"

"I've got some Gatorade over there in that ice chest, and in this box, I've got some sardines and Spam," I said.

This guy looked at me and said, "Young man, let me tell you something, Cajuns will surely eat just about anything. But we're just not that desperate! There's plenty of dead things floating by out here that we'd rather eat. But I wouldn't mind having that Gatorade."

Then about four weeks later, I had again packed my "emergency food" supply for the Hurricane Rita missions—much to Glen's chagrin. However, Glen fixed that.

We had two ladies down in Orange, Texas that came up to Glen and said, "Mr. Hyde, we've never asked for so much as a toothpick in our whole life, but we haven't eaten for over two days. We're down to one bottle of water. Have you got any food or water on the airplane?"

Glen replied, "Yes, ma'am, we do. How much do you need?" This worked out great because he was desperately trying to get rid of my precious Spam and sardines. He was concerned about me opening the sardines in the airplane. As he saw it, if any of the juice from it leaked down into the floor grates, the smell of it would mess up his airplane forever. Therefore, he jubilantly told the hungry ladies, "I've got some sardines and some Spam. Would you like some of that?"

They said, "Oh yeah! We like that stuff."

Relieved, Glen told them, "Great! It's yours! Also, I've got some soft drinks. You want one?" Of course, they did.

So, Glen got each of them a cola with ice out of the coolers. There are so many things that we take for granted on an everyday basis. If we want a cola, we stop at a local convenience store and get one. If we need gas, we stop and get some. However, people affected by these disasters do not have hardly anything. Even a cola is a miracle to them!

Well, anyway, after Glen gave those ladies each a cola "on the rocks," he grabbed my box of goodies from the cockpit and carried it back toward the cargo door to give to them.

Glen gave away my surf and turf! My sardines and Spam! I said, "Glen, you're not going to give away my sardines and Spam are you?!"

He told me, "Absolutely, Denny! They need it a lot worse than you need it." Well, I could not argue with that—even if Glen did have some ulterior motives.

Rich's Note: It is often true that when one is busy ministering to others in need, they may not give their own requirements a second thought. Denny did not mind Glen's giving away his "surf and turf" at all.

Moreover, often those serving others will endure tremendous circumstances while they provide the needed aid. This is one of the noble characteristics of selfless service.

For example, the heat and humidity in Louisiana during the time frame of the Katrina relief flights was dreadful. For Denny Ghiringhelli, this meant that his unloading and maintenance labors throughout the mission kept him bathed constantly in perspiration. (Hence, the Gatorade supply he kept on board the airplane.) However, it also meant that he did not realize how "ripe" his selfless labors made him—as he illustrates in the following story.

Lookin' Purdy!

We had been in Fort Worth working long and hard to get the prop seals and a few other items fixed. So by the time we landed back at Copeland Field, I was covered from head to toe in engine oil, dirt, sweat, and grime. We had just begun fueling and loading for the trip to Slidell, and I commented to JP that what I really needed was a shower. "Denny," said JP, "I agree – and we just happen to have one in the hangar."

"Oh, I'm alright…" I told him. "Besides, I think all my clean shirts are in Lafayette."

"I'll take care of that," said JP. "When you get out of the shower you will find a KCM T-shirt and some other things we gathered up for you. So climb down off the wing and get to it."

So, I climbed down off of the airplane and headed for the shower.

Glen came out to the airplane a short while later and found me freshly bathed—and dressed in a KCM partner T-shirt and the other clean clothes the mechanics had scavenged together for me.

"Well, you're lookin' clean and fresh! I hardly recognized you!" Glen laughed.

"Yeah, yeah," I laughed back.

The T-shirt had KCM in bold letters printed across the back. There was a photographer there that day, taking pictures that would eventually be posted on one of the KCM websites. It just happened that in every picture I was in, I had my back to the camera – fueling, oil servicing, whatever. In addition, the photographer did not know my name. Consequently, when the pictures went up onto the website, they initially had me on there anonymously, working diligently with "KCM" plastered across my back.

It was not long before Glen and Melvin started calling me "KCM Boy." In fact, by the time the Katrina and Rita relief missions were all over, I had acquired quite a collection of KCM T-shirts.

Rich's Note: Denny's reflections on how the entire operation affected him personally are profound. Thus, it is proper we should finish this chapter with these as his final thoughts.

Observations of the Relief Effort

Over time, I would come to better understand some of what I saw and experienced during the Angel Flight 44 relief effort. After seeing firsthand the death and destruction of something as powerful as Katrina, I am sure my question was the same as that of many others: "Why?" All I can think is Mother Nature is a force that is a part of our lives and we must deal with it—good or bad, creation or destruction. The same sun and rain that together grow crops and give us life can bring drought and floods that lead to death. However, it is not what nature does, but what we do.

I think back to what my wife said about God giving people the opportunity to do the right thing, and reflect on what I saw. I think what I saw was strength—the strength of a hurricane uprooting trees, blowing a house into a million pieces, and discarding those pieces into oblivion. Trailers, cars, trucks, and buses cast about like children's play toys...and the tragic loss of life. The strength of a wall of water so powerful it lifted houses off their foundations and boats from their moorings and discarded the remnants miles inland. We will never know what—or who—was swept out to sea. That is the strength of the destructive force of Mother Nature.

By the same token, I also saw another type of strength: I saw the strength of people who had just lost everything. Yet, they were not standing around asking, "Why me?" but were, instead, moving ahead—confident they would get through this. I saw people not looking for who would help them but for whom they could help. I saw the strength of a young boy whose only request was to help his dad. I saw the combined strength of the members of KCM contributing to help those in need, the staff and volunteers who gave so unselfishly of their time—all to help people they neither knew nor saw.

I also saw the strength of Kenneth Copeland, who told his staff to "make it happen." I saw the strength of faith. Kenneth Copeland, I thank you, too, for the opportunity.

Captain Denny Ghiringhelli flashes a smile as he pilots the Super-3 during a post-Katrina flight. Photo by Rich Vermillion

CHAPTER 17

McKesson Pharmaceutical

The phenomenal testimony of how Glen Hyde and Denny Ghiringhelli walk up to the four McKesson guys at the airport in Lafayette is nothing less than truly amazing. The "behind the scenes" details provide an extra dimension to marvel over—especially once one realizes how many pieces the Lord must bring into place for the puzzle to be completed.

Pre-Storm Challenges

At this time (prior to Hurricane Katrina), McKesson Pharmaceutical has distribution centers all around the country, including one located in Slidell, Louisiana. The Slidell distribution center provides pharmaceuticals to facilities in Louisiana, Southern Mississippi, and Southern Texas—and is directly in Katrina's path. In preparation for the storm, some of their inventory has been moved to Memphis. However, all other assets have been left behind to weather the storm.

As Hurricane Katrina comes rolling into the Gulf of Mexico, the Slidell facility is in the process of closing, as is their Arlington, Texas location. The company has built a brand new facility in Conroe, Texas to replace these two. Nevertheless, the hurricane occurs right at the same time that they are getting ready to shift their customers' deliveries to begin originating from the Conroe distribution center. The delivery process necessary to get product out has not yet been implemented. In other words, this storm is definitely hitting McKesson during a vulnerable moment of transition.

With the storm raging off the Gulf Coast, McKesson's management team realizes that they need to pause in their efforts to transfer inventories to Conroe, and they shift their focus toward stocking the hospitals in the storm's path with emergency supplies. They begin to implement their emergency stocking procedures on behalf of the hospital pharmacies in the New Orleans area.

McKesson's standard emergency plans originally called for an influx of product into the storm-threatened areas forty-eight hours before expected landfall. However, after an extensive delay that still baffles most people today, Mayor Nagin of New Orleans waits until just thirty-eight hours before Katrina would make landfall to call for the mandatory evacuation of the city—and, consequently, the two efforts collide. McKesson Pharmaceutical finds their efforts to enter the area opposed by a massive last-minute evacuation effort going the opposite way.

Slidell Distribution Center Takes Major Hit

The rain and wind are merciless. The subsequent power loss and potential flooding in the distribution center area causes all the personnel to flee for higher ground. The couriers that McKesson has been using for deliveries have also all left for safety.

John Brannan, McKesson Health System Account Manager for Louisiana, had hunkered down and ridden out the storm in his Baton Rouge home. After the storm, he drives to Slidell to evaluate the damage. Before he can get as far as the facility, however, the high waters force him to park the car and continue on foot. Wading through water the last four blocks to the distribution center, he arrives to discover the distribution center somewhat intact—but completely inoperable.

Later John comments, "It looked like a war zone. Trees were thrown everywhere, power lines were down, water was knee-deep in places…and it was quiet. Real quiet."

Since the day the hurricane touched down, McKesson has been conducting two conference calls per day to accomplish two things: to try and locate employees to see how they could be helped; and to repair the distribution network that had been in place for years that had now been destroyed in one night.

On the August 29th morning conference call, John gives a report on the Slidell distribution center: "I had to park four blocks from the building due to high water. I managed to wade the rest of the way where I found the front offices having part of the roof peeled back, which has allowed for rain to pour in. There is no power. The rest looks to be in pretty good shape." Then he asks, "What are we going to do?"

Behind the scenes is a task force trying to answer that very question. The network which has been delivering drugs to hospitals in the area has now been decimated. McKesson is covering the delivery routes via their Arlington, Texas; Atlanta, Georgia; and Memphis, Tennessee distribution centers. However, even that contingency arrangement does not go as planned.

The destruction of bridges and roads adds hundreds of miles and hours to deliveries. Hospitals in New Orleans cannot be reached by ground at all; the flooding caused by the breaking levies has made the roads impossible to drive on. At the end of the day, hospitals are in need of drugs for patients, victims, and support personnel; and McKesson must find a way to get them in.

Trying to Leave Lafayette

John, along with Mike Callahan (the Health Services Account Manager for South Texas), Brian Gore (the McKesson Health System Account Manager for Southern Mississippi, Southern Alabama, and North West Florida), and Larry Alexander (the Retail Account Manager for South Texas) leave Slidell, contemplating how to resolve the massive logistical problems. The needs of the hospitals in the South are changing by the hour, but McKesson is hundreds of miles away. "How do we fix this?" they keep asking themselves.

That single distribution center has been serving all of Louisiana and western Mississippi. Consequently, at this point McKesson has no access to pharmaceuticals and supplies with which to stock the hospitals that they normally service in the Louisiana and Mississippi markets. The loss of that center has created some definite needs in those areas.

McKesson has a hospital that they service in Lafayette, so John and his party withdraw from the crippled Slidell distribution center back to that city. Once there, they decide to head over to the airport to see if they can make arrangements with anyone to fly supplies into the Slidell area.

John and his group then stumble across the folks from Acadian Ambulance & Air Med Services (AAA). While the others wait outside, John walks in and introduces himself and explains the urgent need. Regrettably, Acadian has already signed a contract with FEMA and is subject to the grounding order that had every available plane just sitting on the Lafayette airport flight line—*useless*.

They then find that other pilots they investigate are bound by the same restriction. Calls made to trucking companies also turn out to be dead ends. Even the couriers who have driven their four semi-trucks of supplies from Arlington refuse to go any further than Lafayette. Nobody is available to transport the critical supplies they have parked there. They are either prevented from doing so due to the FEMA shutdown, or they are unwilling to do it due to the looting and violence reported by the media.

Dejected and nearly hopeless, the McKesson men now just stand there outside of the Acadia facility at the Lafayette airport this Saturday afternoon in a huddle—trying to figure out what to do next. It is at this point that they hear the delightful query from a pair of Super DC-3 pilots, "Who here needs to go to Slidell?"

Taking Action

Mike Ripple, a McKesson Health Systems National Account Manager, is responsible for numerous accounts—some of which are ones that have been affected by Hurricane Katrina. On Saturday, September 3rd, at approximately 5:30 p.m., he receives a call from Shane Withers, the McKesson Health Systems Account Manager for North Texas, concerning the Katrina after effects. It is a call Mike has been praying for. Shane informs Mike that he will be leaving the next morning to help in the aftermath. Mike agrees to go with him. Shane and Mike volunteer to go down to help wherever they are needed.

Connecting with the DC-3 Duo

Sunday, September 4th, 2005

At approximately 6 a.m. the next day, Mike and Shane leave Frisco, Texas and head to Lafayette. They have packed the car with as little as possible in order to save room for something else—they just are not sure what. They receive an answer to that question four hours later, when the phone rings.

It is John, who instructs them, "Stop on your way down here. We need some things: shirts, socks, underwear, air mattresses, baby food, baby formula, diapers…" The guys make a quick call to their vice presidents, who confirm that McKesson is willing to purchase and donate these items. So Mike and Shane pick up the things requested and fill up the car to the roof.

That afternoon, they drive into Lafayette and meet John. There, they exchange the car for two cargo vans and leave for Slidell. On the trip down to Lafayette, Mike Ripple calls back to John on his cell phone, who then explains further about how he ran across a guy named Glen Hyde—who is in the air at that moment with Larry Alexander, on a mission to pick up much-needed medical supplies from Grand Prairie. After getting further details, Mike then hangs up the phone to concentrate more on driving. Meanwhile, Glen and Denny leave Larry Alexander back in Grand Prairie as they fly the supplies to Slidell.

By the time Glen and Denny land, they find Mike and Shane on the receiving end. As Mike later shares, "It worked out perfectly! Shane and I drove in from Dallas straight to Lafayette that Sunday. We picked up the vans at the Acadia offices and drove to Slidell. We weren't there five minutes and here came Glen and Denny, almost as if we had planned it that way."

Becoming Acquainted

The next day, Monday September 5th, finds the McKesson guys back at Lafayette Airport. John touches base with Glen to confirm that the Super Gooney is available for a supply run. Mike and Shane advise the Arlington distribution center to prepare the shipment because the DC-3 would be coming in for a pickup in a few hours back at the Grand Prairie airport. Moreover, Mike Ripple decides, with the group's approval, to join Glen and Denny on the next flight to the distribution center.

Since this is the first time Mike has met the two pilots, they get to know each other during the flight. On the journey, Mike learns about Glen's USMC pilot background, and that Denny flies professionally for American Airlines. Interestingly, the two pilots meet Mike hundreds of miles from home, but they are all practically neighbors. It turns out that the three all live in North Texas within close proximity of each other. But now God had brought them together at the right *place* and at the perfect time for a special purpose.

Continuing to learn about the background of these two expert pilots, Mike now shifts himself into learning mode, feeling completely at ease in their hands. He learns that Glen has flown the same type of plane in the U.S. Marine Corps during the Vietnam era out of El Toro Marine Corps Air Station (MCAS) in California. He also learns about Denny's years of professional flight experience, particularly with American Airlines. Mike enjoys listening to the stories and tales of Glen and Denny's twenty years of flying together. He is also intrigued by their ingenuity when it comes to improvising methods to safely operate the aircraft.

As Mike later recalls, "I kept watching these guys measure the sunrise, or I guess the horizon, by their fingers, to determine how much time they had left before sunset. Denny would also flip a bottle of water upside down to use it as a sight for determining if the clouds ahead of us were above or below our aircraft at our current altitude. I probably learned more about flying in those two days then I have in the last thirty-five years.

"It's like I told John Brannan later, you just immediately have got to trust. I had never met Glen or Denny before Katrina, and it was just like, 'we've got to go,' and we just went. We did not have time to sit down for a few days to share dreams and food together and get to know each other. You just went. It was great. It worked out great. We got a lot of medications to people who had a lot of great needs."

Not only does he get to know these two top-notch pilots, he is very helpful to them. Mike has his own role to play during flight operations. With Glen's help, he quickly learns how to operate a satellite phone (satphone) and takes over airborne logistics communication for Angel Flight 44. Whenever necessary, he makes calls to Pastor Terri Pearsons (EMIC), Ron Oats (OBI), and Chris Clem (KCM) to give them progress reports. Mike does not have any idea who these people are, but when Glen says to call, he dials them up—no questions asked.

Looking back on how well Mike Ripple integrated into the flight crew whenever he was aboard, Glen explains, "Mike was great. He took over satphone operations for me. He got on it and figured it out. He was able to make a lot of our contacts airborne to let them know we were coming, when we were going to be there and what we needed. It was a major blessing. Since it was just non-stop from daylight to dark for fourteen days, Mike's help in that area was a big asset."

Landing in Grand Prairie

After landing in Grand Prairie that afternoon, they meet up with Nick Rutledge, who manages inventory at the McKesson distribution center in Arlington. He has driven in the product from the warehouse and has it staged at the airport. They load the cargo into the plane and fill her up near to capacity. Glen and Denny give Mike a crash course in securing cargo, and in fifteen minutes, he becomes an honorary payload master.

The medical supplies that are being loaded include orders from hospitals and retail stores from the Louisiana market. Additional items are included in the load as well—specifically, boxes and boxes of donated product from McKesson. All of the supplies are packed into totes, generally 24 inches square by 8 inches high. They stack up perfectly inside the Super DC-3. Loading up the Gooney Bird to the ceiling, they leave just enough room for Glen's white OCC chair in the back.

"Between the multiple flights with the DC-3, cases upon cases of tetanus vaccines, creams, antibiotics, and other drugs were brought in along with personal care products in order to support the area," Mike later comments. "Hundreds of thousands of dollars of product were shipped in for sites located from Slidell to Lafayette. This helped scores of people. The McKesson delivery area affected by those supplies we flew in by the DC-3 covered stores over a territory that spanned 150 miles wide and fifty miles north to south."

Heavy Takeoff

Taking off from the airport in Grand Prairie that first time is truly an experience—and one that Mike Ripple will not quickly forget. The crew takes off for Lafayette at 2:00 p.m. and needs every bit of horsepower to get over the tree line.

"We were loaded down pretty heavy," he later comments. "Here we were rolling down the runway to take off…and the trees kept getting bigger and taller. I also noticed that the flight deck was silent while Glen and Denny worked the controls to gain altitude. The two pilots were pretty quiet, which was not like them."

"After we got off the runway into the air and cleared the trees, Glen asked me, 'Were you scared?' I said, 'No, I figured you two knew what you were doing. If you two guys were going to make it, I was going to make it too.'

"Then Glen said to me, 'Well, Denny and I were scared!'

"That's when he really got my attention. I suddenly realized that we certainly didn't pass those treetops by much."

Looking back on the incident, Glen explains further, "We were joking with Mike when we said that. It was certainly a tight operation, but we both knew we were going to be fine. We have both been flying big airplanes for many years. But, it was tight.

"We went all the way down the full length of that runway. Denny's looking at me and I am looking at him. We just kept pushing up the power and holding it. It wasn't until we came right off the end of the runway that we finally got airborne. We wanted to use every available inch of tarmac before lifting off the runway. This was partially because of the fact that it was hot—it was what we call in aviation a 'high-density operation.' We also had the weight of full fuel tanks and a full load of pharmaceuticals. We were just loaded to the gills. That's why it was so tight.

"To make it even more complicated, we also had a ninety-degree crosswind of about fifteen to twenty miles per hour…on a short runway…on a hot day. Nevertheless, we lifted off and went non-stop to Slidell. We were there in two hours and thirty minutes, give or take."

Return Flight to Lafayette

The Super DC-3 is in the landing pattern for Lafayette. The tower gives immediate clearance from the West, and a commercial airliner is held back in order for Angel Flight 44 to land. This provides a glimpse into the priority that is placed on humanitarian efforts coming and going. The jet has ample time to taxi down the runway, but the tower allows the Gooney Bird to land first.

Out come the vans, and the precious cargo is sorted by destination. Along with the drugs are boxes of donated items for personal care. Items such as shampoo, soap, toothpaste, toothbrushes, and other necessities are stacked up by the case.

There is too much product to fit into the vans, so Mike makes the decision to stay back with the extra product to allow more totes in the van. Glen and Denny are already getting to work on the engines. In minutes, they are up to their elbows in grease and getting dirty and sweaty in the afternoon heat.

The vans return to the airport and are immediately loaded up with all the remaining items. The group shakes hands and with a nod, says, "goodbye." It is now about 7 p.m., and the rest of the product needs to be delivered that night by the van drivers. The demand for medical supplies is too high for the drivers to wait until the next day.

Transportation Challenges

In partnership with Angel Flight 44, McKesson Pharmaceutical is able to conquer both space and time. Prior to that, their transportation dilemma has been huge.

"The traffic and road conditions were changing so fast and the demand for supplies was constant," Mike Ripple recalls. "We were trying to service the Louisiana market out of our Memphis, Tennessee location. The National Guardsmen would not let them through. They could not tell the looters from others, so all the couriers were getting turned around and sent back. So, on the other end, we had hospitals starving for drugs. There were patients who had been evacuated, but they were in bad need of basic maintenance medication—such as insulin for diabetics and things like that.

"The best way we found to get the supplies there was by Glen's plane. By truck, I think it was about 225 miles from our distribution center in Arlington to Shreveport, where the trucking company we used has a dock, where the products would be re-sorted onto trucks headed for southern Louisiana—which would then mean another 250-350 road miles, depending on the destination. All together, this made for a ten- to twelve-hour trip by semi-truck or van—if you could get one through.

"But by plane, we were able to do it in a couple hours each way, which was great. We had two vans on the distribution side on our end. As soon as the plane got in, we could load the stuff up on the vans and take off in different directions. So, it worked out really well.

"For a period of time, Glen's DC-3 was the only reliable source of transportation we had for distribution. With people being turned around by the National Guard and needing 'papers' to get by, it was pretty hairy for a number of weeks of trying to get a smooth courier service into that area."

Safety Precautions

Delivering drugs and medical supplies into a disaster torn area is no easy task. Neither are the conditions generally considered safe. Nevertheless, the supplies must get to those who need them, so the McKesson Pharmaceutical men rise to the occasion to make it happen.

As Mike describes, "The traffic was amazing. It was taking us a couple of hours for us to get from Lafayette to New Orleans on the causeways. Then once we would get to the hospitals, sometimes we had to go through one or two roadblocks so they could make sure we had a need or a reason to be there. The highways were dark and the roadways were dark. Each hospital was under lockdown, so you had to go through security to get into the hospitals.

"For safety, we always traveled in two's at a minimum. We also traveled in unmarked vans. In New Orleans, there were reports of people taking over vehicles. So when we went down there, we made sure we had *no fewer* than three in the van.

"A lot of our traveling we actually did in the late afternoon and at night, when the roads were less traveled, which gave us more opportunities to go in and out. John knew the roads pretty well, so that helped. And once we got into the hospital area, it was very safe."

God's Provision for McKesson Personnel

Back in Lafayette, the Acadian hangar has become a hub for relief efforts, and Acadian Air Ambulance has allowed McKesson to utilize a conference room.

Mike later ponders everything this place had brought together: "In the terminal were top pilots from many various agencies along with support personnel. All egos were tossed aside as teams were formed for different missions and needs. Maps plastered the walls because most all of the LZ's [landing zones] were dark due to no power; and maps printed from the Internet and night vision goggles were the only way to fly in at night.

"Trust was a big factor. The hangar was filled with all kinds of goods. One side was assigned to specific destinations and the other was to be given to those who could use it. Sheila Hebert at Acadian was fantastic in allowing McKesson to utilize a fax machine, and to let us print out orders so John and I could see what was coming in.

"The willingness to help was also present. Tables were full of food and cases of water littered the floor. Meals always managed to show up around lunch. There was no fan fare—no one waiting for a pat on the back—just everyone giving what they had to make it all work together. God had provided."

"In fact, we found just about everyone was willing to help out in some way. One time we were landing in Lafayette. Glen got on the horn to the controller and said, 'Hey, can you patch me through to a mechanic? I need a truck and this is what I need on it (wrenches, etc.).' When we landed, the truck was sitting there, full of tools. There was no, 'Please return to such and such,' or 'Here's my invoice. Call me.' It was just there. A lot of times, if we needed something, there were enough guys there in Lafayette to just make it happen."

That same type of "just-make-it-happen" attitude is present in the financial arrangements between Angel Flight 44 and McKesson. As Mike later explains, "Glen and his group were great for us because they were a reliable source. They would show up when they said they would. They got it done. No questions asked. A lot of stuff we did we took care of on the backside—which was great. It was not 'sign this, sign that.' It was a matter of making it happen and figuring out the paperwork later."

Glen Hyde also adds, "One of the first things the McKesson guys said was, 'We don't know how we're going to pay you.' So, I said, 'Don't worry about it. We'll figure that out later.' Later on, they cut us a check for our expenses—for gas and oil. We did not charge them anything for the use of the airplane itself, or for our time flying it. We just wanted to help those people down there, and they needed the supplies that McKesson could provide."

Preparations for the Future

With the experiences of Hurricane Katrina, it is easy to understand how any company would find it beneficial to debrief their field staff, examine their procedures, and discover what could be done to prepare for any future natural disasters. McKesson Pharmaceutical is no exception.

As Mike Ripple has learned, "All of the knowledge we gained from Katrina has allowed us to tweak our distribution centers' business continuity plans. We have done more in-depth preparations with our couriers and other critical vendors. They are plans we hope we will never need, but it is good to have them just in case.

"However, all you can do is prepare the best you can and react to whatever it is that nature presents. Glen, Denny, and the Super DC-3 helped us out tremendously in our time of need. The knowledge we gained has found its way into our preparation plans: we now ask our field personnel to know where the closest airport is and what is the length of the runway, how wide it is, and whether or not the airfield has aviation fuel."

In conclusion, Mike adds, "God was always with us. He was our security the whole time we spent in Katrina's aftermath. We were put into some unique situations, sometimes at odd hours of the night and never once faced peril or felt threatened. I believe the Lord was with us and protecting his servants, both in the air and on the ground. It was amazing how He led me to Glen and Denny hundreds of miles from home, yet coming from the same part of Texas."

Mike Ripple swaps more Katrina stories with Glen Hyde. Photo by Rich Vermillion

CHAPTER 18

Roques of Gibraltar

Rich's Note: Pastor Larry Roques (pronounced, "Rock") of Joy Fellowship Church in Slidell, Louisiana and his family are key figures within the Angel Flight 44 saga. The miracle of how he met Glen and Denny even forms the "bookends" of the account earlier in this book. However, we had to leave out many particulars in the main narrative. Consequently, we wanted to include these "extra scenes" in this portion of the book to give our readers a more comprehensive view of the story. His perspective also provides greater detail as to the living conditions in Slidell post-Katrina.

*The citations that follow are derived from the interview I conducted with Larry in Slidell, Louisiana in April of 2006. Therein, Pastor Roques describes many of the ministry efforts that were occurring at that time. Most are still underway even at the time of this writing, in October of 2006. The aftermath of Hurricane Katrina is still ongoing. What you are about to read is **in the voice of Pastor Larry Roques**.*

Extreme Broadcasting

I was in the broadcasting media for a living for twenty-some years before I went into the ministry. In all of those years, I can never remember the Emergency Broadcasting System ever being activated. It was frequently tested. But to my remembrance, it was never used. Well, we used it this time in Louisiana. Every station was broadcasting the same thing.

Warnings of pending destruction were ringing out from all quarters as the hurricane strengthened, even as high as Category 5. Yet, despite the tremendous alarm being expressed by local, state, and federal authorities, I had not yet fully realized the potential impact of the looming storm.

I still had not connected the dots. I knew this thing was bad. I knew this was a horrible storm. I knew it was out there. But really...I was one of those last-minute evacuees. I told my wife, "I lived through Hurricane Camille in 1969. I have lived in that town all my life—in fact, I have never lived anywhere else except that general area. I was born in New Orleans, but I have always lived in Slidell. So I can assure you that Slidell has never flooded. This is a high town! We are higher than New Orleans. Sure, New Orleans might get beat up, but we are going to be just fine. Let's just stay here instead of risking our lives traveling down the highway with no place to go."

At the last minute, my eldest daughter talked us into leaving with her and her husband. She called us at 6:00 Sunday morning and said, "Dad, you've got to leave. You have got to come with us. We are leaving now. This thing is headed straight up there—straight up the mouth of the Mississippi River!" That's what the weather forecasters thought it would do.

To the forecasters, that was the worst possible route the storm could take since it would remain over some water much farther inland—making the potential devastation of river waves immense. However, at the last minute, Katrina took a slight northeast turn. When it did, that automatically made the towns of Slidell, Bay St. Louis, Waveland, and Gulf Port, all "ground zero" targets for the storm.

Slidell was particularly hard-hit. That "high town" received the massive—and completely unexpected—storm surge from Lake Pontchartrain. A thirty-five-foot wall of water came ashore from the lake to spread colossal destruction as it moved inland.

I still break up and get upset about it. I don't *think* I have Katrina Post-Stress Syndrome, or whatever they call it. I think I just have the realization that God is a good God—and that He has brought us through this thing. That's it, I believe... it's the realization that God carried us through this thing. But when I talk about it, it's still easy for me to get caught up in it.

Thankfully, my wife and I were there for each other. When one of us would start to get overwhelmed and just collapse, the other one would sit there blowing in the other one's face saying, "It's alright. It's okay. Snap out of it."

Lack of Exposure

We eventually landed in Saint Francisville, Louisiana, north of Baton Rouge after riding the hurricane out in Laurel, Mississippi Sunday night and Monday. The storm had hit Laurel really hard as a Category 3, and caused a lot of damage in that area, too. Power was out, and the hotel was badly damaged. The ground floor had even been flooded. Consequently, when the police gave us the go-ahead to leave Laurel on Tuesday morning, we left. We headed west on a small two-lane road toward Jackson, Mississippi because the southbound roads were all wiped out.

As we headed west on this little road, we caught up with the tree-cutting crews who were clearing the roadway, and we followed them all the way into Jackson. A trip that normally was about an hour and a half actually took several hours with all the trees down and storm damage littering the roadway.

We did not find any open gas stations until we got to Jackson because power was out everywhere. Even half of Jackson was without power. So we gassed up the mini-van and were planning to head north to Memphis to stay until we could determine when we could go back to Slidell. Just before we left Jackson, though, my son-in-law, Steve Morris (who was also with us), got a message on his cell phone that had been left by his grandmother in Saint Francisville, Louisiana. She had found out we were all looking for a place to stay, and she was trying to track us all down to tell us we could stay with them at their house until we could head back to Slidell again. As a result, we changed plans and headed west to Saint Francisville instead of Memphis.

During this time of evacuating from one place to another, whenever we were able to watch a TV, we noticed the media was not talking about Slidell. *Nobody* was talking about it. Nobody would even *mention* it. They did not show any pictures of Slidell. All they would show was New Orleans and some of the Gulf Coast. I was becoming really irate. I said, "Why aren't they talking about Slidell? That's a huge residential area." But then I went into denial and started saying, "Well, you know why they're not talking about Slidell? It is because everything is okay. Everything's fine. We're going to be alright."

My eldest son, Joshua, somehow got past the National Guard about five hours after the storm made landfall [Monday], and drove from Pineville, Louisiana, into Slidell. He parked his car outside the city limits and walked into town. He then met somebody who stayed in a car, who then took him around to go check on stuff.

He went first to our house, then text messaged me later because he couldn't get a phone call out—too many cell phone towers were wiped out. It was Tuesday before I got the message, though, and the message said, "Dad, your house is real beat up. Can't even get to mine. Too much water. Can't get to Steve and Mikhael's (my son-in-law and daughter). Too much water. Maw Maw's (my mother) house has six feet of water." We just began to get these reports back. That is when I knew something really bad had happened there.

Then I saw the first aerial shots of Slidell on CNN. They did not even use the town's name in the report. They said something like, "We're coming into an area north of Lake Pontchartrain. Now we are following along the Interstate 10 twin spans, and we are looking at an area…we do not know what it is, we are going to find out more about it. But we're looking at an area that was apparently a residential area that was waterfront. It's been utterly obliterated." It looked like a bunch of matchsticks thrown against the shore. That area where they were videoing was the Eden Isles/Oak Harbor area—a very ritzy area…for us anyway.

The "matchsticks" of the Eden Isles/Oak Harbor area seen by Pastor Larry on CNN—as seen from the air over Lake Pontchartrain eight months later. Photo by Rich Vermillion

Rich's Note: *That area Larry and his family watched that night on CNN was the same area that Glen and Denny had seen from the air in the Super DC-3 a few days later. "That's the area that we kept looking at that I thought had been fishing piers," Denny later said. Of course, he now realizes that these are the remains of homes formerly built over the water itself, with piers leading from the shore out to them.*

Death Toll?

There are varying stories as to how many people died. The official count for the entire parish was about one hundred and two. For New Orleans, the official count was much higher—several hundred. But I think all of those figures are diminished greatly for the media's sake.

In fact, I was out at North Shore, which was an area that got hit really hard by the storm surge, and there was an apartment complex nearby where we were. I was leading a tour for a group from World Vision to show them some of the devastation out in that area. While we were there, Federal authorities were quarantining off one of the apartment buildings. They had just found seventy-eight bodies in a single apartment building of that complex. They said they think the people were having a hurricane party, and that it was probably a complex-wide party because it seemed like none of the people who lived there left.

So, in just one apartment building there were seventy-eight dead. Just down the street from there is another family of five whose bodies have not yet been recovered from their sunken home because of the hazards that make recovery nearly impossible. Add to that the fact that over thirteen hundred people are missing from the Slidell area alone—and does anybody think that one hundred and two is a realistic number of fatalities?

Returning to Slidell

When we made it back in on Wednesday to check things out, I still hadn't put two and two together. I still had not figured out exactly what was going on. I told somebody, "We're going to go down on Wednesday, and we're going to go see what's left."

So we drove in Wednesday from Saint Francisville. I went to my house to see it for the first time since the hurricane hit. It was a pretty big shock when I saw it. Then, when I finally got over that, I tried to investigate other houses in our family. I could not get to my mother's home because of the water still in the streets. I passed by the church, and it was still standing. It had trees all over it, but, thank God, it was still standing.

Once I got back to where we could get cell phone service, I got a hold of my wife to fill her in, and then I told her, "Well, you know what we've got to do."

Rich's Note: Pastors Larry and Leslie Roques sensed in their hearts a divine call to duty. While others were leaving the disaster area, they were heading back in. The courage and compassion of this family cannot be understated. Many are alive today because of this family's selfless efforts, faith, and personal sacrifice.

So, when I came back to Saint Francisville, we packed up the kids and headed back to Slidell the next day. On the way, we stopped off in Baton Rouge and bought $200 worth of groceries. We moved into the church since it was somewhat habitable and our house was definitely not. On Friday, we began feeding whomever we could, and for a couple of days we fed every church member still in the area until those supplies ran out. Some people had come back as we did from wherever they were scattered, to help us. We all slept there and lived there. We lived on peanut butter and crackers—stuff we did not have to refrigerate. It was a pretty "gamey" food selection after a couple of days.

We eventually got our generator in place and were able to run some lights. But we still had no air conditioning or water. It was still miserably hot everywhere. There was unbelievable damage done to the town. There were no lights at all. At nighttime, it was eerie to walk outside and just see the level of blackness.

In the beginning, when we first came back, the state police told us, "You're here. Do not go anywhere. The area is under Martial Law, and we don't want you doing anything." So we were stuck on the property. After a week, we were able to venture out a little bit. We began to use some people's houses that were on city services for hygiene and such. You could not drink the water, but you could take a bath in it and use it to flush toilets. We would go to different houses every night to use somebody's toilet or their shower or something. We found somebody who had gas water heat. Therefore, we were able to use their hot water to get a hot shower every couple of days.

About this time, I was finally beginning to put two and two together. I was sitting in my office thinking. I could not get my computer running to read my notes, but I just started looking them up in my Bible. I read the one about ministering to the families. I read the one I had given to the worship team about being joyful and not complaining, about not lamenting on your bed and being an encouragement to the Body. Everything began to come together for me about then.

Becoming Somewhat Functional

About six or seven days after the storm hit, we started going out to the airport. That is when we started working a little with the organization *Thirst No More*—a few days before we met Glen and Denny.

So we showed up, really as a favor, to help *Thirst No More* get some of the food off of some of their little planes. They told us that if we would help them, they would give us some of it. At first, we were okay because at that time, we did not have the long food lines that we ultimately did. So we would take food boxes back to the church, and people showed up to get it. It was very sporadic and unorganized in the beginning.

After another week [about two weeks after the storm], the Salvation Army showed up and started to cook some meals. It was great to have the meat of a *real* hot dog. They had their own refrigerators on their vehicle and were self-sufficient, so they did not need any outside electrical power. It was great!

For fuel for our cars, we had to have gasoline trucked in from out of state in covered vehicles because they were literally hijacking trucks with gasoline. They did not do it to us, thank God. In general, however, if they knew someone had gas they would try to hijack them. Then the hijackers would go and sell it since you could not get gasoline anywhere at that time. I think our first delivery of fuel was three fifty-five gallon drums. With that, we filled our vehicles so we could get around some. We used it for our generators, and we also gave some of it to the Salvation Army to keep their units running.

We have a well on the property. When we finally got a couple more generators up, we managed to get the pump going on the well. We then had active toilets going and clean drinking water since the well water was not contaminated.

We also made a makeshift shower out on one of the fire escapes of the church—which consisted of a blue tarp and a sprinkler head that we found. The bad news was that we were right underneath the flight plan for one of the hospitals. If you were above, you could look right down into that thing when you passed over. Therefore, women would not use that shower because choppers were passing over it all day. For a man, it's simply a "two-hand scramble" when you hear a chopper coming—and you are covered up. However, it is a little harder for a woman. It's almost like these choppers figured that out, and were flying low on purpose.

Overall, with the help of some outside Christian organizations, we were able to become more and more functional. And we were able to help meet more of the community's needs as a result.

A Hand Up

However, while we were whole-heartedly doing what we could to minister to our hurting area, I soon realized that not everyone understood the Gospel as I did.

I actually had another pastor in Slidell that came up to me and said, "Why don't you quit doing this? Why don't y'all just stop it and let people go and take care of themselves?"

But I answered him, "Haven't you figured it out? Most of these people do not have jobs to go back to. How can they take care of themselves?"

Then I said to him, "Hmm. Let's consider what you just said. Let's say I am an engineer for an oil company. My usual income of six digits, about $120,000 a year, has been severed for a while. But I am getting about $550 per week from my unemployment. Since I do not have a whole lot of expenses anymore—because I do not have to drive into the city every day and do a lot of things every day—I can make ends meet…with a little help. If I go through Joy Fellowship Church's food line, they help me take care of my groceries every week. That way, I could just live on my unemployment and work on my house—and get my life *normalized*.

"Or, I could take that good pastor's advice down the street and go get myself a minimum wage job at Wal-Mart and get yelled at by a manager—who is a kid with half the education I have—and my house goes un-repaired for lack of both time and money. Listen friend, I'm not interested in having these people humiliate themselves worse than they already are. I would rather just help them and meet them at their point of need and trust God to bring back the local economy in due time."

It is true that even the Burger Kings in Slidell were offering a $6,000 sign-on bonus for anyone willing to work for them. The problem was that the people who were left in Slidell were mostly those who had evacuated New Orleans and the other areas, and so they had no real permanent address. Therefore, they could not get a job because nobody would employ someone that has no way of being contacted. They need to know where to mail W-2's. So, there were so few people that were hirable in Slidell, that even Burger King had to offer sign-on bonuses to attract a few of those who were! This is where the 444 messages I received from the Lord months before make even more sense.

Feeding the Multitudes

The population of Slidell pre-Katrina was about 35,000—a nice little suburban town. The last numbers we heard, however, the number of people living in Slidell post-Katrina had grown to about 110,000. Those extra people came out of New Orleans and all the surrounding parishes. Hence, the "444" words—ministering to 3,200 families. We are definitely seeing that in our church now. We are actually in the midst of that message I received in May of 2005! In fact, I think we have actually surpassed that figure—at least in numbers of people to whom we have ministered. They come with sometimes two families in one car. Sometimes it is one person picking up food for the whole family.

However you slice it, they're coming from all these different places—and *every one* of those families is being witnessed to about the Lord. We are sharing the Gospel with *everyone* that comes on our property. Kenneth Copeland Ministries has provided us with literally truckloads of Bibles and materials. We make these little bags with all these Bible-based materials in them because a lot of these people are wondering why they are going through this tragedy. There are no real answers for them outside of the fact that, with God's help, we can all get through it. So through these bags of KCM materials, we can offer them a source of comfort.

To tell you the truth, there are people who would have spit on our property before this hurricane happened. But now that it has, these same people have been brought to the place where they've had to pull their cars onto our property to get what they needed to survive. Once they get there, I believe the presence of God pulls their hearts in. It's just like bait to a starving catfish. They want answers and we have one in Jesus—so we just use that to "reel them in."

Interestingly, just before the storm, we had developed a church logo with a fish hook that represents being "fishers of men." [Matthew 4:19] So, the hook was crafted more closely into the shape of a "J" for "Jesus." The fascinating thing, then, is that when we devised that logo, we had no idea how relevant it was going to be. Right now, we are literally fishing in a stream that has hundreds of fish that swim in to us every day. We drop the hook, and they bite down hard. They are people who are hungry for answers.

We are ministering to hundreds daily who come in there. They start lining up outside the parking lot at about 11:00 a.m. at our gate. They are coming for a box of food at lunchtime. As they come through, they go through different stations. At the first station, they will get bottled water. At the next station, they will get a box of food to take back to wherever they are staying. Then they will get cleaning products at the next station. Then they get hygiene products. Then they receive a hot meal for lunch. At the final station, they get a bag of Bibles and Bible materials that we give them—and then we have an opportunity to pray with them.

The food line outside of Joy Fellowship Church, eight months after Hurricane Katrina.
Photo by Rich Vermillion

It has been such an opportunity for us to share the gospel. The whole miracle of this thing for me began back in May of 2005, when I began to hear those words about getting the place ready—such as cleaning out all the closets. We need every square foot that we have in our building right now. It is only about 10,000 square feet total. I used to think that was a nice-sized building. Now, it is half full of food, and coats and blankets are filling up half of our sanctuary.

Church Note Due

In the midst of us reaching out to help the community as best as we could, we were also aware of the fact that Joy Fellowship had some needs of its own.

Pastor Larry Roques and Glen Hyde stand among some of the provisions stored inside of Joy Fellowship Church's building. Photo by Rich Vermillion

By the time I met Glen, Denny, and Chris at the airport for the first time, it had been two weeks since we had taken up an offering at our church. Basically, the church had no income—and we had a bank note coming due for our building. We did not have a congregation there to support the work because most of our congregation did not come back for a month. We had about twenty people living on the property, and those people were just surviving. They were people who could not afford to live in a hotel or somewhere. Some of them came back to help us feed people.

Out there at the airport that first day, Chris Clem from KCM said, "Look, we've brought some money. Do you need some? Do you need some cash to take care of some things?"

I had just found out we were getting that entire load of relief supplies, so this new news was just as shocking. After I blinked a few times in wonderment, I told him, "Well, I don't know if you can help me tonight, but we have got our church's bank note due as soon as our bank opens its doors again—which will be pretty soon. When they do, we are going to be required to come up with that money."

Chris then said, "Brother Copeland has given us an amount of money to carry with us in case someone needed some cash right away. How much is your note?"

"Almost $2,500," I said.

Chris gave me $1,000, and then Glen told me, "I've got the difference on the plane. Kenneth gave me some money too—just a couple of days ago."

So, thanks to the Lord using Kenneth Copeland, Chris, and Glen—our note was paid. When everything reopened, we had the money. KCM even helped us later to pay our building insurance premium when it came due. Without question, KCM was God's channel of provision for us…and the thousands we now minister to daily.

The Great Equalizer

The thing I have noticed about this whole operation we are involved in is that it has been *the great equalizer*. By that I mean, we see the people who come through our line—we see the soccer mom driving a late-model Lexus right behind the poor mom driving a '79 Buick. It is the great equalizer. Everybody was affected.

There have been people who have said, "Why in the world are we giving food to this person in the Lexus?"

I said, "Because that's all they've got left. They managed to get it out of the driveway of their home before the storm surge took the house off the foundation. Right now, they are in no better shape than the lady who had lived in the house trailer and now only has that '79 Buick. Neither of them has a place to live anymore." Thus, it has been in so many ways, the great equalizer. It has really put humility in a lot of people's lives—humility that was not there before Katrina.

Joy Fellowship and the Roques Today

Within a few months after Katrina, Larry and his family were able to move back into their home. However, even at the time of this writing, there remains damage to the house that has not yet been repaired. Also, his son, Joshua, and his wife lost their home entirely in the storm. The combination of flood waters and tree damage essentially obliterated it. Thus, they had to move in with Larry and Leslie, and at the time of this writing, were hopeful to move into a new home sometime in early 2007.

What about the church? Since those early days after Katrina, much has evolved around the ministry and purpose of Joy Fellowship Church. Pastors Larry and Leslie Roques and their congregation have witnessed a paradigm shift in the way they "do church." The little congregation that so humbly welcomed the opportunity to be used of God as a mighty disaster relief center is now seeking the Lord about doing more. "The one thing that we knew was that with God's help, there was nothing we could not do," said Pastor Larry. "It almost became a daily adventure to see needs presented by our situation, and then supernaturally met by the awesome power and provision of God."

Presently, Pastors Roques has stepped out in faith, hearing the voice of the Lord to "stretch out their tent pegs." They have just begun a new outreach work in the hardest hit area of New Orleans. The eastern bank of the Industrial Canal is the sight of the now famous Ninth Ward, where flooding exceeded twelve feet in some areas. It is a neighborhood that is only minutes from Joy Fellowship's facility in Slidell. Joy Fellowship Church answered the call of God to go into this devastated area and begin a new church work amidst the rubble and ruin. In the true tradition of Nehemiah 8:10, "The joy of the Lord is our strength," they intend to see "God raise up the walls" of the city from destruction.

Every Saturday, rain or shine, volunteers and discipleship students from Joy Fellowship Church load up "Peacemaker 44" (their KCM-donated Chevy Suburban) and attach a trailer loaded with boxes of food, hygiene articles, and bible packs, a small PA system and a gasoline- powered generator. They set up on a vacated lot in the Katrina-stricken Ninth Ward, only feet from the levee breach, and "have church." After an encouraging message by one of the team, they then get to the work of distribution of the much needed food and supplies to the hundreds of families who have returned to not much more than a vacant lot where their homes used to be.

For Christmas 2006, Angel flight 44 airlifted over one thousand toys in to the Slidell Airport, delivered to Joy Fellowship Church for distribution to hard-hit families in Slidell, as well as its new work in East New Orleans.

Most recently, Joy Fellowship has located a property that it hopes to call "home" for its New Orleans relief center and church campus. The building (a former church) has been abandoned by its previous occupants and congregation. It has now become available at an extremely low price. It has already been restored from the effects of the floodwaters, and is even equipped with a soup kitchen and life center already in the facility.

"Why was it abandoned?" you might ask. Many of the pastors and congregations of the approximately sixty churches that existed in the Ninth Ward just decided not to come back after Hurricane Katrina. At the time of this writing, there are only two churches getting ready to reopen of all of the old ones that were previously there.

The Lower Ninth Ward was the site of the highest crime rate in the entire city prior to Hurricane Katrina. Now it is just a shell of its former self, destroyed in many places beyond repair. "At this point, we are believing God for the finances to purchase the old church and see the miracles happen as the Ninth Ward comes back to life, too…and with life more abundant this time."

(To learn more about Joy Fellowship Church, their Katrina relief efforts, the Roques family, and the latest updates regarding their ministry, we encourage you to visit **www.joyfellowshipchurch.com** today.)

CHAPTER 19

Taking Care of "My" Marines

There is another intriguing aspect of the Angel Flight 44 story—one that involves a "few good men." Early on in these humanitarian aid flights, the U.S. Marines move into the Slidell airport to begin enforcing Martial Law. However, the Angel Flight 44 team—partnered with Kenneth Copeland Ministries—find themselves ministering to them as well. In other words, they have to help take care of the Marines...and gladly do so.

During the operation, Angel Flight 44 receives assistance from the Marines with debarkation (i.e., unloading the aircraft) and security. On the other hand, the Angel Flight 44 team provides the Marines with those things that they are lacking through their own logistics. It becomes a truly symbiotic relationship.

Chris Clem is one of the executives on staff at Kenneth Copeland Ministries during the Katrina relief effort. He and Dennis O'Brien are the two most involved in the operation. Chris later comments, "We were providing logistics to Pastor Larry's church in Slidell, to another church, support for Operation Blessing as needed, and then also for the Marine Corps. I mean, a significant part of what we brought in was for the Marines.

"What had happened was that the Marines had enough medications to treat a number of disaster victims, but not enough really to treat their own men. In fact, they were sent to Slidell without any of their vaccinations. We talked to Kenneth about that and he said very firmly, 'That's not acceptable.' Consequently, we got busy and did something to help those Marines."

Glen Hyde "introduced" himself to the nearly 700 Marines the first day they began to move into the Slidell Airport. Earlier in the book, we relayed the story of his initial conversation with the young second lieutenant regarding the availability of the airport for Angel Flight 44's continued flight operations. That incident helped set a "cooperative tone" between the two groups—especially when the young officer found out who Glen's old flight buddy was...General Bill "Spider" Nyland, Assistant Commandant of the Marine Corps.

Nevertheless, the old axiom continues to prove true, "Once a Marine, always a Marine." Glen's love and affection for this new generation of "Jar Heads" quickly becomes evident. The former U.S.M.C. captain essentially "adopts" these men and, with the enthusiastic backing of Kenneth Copeland and the entire KCM team, they do whatever they can to bless them. In Glen's mind, those are "his" Marines.

Shots

As Glen later recollects, "We had everything. We were bringing in food, water, medicine, generators...you name it! After a short while, though, I started to wonder if my Marines needed anything. After all, they unloaded the DC-3 every time we landed, transported the supplies wherever we needed them, helped to provide us with security—and they even removed truck loads of trash from Pastor Larry's church parking lot when it had built up from all that they were doing. There was no trash pickup service in operation in Slidell, of course, and when those Marines found out about the problem—they showed up and did something about it! So, I started to think, 'Now, what can we do for these guys?'"

So on one trip, Glen walks over and starts talking with a Marine sergeant to ask him how he is doing.

He replies, "Well, I just got back from my third rotation overseas—I had two rotations in Iraq right on the tail end of one in Afghanistan...and now I'm here. With this disaster, I was not able to get any leave time as was originally planned. They didn't even send us down here with our shots."

Glen is shocked at the last part. He quickly decides to press him for more information.

"Wait a minute. What do you mean you don't have your shots?"

The sergeant explains, "Well, we didn't have our shots before we came here. As you know, there's a lot of bad diseases down here right now with all this stuff going on. There's a lot of dead bodies floating around, and swamps that have been turned over, and bad mosquitoes. There's typhoid, diphtheria, black water disease, and everything else—things we never got inoculated for before we came."

Glen then asks, "Well, who's your corpsman?" (This is the Marine Corps' version of a "medic.")

"Chief Drennan," he answers.

"I've talked to him a few times, but he didn't say anything about shots. Get him on the radio. I don't have any transportation or I'd go over to him. So, can you get him over here? We're leaving in about twenty minutes, and I need to talk to him."

"Sure," he replies. He grabs his radio and locates the corpsman.

Once Chief Drennan comes over, Glen quizzes him about the inoculation issue.

"Chief, you know, 'Once a Marine, always a Marine;' and I understand that *my* Marines don't have their inoculations. So, what's the deal with the shots?"

"Well, they sent us down here without any to give them."

"Why don't you send them over to the hospital? You can get them their shots over there."

The corpsman's countenance drops slightly, and his tone becomes more serious as he answers, "Well, they won't take them over there."

Glen is somewhat astonished. "Why not?"

Chief Drennan explains, "They told us that we're 'government employees'… that we're not *their* responsibility."

Chief Drennan had called the hospital earlier in search of inoculations for the over 700 Marines encamped at the airport to perform security and humanitarian aid to the community. The hospital officials told him they did not have enough for the Marines. Actually, they had plenty on hand to supply nearly all of southern Louisiana…thanks to Glen and his Super Gooney.

However, the hospital has also become a distribution center for the other hospitals because of the abundant shipments coming in to them via Angel Flight 44. They simply do not want to use up any of that supply on the Marines—who they say are the "government's responsibility." This attitude displays a significant lack of understanding on the part of the hospital staff as to where and how those meds are coming to them.

Upon hearing of this, Glen's "feathers" become quite "ruffled." His indignation becomes readily apparent in his tone of voice as he replies, "Do you know that hospital wouldn't have any pharmaceuticals if wasn't for us supplying them?! We're supplying that hospital with that DC-3 right there," pointing toward his Super Gooney. "I tell you right now that we're going to fix this situation without delay. What do you need?"

131

Chief Drennan responds, "We need about five shots per Marine. We've got typhoid, diphtheria, black water disease…," and lists two other diseases with names too long to pronounce.

"Write them down. I'll make a couple of calls," Glen assures him.

The corpsman makes a list and hands it to the former Marine Corps captain. Glen then walks over, sits down in his OCC chair under the wing of the Super DC-3, and calls John Brannan. He is the local rep for McKesson Pharmaceutical, and Glen wants him to contact the hospital about this matter immediately.

Once Glen briefs him on the situation, John replies, "Glen, just tell them to go over to the hospital and get their shots. They've got plenty over there."

Glen explains, "They won't give them to them because they say that the Marines are not the hospital's *responsibility*. But you ask the head nurse there this, 'Is it Glen Hyde's *responsibility* to furnish free air transportation to keep that hospital open without receiving compensation for all those thousands of people that are being served there?' We're furnishing our own airplane, our own fuel—so the Church is essentially furnishing all these medical supplies. Furthermore, we're loading and unloading this stuff through these Marines over here. They wouldn't have anything at that hospital if it wasn't for my DC-3 and these Marines."

"They said what?! I'll call you back," John replies, and then hangs up the phone.

John Brannan calls the hospital and gets a supervisor on the phone to discuss inoculations for the Marines. She tells him the same thing she had said to the corpsman before—that the Marines are not their responsibility.

John then counters, "Listen, do you know where all your supplies are coming from? A former United States Marine. They have a saying, 'Once a Marine, always a Marine.' To Captain Hyde, those young Marines are *his* Marines—and you have already stepped on his toes by refusing to take care of those men. He flies those supplies in on his own personal DC-3, and then those same Marines unload them for transport to your facility. In other words, you are biting the hands that are feeding you! If you want your hospital to continue to be supplied, you'd better change your policy *real quick* and take care of *his* Marines!"

She quickly replies, "Oh, my! I didn't realize…uh…good point! We'll take care of them!"

After he signs off with the hospital, John calls Glen back about fifteen minutes later. "I *explained* things to that supervisor, and she is very cooperative now. She said, 'Bring them on over! Just please send them in groups of only fifty and line them up. We'll take care of them.' So tell Chief Drennan to send them over."

Glen is very appreciative of John's assistance, and his temper immediately subsides. Standing up from the OCC chair, he heads over to the chief and the Marine officer in charge to give them the good news. Elated, they immediately begin to send the men over in groups of fifty, as requested.

Sometime later, the corpsman informs Glen that there are a few types of shots that his men need but are not available in the hospital's inventory. He replies, "We'll get those shots."

He sits down in the OCC chair again and calls back to a contact over at McKesson's Arlington, Texas distribution center, and puts in an order. It is about 9:30 a.m. when he makes the call.

After informing Chief Drennan that the order has been placed, the corpsman asks, "When are you going to be back with the supplies? Tomorrow?"

"No, we're going to be back today."

"Today?!"

"Yep, today," Glen smiles. "This is not a picnic. We've got a hurricane situation here. This is a job, and we're going to do this job. We are taking care of my Marines today."

Showers

Now that the inoculation issue is resolved, Glen then wants to know what other services he can provide for his Marines. He turns to the lieutenant and asks, "What else do you Marines need?"

The officer answers, "Well, sir, my Marines have not had a bath since they have been here…over a week now. In this heat and humidity, they're starting to get quite ripe. Do you think you could find some portable showers for us?"

"How many do you need?"

"Could you maybe find us two or three?"

Glen chuckles and replies, "Two or three? For seven hundred Marines? Lieutenant, the Marines have certainly mastered the art of doing 'so much, for so long, with so little—that they have become masters of doing the impossible with nothing, forever.' If you're asking for two or three showers, I know you *really* need ten to fifteen. We'll get them. What else?"

Somewhat embarrassed, the officer answers again, "Well, sir, my Marines don't all have enough sleeping bags, or tents, or…"

Glen is amazed at what the young officer is telling him. The U.S. government is overwhelmed by the size and scope of the catastrophe. Coupled with their overseas commitments to the War on Terror, their logistics are apparently beleaguered by the situation. Consequently, the military forces sent into the Hurricane Katrina disaster areas are poorly supplied and equipped. Even the essentials are lacking.

After taking notes, Glen has a list of gear that the Marines need. He heads back over to his OCC chair under the wing of the 'Gooney Bird' once more. Glen calls Chris Clem, who was, at the time, in his office back at Kenneth Copeland Ministries.

With a shopping list in hand, Chris quickly joins up with Dennis O'Brien and the team. They head off to one of the world's premier hunting, fishing and outdoor gear suppliers, Cabela's. They have an impressive showroom just north of Fort Worth, Texas. After Chris and Dennis explain to the manager why they need the fifteen portable showers, the manager gladly supplies them at a heavy discount. He wants to help the ministry with its Katrina relief operations. Sleeping bags, tents, and other necessary "camping" supplies are also obtained, per the lieutenant's request.

The Super DC-3 lands later that day back at Copeland Field to load up the custom-order of pharmaceuticals for the Marines—now in transit to KCM by courier from McKesson. As they taxi to the hangar, Glen and Denny discover that the showers and camping gear are already staged and ready to be loaded for the next flight.

"Man, these guys are on the ball," Glen comments to Denny with a grin.

They park the aircraft and shut down the engines. While the volunteers are busily loading the precious cargo, Denny begins checking the oil and overseeing the refueling of the aircraft with the help of David Orozco—a veteran pilot and airplane mechanic who has volunteered his time to help with the relief operations. As the two work, Denny overhears Dennis O'Brien talking to Travis Clay, the manager of hospitality at Kenneth Copeland Ministries:

"Travis, there is a courier on his way over here from McKesson with a custom order for the Marines. I don't know if they are donating them, or if the order is being paid for by the Marines, or what. But, if the courier hands you an invoice, *pay it*—no questions asked."

Travis responds, "You bet."

"Wow," Denny thinks to himself. "These guys here at KCM are really top-notch. They don't care about paperwork or getting reimbursed...just about helping people."

The courier arrives a short while later with the much-needed vaccinations for the Marines. Travis Clay discovers that McKesson has actually donated the shots in support of the relief operations, and he simply has to direct the courier to the appropriate place to unload his van.

Once everything is loaded and secured, Angel Flight 44 takes off again non-stop for Slidell. By 5:00 p.m. that afternoon, the teamwork between Angel

Flight 44 and KCM, along with the generosity of McKesson Pharmaceutical and Cabela's, has resulted in the Marines receiving their remaining shots, badly needed showers…and some *very nice* camping gear.

CHAPTER 20

Impacted

There is a consistent sentiment expressed by those who personally witnessed the aftermath of Katrina: "It just impacted me." The sheer shock factor of seeing so much devastation is huge. Believe me, I know this firsthand. Beyond that, the realization of the goodness of God in the midst of such catastrophe is ultra life-altering. Thus, I thought it appropriate to include this chapter in the overall text to highlight these facts.

We will begin with my own (Rich Vermillion's) experience visiting Slidell to conduct research for writing *Angel Flight 44*. Then, we will read Chris Clem's impressions from his participation in the relief missions. We will subsequently end this chapter with Glen Hyde's story about how one of the relief aid vendors was personally impacted when he visited Slidell. As you read these accounts, you may find yourself "impacted" by them as well.

My Experience

As the writing author of this book, I felt the need to fly down to Slidell myself to see what the area looked like, and to put some faces with the many names of this story. Therefore, in April of 2006—about eight months after the hurricane—Glen and I flew down there in a Cessna 210 (which Tom Westberry generously loaned to us). We met with Pastor Larry Roques and his church, and with Bill Horan and the Operation Blessing team in Slidell. We also toured the entire area, including the waterfront areas of Lake Pontchartrain.

I have to admit, I was quite shocked at how evident the devastation still was—so long after the event had occurred. Of course, by then we did not see bodies floating around in the streets. However, you could still see much of the *effects* created by the storm surge eight months after the event. Moreover, it became progressively worse the closer you came to the lake.

Pastor Larry and his family toured us through the area. At different points, I would say, "Stop!" and jump out with my camera to take a few digital shots of the wreckage I saw. He showed us the commercial buildings, shopping centers, malls, and fast-food businesses that were all flooded out—several miles inland. Each of those buildings must now be demolished.

We toured the downtown district where the government buildings are. Some had already been renovated and reopened. Others remained unusable with the watermarks still showing on their exteriors six to eight feet high. Many houses and business around that area had been abandoned by their owners—some intending never to return.

The most remarkable examples of damage and destruction are at the waterfront. Some were houses with boats stuck in them; one had a car intertwined within the debris. Several were homes that had been flooded, but looked as if they could be repaired and made habitable once again because the structures were intact. Others were devastated beyond repair. In fact, one house in particular still impresses my memory so clearly today…

Just a hundred feet or so from the lake and a smaller bridge that is west of the I-10 twin spans, was a lagoon of sorts. It was off from the lake and connected by a small canal. On the edge of this deep lagoon was a house that had been knocked completely over into it by the storm surge. All you could see of the house was the roof. It had apparently been built on piers with the lagoon to its rear, and the roadway to its front—facing the marshes of the lake beyond. When the wall of water struck it, it smashed over into the lagoon and sunk. All that was now visible was this roof.

There is another small road that passes this house on the backside. It is on the opposite side of the lagoon, and we were using it as a shortcut to the lakefront. As we passed by, I laid eyes on this wreckage. I seemed drawn to it in my spirit. Intrigued, I again said, "Stop!" to my gracious host—who admits that he often forgot that I might want to look at something before he whisked by. Jumping out, I walked over toward the lagoon from the side opposite the remains of the house.

As I approached the water's edge, something rather large moved in the water as if startled by my presence. I then remembered I was in alligator country. Consequently, I warily stayed back a few yards from the water's edge and kept one eye toward the water's surface—just in case.

The wreckage seemed so surreal. I snapped pictures of the strange sight. Behind me there was a conversation occurring in the Suburban between Larry and Glen. However, I could only hear the sound, not the words being spoken. I really was not paying attention to them at all, but only to the task at hand. After I had taken all the pictures I wanted, I returned to the vehicle and climbed in for the remainder of the tour.

Sometime later, Glen shared with me, "Do you remember that sunken house in that lagoon thing…the one with only the roof sticking up?"

"Very clearly," I replied. "That thing just sticks out in my memory. I can see it in my mind right now, in fact."

"Well, Larry explained to me that a family of five—two parents and three kids—were in that house when the storm came. They had planned to ride out the storm there. When that wall of water hit, all five of them died in that house—and their bodies have never been recovered. With all that wreckage, the conditions are too dangerous for divers to go in there and pull them out. And they can't get a crane big enough to pull that house up out of the water, near enough to do it."

The sunken house. Photo by Rich Vermillion

My heart sank. I had felt strangely drawn to that submerged house before. Now, I realized that the bodies of that family are still entombed inside. When I look back on that day in Slidell, it was as if my own born-again spirit was telling me at that water's side, "They're still in there, and it's just not right that they stay there." Yet, at this point, there is nothing anybody can do. Sadly, the only ones who could have done something about it, died therein.

The stories like this are almost endless. It is no wonder that every person involved in the relief effort said to me, in one form or another, "I was profoundly affected by what I saw." I can now certainly relate—and I was seeing it eight months later. The thing that strikes me so profoundly about it is that much of the loss of life could have been prevented. If the government in New Orleans had reacted sooner, lives would have been saved in that city. If people had heeded the many other warnings and pleas from the federal government and state authorities in Louisiana and Mississippi to seek safety, even more would be alive today.

Despite the magnitude of the destruction, however, I want to emphasize God's kindness. Without question, the goodness of God that manifested in the midst of such tragedy is the most impacting. The majority of *Angel Flight 44* is devoted to calling attention to these tremendous stories of His grace: the babies who received their insulin and lived through it as a result; the storm victims who were treated because of the emergency medical supplies flown in from McKesson; the hungry pastor whose church became an overnight warehouse that fed the entire area. These demonstrations of God's loving care are what truly change a life forever.

I trust that you also have been blessed by these stories through *Angel Flight 44*. I can assure you wholeheartedly that I have been forever changed by researching them, and writing them for you to read. Can you imagine what the effects have been on Glen Hyde, Denny Ghiringhelli, Larry and Leslie Roques, and the many others, for having lived it? I can…just a little, anyway.

Chris Clem's Impressions

Chris recalls, "Glen said to me, 'You've got to see it.' So I flew out there on mission number three. That first time out there was certainly something I will likely always remember.

"From the air, you could see the trees and houses. It looked like a war zone. We landed in Slidell. My first impression was, 'Where is their control tower?' because I heard this Marine talking in my headset, and I did not see a control tower. Well, the control tower looked like a [truck] with two Marines sitting on it with walkie-talkies—and you had to be within a couple miles to be able to communicate with them.

"The other thing I noticed was helicopters everywhere. This was a small airport. I was looking at airplanes upside down. There was a hangar where three quarters of the sheet metal was gone, and inside of it were crushed airplanes on top of each other. There were piles of sheet metal stacked up that apparently had been bulldozed by the Marines or whoever to clear the runway and things like that.

"It was what I imagined from when I had seen pictures of war zones. It just looked like the place had blown up. There was a lot of it still standing, but there was a lot of it torn up. There were helicopters literally lined up hovering behind each other—two, three, or four in a row—that would come in; their engines would stay running as they would fuel back up and take off.

"I would not say I was in shock because I had prepared myself emotionally. You just knew you could not get emotionally involved because you would not be able to function. I knew that. It was tough. It would be when we were flying back that the emotions would hit. I would be in the jump seat behind Glen and we would be talking…then the emotions would hit. Of course, then you are talking about it, which is good because you get to release those emotions. But while you're there, you're accomplishing a mission—so you can't afford to get emotional.

"I remember flying down there with Glen and I was looking down at these trees, and two hundred yards inland was a sailboat. Denny said to me, 'Look at that, Chris.' And there was this huge sailboat there in the middle of the woods!

"There were lots of things like that. Looking down from the altitudes we were coming in at, you could see the paths of the wind patterns, the vortexes. You could see the vortex patterns on the trees. They would all be blowing one way for a quarter of a mile, and then in another spot, you could see where they were blowing a different direction for a quarter of a mile.

"Once we would land, the Marines and Pastor Larry were there. The Marines, Pastor Larry, Ron Oates [with Operation Blessing], and everybody else I initially talked to was focused *on other people*. The attitude was, 'We've got to get water to people, we've got to get food to people, we've got to get diapers'—whatever the list was that day. Literally, it changed almost every day. Every couple of days, you could see the situation changing based on what people requested.

"I knew it was going to be important to minister to Pastor Larry whenever I was out there because he was pouring out so much to others. So we really tried to take a very personal interest in what we could do for him and his family. The ladies here put together a gift basket for his wife, with soaps and bath type of items.

"I was given instructions when my assistant, Vanessa, handed me the gift basket that the women had put together for Pastor Larry's wife. I was thinking about everything going on and was not altogether 'there' at the moment—and she *knew* that. So she grabbed me by the shirt and pulled me down (she is a little bitty lady), and said, 'Now look at me. This basket has got to get into his wife's hands. Do you understand me?'

"I said, 'Yes, ma'am! I understand you.' I knew I didn't want that kind of trouble!" Chris says with a chuckle. "That same day we gave Pastor Larry some more money to help him with some other things—and we got that basket to his wife to try to minister to her personally.

"So, again, while we were reaching out to a lot of people, it was those kinds of stories that I remember the most—of trying to minister to them one-on-one."

Vendor Impact

Glen and Denny had several representatives from different vendors who rode down with them to Slidell in the Super DC-3 to get a firsthand glimpse of how their donated goods were being utilized. On one occasion, an executive from one of the vendors rode along. Before the trip, someone warned Glen that the man was a non-Christian with very little use for "religious" things. To which Glen replied, "Oh, really? Well, that may be so...but there are many 'heart strings' within a man's heart that the Lord can 'pull' to get through to him. I think we'll see a few of them get pulled today."

As Glen elaborates, "He was a non-believer. When he got on the airplane, he was joking about things, laughing, and having fun. I got in the cockpit and I said to Denny, 'I wonder what is going to happen to that guy when he sees that food line down there a mile and a half long.' Well, by the time we got there, it was two and a half to three miles long—full of people who had not eaten anything in two or three days, including entire families.

"This guy followed Chris and a couple of Larry Roques' volunteers way down the food line and watched them as they tapped on this one windshield of a car. It had a guy in it with his wife, and three kids in the back seat. They asked the guy, 'When have y'all eaten last?'

"The man said, 'Well, we ate about three days ago. The kids ate a little bit yesterday, not much, but they really have not eaten anything significant in two days. And we have one bottle of water left.'

"'How much gas have you got in your car?'

"'Close to none.'

"(Now, the food executive was watching and listening to all of this.)

"Then they got on the walkie-talkie and called back up to the church to get them hot meals sent down. They fed them right there, and filled up their trunk full of food and their gas tank full of gas.

"Then, they went to another car and another and another. It was a different story with each family all the way down. All the while, this guy is following them around taking all of this in.

"The man comes back to the airport where Denny and I have been supervising the unloading and prepping the DC-3 for the flight back. He gets back on the airplane after all of this, and just sits down in one of the passenger seats we had left bolted into the cargo area for the occasional passenger. He does not say a word to anybody. No smile, no laugh—just sits there with his hand on his chin thinking.

"After we get airborne and get to our cruising altitude for the flight home, I tell Denny, 'Take the controls. I'm going back there for a minute to check on him.'

"So, I head back and plop down in the seat next to him and say, 'Are you alright? What's going on with you?'

"He drops his hand from his chin, looks at me, and says, 'Mr. Hyde, let me tell you something. Anything you all need for those people back there, you have got it. Our company will supply you anything you ask!'

"The man is now a different human being. He realizes that this is serious. People just walked out of their homes one day with what they were wearing, and what they have got now is all they have. Their whole life went down in one swoop. Everything behind them is gone. There's no sense in going back home because there is no home there anymore. There's no job anymore. There's no money there anymore. There's no food there. So there is nothing to go back to. They went from being upscale, hardworking Americans to basically beggars at the snap of your fingers.

"This man saw that for himself on that trip…firsthand…and he'll never be the same again."

Changed

Whether we are discussing the vendor, Chris, Glen, Denny, or myself—we have all been changed by Katrina. For that matter, anyone who has had an opportunity to view the damage firsthand has been altered thereby. Obviously, the people whose lives have been directly affected by the storm—those who lost family, friends, and/or possessions—have experienced the most impact from this event. Nonetheless, just observing the aftermath personally is sufficient to make an impression on you that will last forever.

Then there is God's loving grace…

Oh, what a difference His grace has made! Thank God for the many people who heeded the call to help. I thank God that Kenneth Copeland obeyed the Holy Spirit, and got involved. I thank God for Bill Horan, Jody Herrington, and the outstanding organization called Operation Blessing, and all they do every day to help people worldwide. I thank God for the Salvation Army and the many other organizations who swooped in to succor those in need. And I thank God for a big-hearted salty ol' former Marine, his Super DC-3, and a willing and dedicated American Airlines captain.

Most of all, thank You, Jesus, for providing all of these. You, most Holy Sir, are truly the Savior…and we all love You for it.

PART IV

Behind the Scenes at OBI

"We are very market-driven...particularly in disasters. We want to go where the hurt is. Wherever the hurt is, that is where we want to be, demonstrating 'Christian Compassion in Action' by providing *relief in real time.*"

–Bill Horan

Pictured above (from left to right): Jody Herrington; Leslie, Larry, and Abigail Roques; Glen Hyde; and Bill Horan. Photo by Rich Vermillion

CHAPTER 21

Oh, What a Blessing!

There are some tremendous faith-based organizations in the world providing humanitarian aid and disaster relief. There are precious few, however, that can compare with the phenomenal work being done globally by Operation Blessing.

Much of Operation Blessing's involvement in the Katrina relief efforts took place after the time period covered by the main narrative in the first part of *Angel Flight 44*. That story covered the time from when Glen first received his "orders" from Heaven to restore the Super DC-3, up to the third day of relief flight operations. Much of Operation Blessing's interface with the Angel Flight 44 flights took place after that.

Moreover, Operation Blessing's relief efforts extend beyond the town of Slidell, Louisiana alone—or even Hurricane Katrina aid in general. Their efforts are continuously happening worldwide. One of the honors associated with being able to research and write this book was the opportunity to see firsthand the work they are doing in Slidell, and to interview Bill Horan and some of his other key leaders. Thus, this section of *Angel Flight 44* is devoted to highlighting the tremendous work these folks are doing around the world, with special emphasis being placed on their Katrina relief efforts and interface with Angel Flight 44 flight operations.

Lessons from the Hurricanes of 2004

Operation Blessing International Relief and Development Corporation (OBI) learned during the hurricane season of 2004 that one of the most effective ways they could help hurricane victims was by fueling the affected churches and church groups with *cash*.

These groups needed ready money that could be spent when the banking systems, credit card terminals, and other electronic transaction devices were rendered useless by the power outages caused by the storms. In our modern economy, *electricity* is often more important than how much you have in your bank account—or your credit limit—when it comes to making a purchase. When the power was gone, the economy in the affected areas quickly transitioned into mostly a cash-only financial system.

Moreover, while food, water and other relief supplies are always appreciated, urgent needs vary according to specific conditions caused by the storm. For example, victims in one area might still be in their homes, but without power. Therefore, generators may be the key. In another area where the homes were destroyed, victims may be huddled in churches or shelters. In that case, blankets and cots are the most urgent necessities. Cash readily converts into what is most needed in almost any circumstance.

Making cash grants was uncharted territory for OBI. Historically, during times of domestic disaster, OBI devoted its fleet of trucks and refrigerated trailers to logistic support of The Salvation Army's mass feeding program. During the 2004 hurricane season, OBI's donors were especially generous and provided funds that more than covered the massive support of The Salvation Army. This enabled the birth of a new fast-track cash grant program.

One reason for the increase in donations is that OBI is able to show proof of performance to donors on almost a daily basis. As the humanitarian relief arm of the Christian Broadcasting Network (CBN), they supplied Pat Robertson and the 700 Club with stories, anecdotes, and actual video footage of what Operation Blessing was doing on the front lines of hurricane relief. As a result, viewers responded to that overwhelming "proof of performance" because they could *see* clear evidence of OBI's good stewardship.

Suddenly, OBI found itself with extra money in the bank, available for innovative new programs to help victims. Bill Horan and his management team decided that a cash grant program—one that put hard cash into the hands of pastors and church leaders already engaged in disaster relief—was the best way to utilize the additional funds. The results were phenomenal, so the program became an ongoing part of OBI's disaster relief efforts.

Operation Blessing's new cash grant program is designed to multiply and leverage the efforts of church groups who are already providing volunteer assistance to victims, but lack funding to do more. OBI staff is anxious to help, but asks many questions before they do. As Bill Horan explains, "We are big on making sure that grant recipients are responsible and have a plan. We ask lots of questions like: 'Are you feeding the people? Are you sheltering them? Do they need chainsaws, tarps, generators, or building materials? Do your people need money to stay in a hotel? Do they need vouchers for groceries or gas?' You could fill in the blank with regard to the need. But the key thing we want to know is how are these groups helping people in tangible ways—*before* we start handing out the cash. We have a huge respect for the intentions of our donors. Therefore, we insist on good stewardship and accountability from those who participate in the cash grant program."

Operation Blessing made hundreds of cash grants during the 2004 hurricane season and distributed over $3 million dollars through the new program.

Quick and Simple

OBI's simple fast-track program allows a pastor or the leader of a faith-based organization to access these funds quickly. They simply fill out a two page application and then show OBI an actual business-like plan. These funds are not given to those who just sit idly by and "hope for the best," but rather to organizations that can articulate a business-like strategy explaining how they are going to help the storm victims. The churches and faith-based groups possessing a plan and applying for funds find that Operation Blessing is very willing to give them some money to support their efforts.

Thus, with lessons learned during the 2004 hurricane season and the phenomenal success of their new cash-grant program, Operation Blessing was in an excellent position to support relief efforts in the 2005 season when Hurricanes Katrina and Rita ravaged the Gulf Coast region. In the case of Katrina relief, OBI made $5.9 million in cash grants to 239 different faith-based organizations.

"There were actually 279 grants made," Bill Horan shares. "But certain groups received more than one grant. We will also continue to issue these cash grants to the faith-based organizations who request them, as long as the well doesn't run dry."

Thank you, donors, for ensuring that Operation Blessing's "wells" stay full. Lives still depend on OBI. Moreover, many more people might need to "drink" from their supply very soon. In fact, the Bible indicates that there will be more natural disasters as we approach the Day of the Lord (but more on that later). Therefore, it is imperative that ministries like Operation Blessing stay fully funded. Donors and their contributions make that happen.

How effective is the cash-grant program? Bill Horan continues by explaining, "What we found in doing these cash grants is that there might be a little church group out in Mississippi somewhere that has got a bunch of volunteers who have a heart to do something good—but there's only so much money the locals can raise. If we can give them some money to augment the work that the volunteers are performing for free, we are going to do that. The cash then acts as a force multiplier, and we get more 'bang' out of each donor buck.

"Our average grant is around eighteen thousand; there have been some for as little as $5,000; there have been a few for as much as $150,000. To distribute the grants, we have developed a huge network of Christian churches—without regard to denomination. The Lord has given CBN a strong voice through the 700 Club, and Christians all over the United States have an opportunity to partner in OBI efforts by sending money—*all* of which will be used for disaster relief, and *none* of which will be used for administration or fund-raising."

Throughout the short history of the new cash-grant program, Operation Blessing has proven itself to be a very good steward. This program has provided clear evidence to the world that Christians are doing humanitarian relief works because they *believe* in it. They do it because their faith dictates that they do this sort of thing. Consequently, the Christians have demonstrated that they are more apt to do a good job than secular organizations.

This solid Christian witness has also provided the Body of Christ *leverage* within these disaster-stricken communities. As the people see believers doing selfless acts of service, providing food and hygiene supplies, repairing homes—and even executing rescue efforts—they are impacted by what they see. People come to know the Messiah, favor is bestowed upon the churches and faith-based organizations within their communities—even among government leaders. Jesus is magnified in the eyes of all.

Thus, a catastrophe can turn quickly into a *revival*.

Hired Just in Time

Jody Herrington is Operation Blessing's Director, U.S. Disaster Relief—and a very godly woman. This "handmaiden of the Lord" has proven to be a tremendous asset to OBI and the community she now serves. Interestingly, she just "happened" to be hired shortly before this disaster struck.

"She's very sharp," Bill Horan comments. "She's only 31 years old and was really thrown into the 'deep end of the pool.' In fact, her first day with Operation Blessing just happened to be the day Katrina came to shore. A couple of months before her first day with OBI, we had planned for her to be with us at our headquarters, but it just happened that her first day was when the hurricane hit. She was supposed to live in Virginia Beach, but she now lives in an RV in Slidell."

Jody has a full-time staff of thirty-one living at OBI's Command Center in Slidell. Besides administration staff, she has a construction coordinator, electrician, several mechanics, counselors, cooks, warehouse personnel, and volunteer coordinators. And in addition to the OBI staff, she also oversees a contracted security team that safeguards the facility.

The warehouse portion of Operation Blessing's Slidell campus is 22,000 square feet. There, OBI is able to store basic tools—ladders, wheelbarrows, shovels, safety equipment, and so forth—and house their volunteers. The main facility has separate sleeping quarters for the men and women, and has had as many as 330 workers operating from that location at one time. By November of 2006, OBI volunteer teams have logged over 146,000 hours of free service.

The volunteers check out tools in the morning and check them back in again in the evening. Jody has a 7:00 p.m. meeting every night with all the team leaders to debrief them regarding work they did during the day, and to issue new work orders for the next day. Everything is organized to keep things safe and simple.

Then at 7:30 p.m., Jody meets with all the volunteers present on the OBI campus. As she shares, "For me, that is probably one of the most important fifteen to thirty minutes I spend during my day. In that meeting, we check on how they are doing, share prayer requests, and determine how we can serve them better. There are things they see that we do not see. That is how I kind of 'steer the ship' and take care of the campus volunteers. I realize that if I miss that meeting, it starts to get 'bumpy' along the way. Besides, the volunteers really appreciate it because it shows we *value* them. So 95% of the time, I conduct the volunteer meeting personally. The other 5% of the time, I make sure that someone on my staff meets with them each night."

Regrettably, volunteer staffing has declined drastically since the Spring of 2006. With the news media reporting less and less on the continuing humanitarian and rebuilding efforts, there has been a decline in the number of churches and faith-based organizations sending groups to help with the endeavor. Nevertheless, the task is enormous, and there is still much work to be done. In fact, at the time of this writing, there were people still *dying* there as a direct result of Hurricane Katrina.

Katrina's Effect on the Middle Class

"In my mind, the biggest thing to focus on is medical," explains Bill Horan. "Katrina is still killing people today. People will die today as a direct result of that storm—*and nobody even knows it*. They are dying because they are out of medicine, they are out of prescriptions, and they do not have anywhere to turn. They do not have any money, and they do not have any health insurance. And I'm not just talking about street people who were chronically poor before Katrina. I'm referring to a whole demographic that we refer to as the 'newly made poor'—people who were not poor before Katrina but are now. These are people who had homes and jobs and health insurance, but now have none of the above...but rather mortgages they can't pay, insurance companies that won't pay, and diseases like hypertension and diabetes that won't go away.

"For example, we had a lady come into our medical clinic two weeks ago. I think it was the day after it opened in New Orleans East. Her name is Darlene. She is a black woman who has been teaching kindergarten in the public school system in New Orleans for twenty-nine years. When Katrina came, her school was flooded—as all of them were—and so it was shut down. Her home was destroyed, and her mother drowned. Then the day they found her mother's body, her sister was overcome by the added stress and dropped dead. Then, when the school system bankrupted, she lost her health insurance.

"She is an educated woman who drives a nice car, has always paid her own way, and has never had to ask anybody for anything in her life. On top of all that, she is also diabetic and has high blood pressure. She no longer had the money or the insurance to buy her medicine, her blood pressure was off the chart, and her sugar was all messed up.

"Thankfully, she happened to hear about our clinic. She came there, our doctors treated her, and we gave her the meds she needed.

"The great thing about this story is that we actually hired her right after that. We were looking for a lady to work our clinic front desk, and I am telling you, the Lord brought this woman to us. She is *perfect* for the position. However, Darlene is an excellent example of one of the 'newly made poor' that I am talking about."

Lamentably, there are tens of thousands of people like Darlene all over southern Louisiana and Mississippi. Many are now living in Baton Rouge, Houston, and other areas. Then there are the elderly poor who have been similarly displaced. Such people now find themselves with no health benefits whatsoever—and no prescription drugs. According to Operation Blessing's clinic statistics, sixty percent of their patients are hypertensive and require high blood pressure medicine. About fifteen percent of the rest are diabetic, and they need insulin or blood glucose testing.

"So medicine and medical services are going to be the main focus of Operation Blessing. Of course, we are going to keep doing the house-gutting and repairs because they are critically important. You have got to light the spark of hope in the hearts of these people. When you've got no money, no possessions, and no job, and your house is still full of mold and rotted sheet rock, soggy furniture—and snakes—it is certainly important that somebody step in there and help you out. So OBI is going to remain in that business as long as the donors support us. However, these people with the medical issues are a real problem. We have got to do whatever we can to get the focus of mainstream America back on the dilemma we have right here in the United States."

Jody Herrington adds, "Beyond the medical needs, we still have some people in dire need of food. Pastor Randy, of one of the churches that we work with in St. Bernard Parish, has probably the largest and strongest disaster relief center in that parish. He has a tent complex set up there. People come through with a grocery cart and pick up their food. I remember seeing a businessman in a suit come through to get groceries. You *know* that had to be hard for him because he never had to depend on free food to get groceries before. But he had to take his lunch break and come and get food—just like everybody else. He's a guy who probably had a great job at one time."

Bill Horan then concludes this discussion by saying, "Operation Blessing has full-time operations in fifteen countries around the world dealing with all sorts of suffering—and I'm not making light of any of that. But my personal focus is on the United States right now. We *really* have to help these folks down here."

Getting Media Exposure

It is obvious that the American public has begun to lose touch with the overwhelming needs still pressing in those areas struck by Hurricanes Katrina and Rita. As world events, economic news, and politics compete for the media's attention, the news organizations have too often departed from the stories of "yesterday" to move on to those of "today." However, the aftermath of these hurricanes still lingers on the Gulf Coast of the United States. It is imperative that Christians everywhere stay informed of current events in those areas—and continue to support Operation Blessing and the ministries still engaged in relief efforts within that region.

One way that Christians can stay informed of Operation Blessing's continued humanitarian relief efforts within the United States and abroad is by regularly viewing CBN's *700 Club* broadcast. Available on most satellite and cable networks, and many local broadcasting stations, the *700 Club* remains one of the most informative Christian resources for news worldwide. The one-hour show is also the primary source for reliable media coverage of Operation Blessing's wonderful humanitarian endeavors. It was even after watching *700 Club* that Kenneth and Gloria Copeland became involved in the Katrina relief effort, by the leading of the Holy Spirit.

Bill Horan states, "In order to keep the public informed, we certainly continue to get our message out through the broadcast—and we show stories of 'Christian Compassion in Action.' For example, we sent a film crew going down to cover the 'mosquito fish project' in detail. (Now, the general media got excited over that project and actually showed up to report on it.) With thousands of abandoned pools in New Orleans, there was a real threat of a West Nile Virus outbreak spread by hoards of mosquitoes that were breeding and hatching. These Gambusia fish eat mosquito larvae. Working side-by-side with members of the New Orleans Mosquito and Termite Board, OBI funded and planted thousands of these fish in over 4300 abandoned pools. And it's not just the fact that we're killing mosquitoes and alleviating suffering. Since the adult mosquitoes carry diseases, we saved lives by killing billions of larvae.

"What is even more exciting to me is that this bug-busting program gained international media attention through NBC, Newsweek, Guidepost Magazine, and others. It brought public awareness of the continuing struggle of folks in the Gulf but did it in a positive way that highlighted innovative action. Sadly, most of the news magazines and networks do not seem to care about how many people are dying every day for lack of their high blood pressure medicine. It is just not interesting news to them. But they were very interested in mosquito fish because it is an interesting story. When I am interviewed by these secular media outlets, it gives me an opportunity to talk about the other things that we are doing down there that are even more important than killing mosquitoes."

Despite the increased media attention Operation Blessing receives through such innovative efforts as the mosquito fish project, the *700 Club* and OBI's website [www.ob.org] remain the best places for the public to learn how Operation Blessing is helping hurting people in need. Thereon, it is remarkable to see the tremendous progress that the donors and volunteers that support Operation Blessing have already accomplished in that region.

What a wonderful reflection of the Savior it is when people look up from their distress to see help coming to them through such a wonderful faith-based organization. For that matter, it is really not the name "Operation Blessing" that impresses these people. Emphatically, it is the volunteers and donors who are making these relief efforts happen…and the victims Operation Blessing assists, truly recognize that fact.

CHAPTER

22

Volunteers and Donors

Since the time Hurricane Katrina first struck Slidell, Louisiana and through November of 2006, Operation Blessing had logged over 146,000 volunteer hours, provided 22 million dollars worth of free medicines to LSU Health System, delivered over 12 million pounds of food and relief supplies, served over 14,000 medical and dental patients, distributed over 27,000 drug prescriptions, and served over 900,000 hot meals. OBI teams have also done countless roof repairs and reconstruction projects with as many as 330 volunteers a day. These diligent volunteers have also 'gutted' houses (removing sheetrock, flooring, insulation, etc.) so that refurbishing could begin.

In March of 2006, Operation Blessing even purchased a fleet of ten school buses, and donated them to the St. Bernard Parish disaster relief board to haul around their volunteers. The transportation tasks had previously been subsidized by FEMA—but the Federal agency had "pulled the plug" and would not pay the bill anymore. Operation Blessing stepped in and now the parish volunteers have a permanent transportation solution.

OBI also opened free dental clinics in St. Bernard and Orleans Parishes, and a free medical clinic and pharmacy in New Orleans East.

As impressive as these accomplishments are, all of this would have been impossible without the generous support of Operation Blessing's donors, and the outstanding turnout of volunteers from around the country. Churches from nearly every denomination have sent teams to Slidell and other disaster areas to help provide humanitarian relief labor.

Help from the Mennonites

One mighty group of Christian laborers has been the Mennonites. These hard-working folks came to OBI's Slidell operation early on. Rotating teams in and out for months, they were a consistent source of high-quality volunteer labor as they worked side-by-side with other believers from around the nation.

Bill Horan elaborates, "The Mennonites have been absolutely wonderful partners. They have averaged somewhere around eighty men on our campus since they moved in. Soon after we set up the Slidell campus, within a week or two, they were there. They promised me fifty men for six months. Then we re-discussed it, when it was evident that we were going to be there much longer than six months. We have had as many as 130 Mennonite men at the camp at one time. And then their wonderful ladies cooked—not only for them, but also for all of our volunteers.

"The problem is that now we are losing them. They told me from day one, 'We're basically farmers and we have got to be plowing and planting in the spring. Consequently, we are going to have a hard time getting people down here.' We are going to lose them pretty much for the summer and they will not be back until fall.

"But, thank God, up until they had to start leaving, they have been with us non-stop. You talk about 'Steady Eddie!' These guys were great. They contributed thousands of hours of volunteerism—and they are just wonderful! We are really looking forward to having them come back in the fall.

"They have even been bringing in brothers from as far as Saskatchewan, Alberta, British Columbia, and all over the United States."

Other Groups

The Mennonites were not the only brethren who answered the call to Christian duty, however. Many other believers took time off from their own personal pursuits to invest their time into helping others in dire need.

Campus Crusade for Christ sent hundreds of volunteers during their spring break in 2006. Multitudes of other church groups from around the country came down at various times, as well—including a contingent from Eagle Mountain International Church, a part of Kenneth Copeland Ministries.

Operation Blessing welcomes volunteers. Anybody over the age of eighteen can stay on the OBI campus—as long as they commit to volunteer for at least a week. OBI will then house them, feed them, and give them tools and work orders.

The OBI staff also goes to great lengths to prevent any of their volunteers from getting hurt. They provide safety training to all incoming workers, as well as appropriate safety equipment for the types of jobs they will be doing. Operation Blessing also has hired twenty-four-hour armed security to protect the OBI campus and its occupants.

Thus, the valuable men and women the Lord provides to help with Operation Blessing's humanitarian relief efforts are treated with great respect and appreciation. The safety and care of volunteers are high priorities to the OBI staff in Slidell—as well as elsewhere where their relief operations continue.

A Call to Action

No doubt, these words are finding their way into the hearts of men and women everywhere who are touched by the pages of this book. As the Lord speaks to your heart, be sure to be diligent to obey the promptings of the Holy Spirit where Operation Blessing, Angel Flight 44, and Kenneth Copeland Ministries are concerned.

There are those whose hearts are stirred to give financially into these tremendous organizations to help spread the Gospel and assist current and future victims of natural disasters. Those who are so moved will do well to visit their websites and find out how they can help. Through our contributions, we are sowing into the lives of our own brothers and sisters in need. We are also spreading the Gospel of Jesus Christ to the world through these humanitarian efforts. Perhaps, we are even sowing into our own future needs, should we or some of our family ever find ourselves in harm's way during a natural catastrophe.

Others reading this can take time off from their busy schedules to donate their time and talents "on the ground" in disaster areas like Slidell, New Orleans, Gulfport, Mississippi, and elsewhere. If you feel the "tug" of compassion stirring you to "put your hand to the plow" where humanitarian aid is concerned, be sure to visit the websites of these wonderful ministries to learn how you can help.

For your benefit, we have provided the website addresses of these organizations within the text of this book. However, here is another quick list for your convenience:

Operation Blessing: www.ob.org

Kenneth Copeland Ministries: www.kcm.org

Angel Flight 44: www.angelflight44.com

Please take the time to avail yourselves of current information available from each of these fine organizations via the Internet.

CHAPTER 23

Faith-Based Success

There have been a myriad of tales of government mishaps associated with Hurricane Katrina relief—especially with regard to the city of New Orleans, the State of Louisiana, and the federal government. With a combined workforce numbering into the tens of thousands, and billions of dollars earmarked for disaster relief, surely the various governments of this nation can handle the job…right?

Apparently not. In fact, those same government agencies that initially asked the faith-based organizations to stay out of their way at the onset of the disaster, soon found themselves extremely appreciative that their requests were largely ignored.

Interacting with the Government

OBI has multifaceted operations functioning in that region—spread out in many parishes, towns, and cities. Thus, interaction with government officials is a necessary by-product of any humanitarian relief operation on that scale. Smaller organizations may slip in "under the radar" here and there as they do local projects and then head back to their respective home bases. However, the sheer size of OBI's operations means that they have to regularly interact with officials on all levels throughout the region.

"We have not had much problem with government because we do not look to government for help," Bill Horan explained. "We are not waiting for food to distribute—and we are not waiting for government money.

"Of course, we try to coordinate as best as we can with FEMA and all other governmental agencies. You cannot have an operation on the scale of ours and not coordinate with the government in various ways. Local officials, for the most part, have been exemplary in the manner in which they have worked with Operation Blessing. They realize we are trying to help the hurting and hungry in their towns and parishes. These are *their* neighbors and constituents. They naturally do everything they can to coordinate with us in that task…most of the time."

And FEMA?

What about OBI's experience working with the Federal Emergency Management Agency? The news has been replete with stories and accounts of FEMA failures and mishaps. There have been extensive federal oversight reviews—and even congressional hearings held—to determine what went wrong, where, and how.

Regrettably, most of the hearings and media coverage have also been filled with political bias and agendas. Many of the mishaps attributed to FEMA have turned out to be actually a result of politically based quarrels, as well as the errors of officials in the State of Louisiana and the City of New Orleans. Some were even problems caused by other federal agencies. Thus, it would appear that in many cases FEMA was made the political and media "scapegoat" to cover many other officials' errors of judgment (although they surely had their share of their own mistakes, too).

Nonetheless, since OBI is a humanitarian aid organization, not a political one, it is extremely interesting to note their experience with the federal organization as they have coordinated with them in an effort to help people in need.

Mr. Horan comments, "Regarding FEMA, I'll make this observation: FEMA has some very compassionate and effective staff on the ground in Louisiana. The FEMA Volunteer Agency Liaisons (VALs) are some very sharp people. Virtually every one of them that I have met also happened to be Christian. Consequently, besides having a job to do, they really have a heart for trying to figure out ways that the government can help victims. The problem is that their superiors are 'handcuffing' the VALs.

"No matter what the local FEMA people want, when an opposing word comes down from Washington, they are outranked. The local FEMA management has been fantastic to work with, but they are very limited in their ability to be effective because of the bureaucrats in Washington, D.C.

"Compounding this problem is the fact that Washington has also been turning over the local FEMA staff frequently. They will leave them in place for, say, six weeks—then jerk them out and then send you a new person. Then they have to start all over again on the learning curve. This creates serious inefficiencies. If they would just leave the experienced personnel there longer, we, and every other relief organization—including FEMA itself—could get more things done more efficiently."

Many Connections

Bill Horan has proven to be both an able leader and natural *networker*, as the President of Operation Blessing. In order to facilitate the mission of OBI in disaster relief operations worldwide, he has connected with many influential government officials and agencies in this continent and on others. He also interfaces effectively with other Non-Government Organizations (NGOs) and Christian and Jewish relief organizations.

Historically, one of the keys to Operation Blessing's profound success in disaster relief domestically and abroad has been its ability to compound its own resources and efforts with those of other ministries. Bill Horan seems to have been able to take this to an even higher level during his tenure at the helm. In addition to working with Kenneth Copeland Ministries and Angel Flight 44, there are many other groups with which they interface.

As an example, Bill Horan elaborates, "We have been working with the White House Office of Faith-Based and Community Initiatives. In early October of 2005, I attended a meeting in the White House. President Bush invited me and eighteen other leaders—the heads of the Salvation Army, Red Cross, United Way, United Jewish Charities, etc., to discuss Katrina relief. The President offered his personal support and opened lines of communication to the White House. That proved to be a big plus."

Fatal Mistake

Despite the bureaucracies encountered when dealing with the government, Operation Blessing just keeps moving forward and getting the job done. As Bill Horan shared earlier, they simply do not allow themselves to become dependent on the government. This allows them the freedom to accomplish their mission without government failures and delays becoming major challenges.

Like Glen Hyde's experience with the FEMA agent at the Lafayette airport, Operation Blessing is also able to say, "We're not a government contractor. Our organization belongs to the Body of Christ. We're moving on!" The grace and power of God, and the participation of generous donors and motivated volunteers, are the key ingredients to OBI's continued success.

However, there were a couple of situations encountered in the Katrina relief effort where the government's intervention actually *prevented* Operation Blessing from accomplishing their intended humanitarian assistance. Regardless of how independent OBI is from the government with regard to their support and logistics, they still have a problem helping people when faced with armed opposition.

"The only *major* frustration for us is what happened in the early days of this disaster regarding access to New Orleans," Bill expresses. "When all those folks were stuck in the Superdome, and when there were people still sitting on highway bridges in New Orleans, we had trucks standing by, full of food and water and blankets and relief supplies. We wanted to go into the city of New Orleans, and we could not go there. *No one* could go there. All the relief agencies were frozen out. The National Guard had sandbags and gun emplacements set up on the highway, and they were not letting anyone in to help those people.

"You just could not get in there—and that was a *fatal mistake* that I'll never understand. They gave us excuses, like 'it was not safe' and 'people were getting shot at.' Nonetheless, we were willing to take the risk and go in there to help those people—and we were prevented from doing so, along with the rest of the relief community."

Taking New Cues

Many mistakes happened at all levels of government during the Katrina disaster. That much is obvious—and completely understandable—given the scope of the catastrophe. However, stories like those above reveal a more dangerous level of negligence and poor judgment on the part of the government.

Bill Horan is actually kind in his comments regarding the government officials and entities with which he has regular contact. However, given the information that I have gathered from some of the other people I interviewed for this book, I have come to the conclusion that if the truth were to be fully investigated and disclosed—some of the government debacles would actually be found to be criminal in nature. The Superdome and I-90 Bridge fiascoes would undeniably prove so.

Nevertheless, thankfully, Bill Horan is quite happy to report that things are already beginning to change for the better. That is, at least on the federal level:

"The Department of Homeland Security (DHS) is trying to figure out how to avoid those problems in the future. I even had a visit with the people from the Homeland Security Institute think tank. Part of the reason for their three-hour visit was to have discussions with us about lessons learned, and about how government could better *synergize* with Operation Blessing and like-minded organizations—not only with this disaster, but also in future disasters.

"They asked Jody Herrington and me to speak at a conference they had in

Baton Rouge the first week of June, 2006. The government is now recognizing the *effectiveness* of the faith-based relief community in the face of domestic disaster. Of course, I was thrilled that they asked Jody and me to participate. Through this, we are getting a chance to help the DHS and its subordinate agencies to change their policies and procedures. Maybe we can help the government figure out how to prevent a situation, like when they banned the trucks from entering New Orleans, from happening again."

Maybe so. To their credit, the federal government has definitely picked the right organization to help them re-evaluate their policies and procedures. With OBI's efficient operations and stewardship of donor funds, every government agency can learn many things from them. There are also some ethical ideals exemplified by OBI which the various governments should learn to emulate.

For example, consider the lengths that Operation Blessing has gone to in order to protect the innocent from exploitation. OBI is certainly an example of how an honest faith-based organization can make all the difference—even when all you need is a "lift"...

CHAPTER 24

Flexibility

Part of the secret to the success of Operation Blessing, in comparison to many other faith-based and NGO humanitarian aid organizations, is that they are *market-driven* in their approach. Bill Horan's business mind will not allow him to run OBI as a bureaucracy. Rather, like an efficiently run business enterprise, Operation Blessing remains flexible in its tactics. This allows OBI to adapt to the unique needs created by individual disasters.

"We are very market-driven...particularly in disasters. We want to go where the hurt is. Wherever the hurt is, that is where we want to be, demonstrating 'Christian Compassion in Action' by providing *relief in real time*. We do not have a fixed template for Operation Blessing relief efforts that we try to 'shoehorn' victims' needs into. Many ministries have a very rigid profile, format, or template that they use. We are kind of the opposite of that. I call it our 'Ask...Don't Tell' policy. We show up and always ask the same question, 'What do you need most?' It is amazing the answers you get. The mayor of Slidell would have a different answer than the mayor of New Orleans, for example...or than the mayor of Gulf Port. And whatever they tell us, that is what we endeavor to do. We now use this policy around the world, and it works everywhere—regardless of what and where the disaster is."

Operation Blessing followed that philosophy in their Hurricane Katrina relief efforts. In so doing, they found themselves doing quite a few things that they never dreamed that they would do.

Commenting on this, Bill adds, "Through the grace of God and the benevolence of our donors, we were funded very well and able to react very quickly to the needs we were presented with. We have no bureaucracy here at all, so we can move quickly—and get things done.

"A good example is when Glen Hyde helped us out in obtaining a crane. The story of how that happened is also an example of Glen's collaboration, and the flexibility—the 'fast-company' sort of action—of Operation Blessing."

Need a Lift?

"When Hurricane Rita was on the radar on the Weather Channel, we were asked by the mayor of Slidell to help with roof repair. After the storm, the FEMA contractors were woefully behind in repairing the roofs damaged by Hurricane Katrina—and, in fact, they could not begin to keep up. There were literally thousands of roofs just in the Slidell area, in St. Tammany Parish, where the houses were not necessarily damaged that badly, and they had not been flooded. However, they had holes in the roofs. And for the lack of a $200 tarp, whatever else that the people had in their homes was going to be ruined when Rita came to shore with torrential rains, unless a tarp could be put in place.

"So, when the mayor made that request, we reacted quickly. I was able to interface immediately with the U.S. Army Corps of Engineers and obtain one thousand and one hundred 20'X100' tarps and mobilize our volunteer crews to do the roofs. But the first day, they came back from the field telling me that maybe twenty percent of the roofs that they went to fix they could not work on—because there was a *tree* on the roof. If there was a tree on the roof, you could not very well patch the hole."

Makes sense.

Alas, the only cranes in the area seemed to be operated by "rip-off" artists. These shady contractors were charging people—even the elderly—as much as $5,000 to remove a single tree. In one case, Bill Horan found out that a particular crane operator charged a "little old lady" $13,000 to lift five trees off the roof of her home. Enraged, Bill notified the local police—describing both the criminal contractor and the location he was last seen operating. The police responded and found the man just a few blocks away from the elderly lady's home. He was immediately arrested.

"But the point is, there was an immediate need for cranes," Bill explains. "So, I called four or five people, including some of my friends that I know from my 'other life' in the contracting business. And one of the people I called was Glen Hyde.

"I said, 'Glen, we need to buy a mobile crane. I need a rough terrain crane,

166

about eighteen to twenty-ton capacity. Do you know anybody over there that might have one? We need it right away.' Glen said he would make some calls for me."

Sold!

Glen picks up the phone to call one of his friends who sells construction equipment—Joe Moody. After he explains the situation to him, Joe replies, "Glen, I don't have anything on the lot, but there's an auction coming up pretty soon at Ritchie Brothers in Fort Worth. I think it's two or three weeks off."

Glen replies, "I don't have two or three weeks. We need a crane, like *yesterday*. If you would, please make some calls and let me know what you find out."

Thirty minutes later, Joe calls back and says, "Glen, you're not going to believe this. The auction is today—it's going on right now! And they've got three cranes down there. Two of them are twenty-ton cranes."

Glen says a quick, "Thanks! Bye!," and runs out the door of his office to jump into his truck. He gives Bill Horan a quick call to update him—and then prays all the way to the auction. Twenty-five minutes later, he pulls up into the Ritchie Brothers Fort Worth auction facility's parking lot.

"I really didn't know if I could even bid at the auction," Glen later explains. "It had been years since I had an account with them—back from the days when I bought equipment to use in construction at my airport. So I didn't even know if they would let me into the auction. It had probably been ten years or more!"

Nevertheless, Glen walks up to the window and says, "I don't know if you folks still even have record of me, but I used to come here years ago to buy equipment, and I really need to get a crane for hurricane disaster relief down in Louisiana."

The lady asks, "What's your name?"

"Glen Hyde."

She clicks the keyboard of her computer a moment and says, "Here you are! Yep, you can bid." He is shocked.

After she gives him his bid slip, Glen is admitted into the auction—which is already under way.

Quickly, he locates the two twenty-ton cranes and checks them out.

Glen and Bill work back and forth together on Glen's cell phone as he checks out the cranes. Only one of the two cranes is deemed a suitable candidate.

As they are talking on the phone, the bidding line is moving closer and closer to Glen. He climbs into the operator's seat of the crane and runs it. Then he tells to Bill, "I'm not a crane man, but it looks good to me."

"Okay," Bill replies. "I'm authorizing you to go as high as $25,000 to get it."

Glen climbs out of the operator's seat, and up onto the front of the crane to wait for the bidding line to catch up to him.

Glen shares later, "I got there about twenty minutes before the bidding line got to me. I was sitting there on the crane, with orders from Bill Horan, who told me that I could bid $25,000 on that crane. I said, 'Okay.'

"When the auction wagon guy was within three spots from my number, my cell phone rang again. It was Bill Horan calling back. He said, 'Glen, you're authorized to go up to $40,000 on that crane. I've got to have that crane!'

"I said, 'Fair enough.' Then the bidding line came up to that crane. One guy from the crowd just kept bidding against me, and, sure enough, that guy bid me all the way up to $40,000—*but no higher*. We got that crane!"

Bill's last minute increase in the maximum bid was certainly a Holy Spirit inspired reauthorization to his man on-site. The maximum price he authorized Glen to bid turned out to be the exact price of the sale.

"We got one for $40,000," Bill recalls jubilantly. "This auction was on a Thursday or Friday. Glen arranged with a trucker on the site to transport it to Slidell, but he could not travel over the weekend because of permits. So the trucker left Fort Worth before the sun came up on Monday—and later that same morning, that crane was sitting on our site in Slidell. That afternoon it was out lifting trees off of people's roofs.

"So there's an example of synergy, between brothers and between ministries. When businesspeople that are involved in this faith-based relief operation get their heads together, two and two sometimes adds up to *more* than four.

"That was just *one* example of how Glen helped us. He arranged the whole deal with the auction and the trucking and got it over here. And then I said, 'Glen, we need some rigging—some more cables and chokers and slings.' So Glen went out and bought all that stuff, put it in his DC-3 over the weekend and flew it over to Slidell on one of his trips. He was able to get us that stuff that was not available locally in Slidell. I cannot tell you how much we appreciated having him—and his airplane—as an asset in our network of relationships."

Glen adds, "If Bill Horan had not called me when he did looking for a crane, and if Joe Moody hadn't called me back when he did to tell me about the auction—we wouldn't have made it to that auction, and the crane wouldn't have been there in Slidell now. That was the Hand of God moving for us again. Every crane within a five-state area had been bought up by other people and sent down there. There were not any more cranes to be had! But God had this one set aside for us."

"But God...," Glen just said. What a statement. The Lord is always greater than the problem. Moreover, He will always help us...whenever we trust Him (Matthew 19:26; Mark 9:23).

Bill Horan and Glen Hyde sit atop one of the cranes obtained for the Katrina relief effort in Slidell, LA. Photo by Rich Vermillion

One More, Please

Glen continues, "Then, two or three weeks later, they needed another crane. So we went down to Fort Worth and bought a *brand new* one—the last twenty-ton crane they had on the lot down there. We then sent it down to Slidell. Now they've got two cranes to help get the trees off of people's roofs, and help those people get their lives back together—without some guy ripping them off for thousands of dollars."

Jody Herrington, the manager of Operation Blessing's Slidell relief operation, adds, "We still have plenty of crane jobs to do, but the hard part is keeping a steady supply of volunteers qualified to run them. Right now, we are in between crane operators, but we're looking for one or more to get the cranes running again."

Money to buy the equipment and qualified volunteers to run them—both are such a necessity. Thankfully, Operation Blessing's donors are proving faithful in their contributions to keep OBI's operations functioning smoothly and fully equipped.

The Lord is also faithful to ensure that adequate volunteers hear the call to duty, and step up to lend a helping hand to those in need.

Again, maybe one is reading these words right now. If so, a quick visit to www.ob.org or www.operationblessiong.org will provide you with the contact information you need to volunteer your time, talent, and services—whatever they may be—to help those who are still in need.

PART V

Behind the Scenes at KCM

"Kenneth and Gloria obviously heard from God in moving and directing things the way that they did. It really blessed me as an executive at KCM to see their faith in us."

–Chris Clem

Pictured above: KCM volunteers and staff load the DC-3S at Copeland Field during the Angel Flight 44 Katrina relief effort. Photo provided courtesy KCM

CHAPTER 25

Establishing Logistics

After Glen Hyde had flown his first mission to Slidell, Kenneth Copeland asked him what KCM needed to do to help. Glen informed him that the primary challenge he and Denny were experiencing was the complexity of doing both the logistics for the aviation arm of the mission, along with the ground logistics.

"We have got to have a ground guy," Glen shared. "When I am flying these missions, I have got to be able to hit the ground running. I cannot do the ground stuff and the air stuff, fly the airplane, load the airplane, put fuel in the airplane—*and* do all the flight planning. It is just too much for me to handle. Denny has his hands full along with me, so the two of us cannot do the whole thing without someone taking over the ground logistics."

Subsequently, Kenneth had a meeting in his office with Chris Clem (Chief Relationship Officer of KCM), Dennis O'Brien (Chief Ministerial Relations Officer of KCM), and Pastors George and Terri Pearsons of EMIC. At this meeting, the problem was solved as the right person stepped up to the plate to take charge of this important aspect of the relief operation.

Well, not quite. Actually…Chris Clem got "volunteered" as the ground logistics coordinator.

Kenneth simply said, "Alright, Chris. Make it happen. Do whatever you need to do." And with that pronouncement, Chris Clem was in charge.

"And I got appointed the 'Ground Operations Communication Control

Commander," Chris shares with a laugh. "It was very interesting, to say the least. Back when Katrina hit, we were doing an emergency response at KCM, as far as putting our plans together on how we were going to do things. However, I did not yet realize then how deep my personal involvement was going be."

Suddenly Logistical

Chris is the first to admit that he was not necessarily the "perfect" choice for this responsibility—according to his natural qualifications.

"I was the Chief Relationship Officer of KCM. I was over the media, marketing, partner development, and prayer departments. The ministry has several other 'chiefs' on the executive team who manage the many other departments—all of whom were far more adept at this sort of thing. Of all the executive staff, I was the *least* logistically inclined. I am a marketing guy! I am a partner developer. I am a 'touchy-feely' kind of guy.

"But, when this disaster happened, John Copeland was on vacation. Our CEO was on vacation. Our COO was on vacation. Our Chief Services Officer—who was over human resources, security, and operations at the facility—was on vacation. So there were three 'chiefs' left in the building: Jan Harbour over Accounting and Finance, Dennis O'Brien over I.T. [Information Technology]… and me. So, when Kenneth looked at me and said 'handle it,' I figured that at that point I was going to quickly become very operationally efficient."

Looking at the situation from a merely human perspective, it may well seem that Chris was somewhat of a ridiculous choice for the responsibility. However, scripturally, it would seem that Chris *was* actually the "perfect" man for the job:

> "Because the foolishness of God is wiser than men, and the weakness of God is stronger than men. For you see your calling, brethren, that not many wise according to the flesh, not many mighty, not many noble, are called. But God has chosen the foolish things of the world to put to shame the wise, and God has chosen the weak things of the world to put to shame the things which are mighty; and the base things of the world and the things which are despised God has chosen, and the things which are not, to bring to nothing the things that are, that no flesh should glory in His presence. But of Him you are in Christ Jesus, who became for us wisdom from God—and righteousness and sanctification and redemption—that, as it is written, 'He who glories, let him glory in the LORD.'"
>
> (1 Corinthians 1:25-31, NKJV)

"They couldn't have picked a better guy," Glen adds. "I think the Spirit moved all those other people to be on vacation—or whatever—to get Chris in this role. The Spirit *definitely* moved on Kenneth to pick him. Our ability to coordinate and work together just blended throughout the entire relief mission… and just made things happen."

No person interviewed for this book in connection with the relief operation remembered there ever being an issue that was not somehow resolved. Of course, there were things that did not go perfectly, at times. However, those involved would simply keep in mind the urgency of the mission—and then just get the job done.

In the United States Marine Corps, we had a motto, "Improvise, adapt, and overcome." Given the similarity of their attitudes, one would almost think that the KCM staff and volunteers had all been Marines!

As Chris comments, "What we did was simply take the same passion that the staff of KCM operates by day in and day out, and redirect it towards the relief mission. We said, 'Now we're going to apply those resources, that focus, that energy towards this thing.' It happened with excellence, and on time."

Chris Clem's "sudden promotion" was obviously a Holy Spirit directed decision. Here was a situation in which a man who seemed to be unqualified for the task at hand was appointed to be the chief of the operation, and then successfully got the job done in the wisdom and anointing of God.

Although this is a prime example of God's doing "the impossible" through someone, there is, of course, also a place for expertise in certain areas. After Chris was appointed, there was a need for someone to handle keeping track of the day-to-day details of such an undertaking. They did not have to look much beyond Chris to find such a person—his wife, Tricia, happened to be the perfect one for the job.

Professional Management

The Thursday following the first relief flight, on September 8th, Chris Clem's wife, Tricia, was assigned to be the project manager of the entire relief operation. Due to the scope of the effort, professional project management skills were required to manage the numbers and details, while Chris provided the leadership and overall coordination.

Since Tricia Clem was already on staff at KCM as a project manager supervising other ventures, she was an ideal choice to take over this crucial role. Subsequently, she worked with her husband, Chris, day and night to see the mission completed with distinction.

"It is amazing how much material—water, food, medical supplies, chainsaws, diapers, etc.—went out from KCM," Chris explains. "Somebody needed to start keeping track of it all. It is all about stewardship. The Lord certainly wants us to be faithful with what is entrusted to us…and that means we must also be *accountable*. That is why we needed to have a professional project manager on the Angel Flight 44 team."

Professionalism/Good Stewardship

Another distinguishing characteristic of Kenneth Copeland Ministries is the fact that they realize the importance of utilizing business people and professionals to carry out tasks that require specific skill sets. Too often, ministries and churches attempt to fill voids with unskilled volunteers or low-cost staffing in order to avoid the expense of acquiring qualified professionals. However, this lack of professionalism can mean not only the potential *failure* of the organization in accomplishing its intended mission, but it can also alienate potential donors as they cannot see an effective management team functioning, nor suitable accountability structures in place.

Businesses, corporations, foundations, government entities, and affluent individuals all want to see effective stewardship before they are willing to contribute to any non-profit enterprise. In fact, *nobody* really gets excited about giving into a ministry or humanitarian organization that seems to be carelessly wasting funds—regardless of the level of the donor's material prosperity.

Consequently, organizations like Kenneth Copeland Ministries, Angel Flight 44, and Operation Blessing, are driven by principles of faithful stewardship and Biblical accountability. That is even why KCM and OBI are managed by former CEOs of multi-million-dollar corporations—Bill Horan at OBI, and Craig Atnip at KCM. Thus, they also seek out other appropriately skilled professionals to ensure the same excellence is evident at all levels within these organizations.

Synchronization

"It was all hands on deck," Chris elaborates. "I ran the ground logistics part of the relief operation using the little bit of military training that I had—which was with the ROTC when I was in college. I would come in every morning with my wife, who was the project director, and with Dennis O'Brien. We would do a briefing. Then we would put a list of things together of what was needed, talk about how we would get them and what was the current status of everything. We did these in the mornings and in the afternoons every weekday.

CHAPTER

26

Partners Make It Happen

The supplies Kenneth Copeland Ministries was sending down to the disaster areas came primarily through the combination of partner contributions and corporate philanthropy. Eventually, KCM partners would donate a whopping $1.7 million towards the new KCM humanitarian relief program. However, with the addition of donated goods and the contribution-matching and heavy discounting offered by vendors, this figure was multiplied many times over "like loaves and fishes" to feed and supply the multitudes.

In addition to the relief supplies, there was also quite a bit of money sent down there to help various people "on the ground" with expenses. In the case of Pastor Larry Roques, KCM not only supplied him food and water and other supplies, but also money to help make his church building payment, to pay his utilities and staff—and whatever else he needed to keep his church and relief operation going.

Dennis O'Brien clarifies, "We were also aware that our partners were responding and donating money toward the operation. We eventually generated over $1.7 million for the mission. At the same time, our revenue to the ministry never stopped. This was above and beyond what KCM's faithful partners normally give. *One hundred percent* of what came in for the relief efforts went right back out to help somebody. We did not use one dime of that money for logistics, administration, or anything else but humanitarian aid. If a dollar came in, that dollar went right back out to help somebody.

"We just gave people the opportunity to give, and they responded because they know that Kenneth Copeland Ministries is a ministry of integrity. They knew that what they gave was going to go where we said it was going to go—not towards administration, not into logistical support…all of it towards relief."

Getting Supplies

It was a miraculous couple of months, in which KCM went from not having *any* response capability, to within twenty-four hours calling vendors—such as Wal-Mart, Sysco Foods, Home Depot, Lowe's, etc.—who would donate things, give them 50% discounts, or would match their purchases dollar for dollar.

Chris explains, "Glen would call me, for example, and say, 'Hey, we need a generator.' Then I would send our purchasing department out to go buy a generator. They would call me from Lowe's and tell me, 'We're with the manager of Lowe's. He said if we buy one, he will give us one.' They came back one day with four generators. We would load what we could on the plane and send the rest on semi-trucks once the roads were back open. I tell you, the corporate sector stepped in and helped every way they could. I do not know of *anybody* that charged us full price for anything.

"Moreover, the team here at KCM did tremendous things. These people are real leaders, who are on staff here. They are people who do not need you to tell them everything for them to function. For example, there is a couple who works in the ministry—Steven Vick, who worked in the Contact Center under me, and his wife Kacie, who worked in the KCM Purchasing Department. They did things to help like go out on their *wedding anniversary* to buy chainsaws for the mission. It was that way!

"I would get phone calls from different people asking me, 'Hey, I am at Wal-Mart and they've got two hundred pallets of water left. How many do you want?' I would tell them, 'Get it all!'"

"Emergency Relief" Ministry

Then Dennis O'Brien adds, "We found that during an emergency relief operation, KCM does not perform any functions that are not part of its normal ministry. The ministry produces TV broadcasts and magazines, processes mail, and takes inbound prayer phone calls and incoming emails. The ministry places outbound phone calls, mails letters and products, and has a corporate infrastructure in place to support all these activities.

"The difference between 'normal' ministry and 'relief operation' ministry is 'the acceleration factor.' TV broadcasts need to be produced overnight instead of over several days. Articles need to be written for publication within four hours instead of in a month. Instead of weekly Internet updates, updates are made twice a day. Instead of purchasing office supplies and ministry books, generators and chainsaws need to be ordered and shipped out within a day. Instead of ministry trucks taking materials to meetings, they are hauling food, water, and urgent supplies two to three times a week to affected areas. Instead of calls for spiritual counseling, our ministers received calls for physical needs."

CHAPTER
27

Slashing the Red Tape

Another tremendous lesson to learn from the example of KCM's humanitarian relief effort is regarding the subject of *bureaucracy*. Regrettably, many churches and charitable organizations end up becoming bogged down with the details of running a relief operation—even those who already *specialize* in providing humanitarian aid of some kind. However, it was critical to the success of KCM's relief effort that they avoid any unnecessary delays. Supplies needed to flow, and the Super DC-3 needed to fly. Thus, "clean and simple" was the rule of thumb for the logistics portion of the mission.

As Chris explains, "It really was so efficient. You know, when situations like that happen, you just have to cut out the red tape. One way we did that was by my going down to the disaster area a few times so that I could have a solid grasp of what was happening on the ground. I do not know how many times I went there…I guess three or four. I even flew a couple of missions myself in a Cessna 210 when we needed to use an extra plane to drop off medical supplies. I am a pilot also, so I got to be pilot-in-command over those missions—which was a thrill.

"But the key was being able to see what was going on down there—very much like a missionary. It was of great help. You know you are sending money over to help, but actually going there and seeing firsthand how we were helping was motivating; for example, meeting the Marines that we had helped with the showers. And it was easier to relay to the staff what was happening down there, to help keep them motivated, too."

"I would get phone calls twenty-four hours a day for two months. Even after the Angel Flight 44 missions had stopped, we were still sending in relief supplies by truck. So, after a while, it got to be consuming. It is what we did for two solid months. Keep in mind, I was also responsible for about eight or ten departments in the ministry—yet, I had to keep my focus on the relief operation during that two-month period. Really, it is a testimony to all the department managers themselves because they just ran things for me and told me, 'You do what you need to do, and we will take care of things here.' And they did. The departments I was responsible for at KCM never missed a beat.

"Furthermore, Dennis O'Brien did a great job. He flew out with pilot John Coon in the Cessna 210 to Hammond, Louisiana once to coordinate with ministries we were supporting there…and then with Glen in the Super DC-3 for a couple Rita missions too. In fact, it worked out well because if I was out in Slidell, Dennis would run the operation from KCM, and if he was in the field somewhere, I would handle things back at KCM."

You've Got Backup

Chris Clem, Dennis O'Brien, and the other members of the KCM leadership had never been involved in anything like the Hurricane Katrina relief effort. It was an experience that none of them would forget. The combination of the *synergy* of the KCM staff and volunteers, coupled with the shear magnitude of the disaster, created a sort of "baptism under fire" for each of the men and women who were engaged in the effort. This was especially true for Chris and Dennis— both of whom were at times at "ground zero" working logistics.

As Chris shares further, "I have never been a part of anything like that. It truly was the Hand of God. Again, Glen invited me to fly on the DC-3 in some missions and I flew the Cessna 210 on a few others—and both types of missions were really critical for me. It is one thing to hear about what is going on, but it is really important that you get somebody *on the ground* from any organization trying to be involved—whether it is a church, or an organization like ours."

However, it is not enough simply to have someone standing onsite witnessing the aftermath of the devastation. That person has to be *empowered* to make decisions. Another one of the key elements that contributed to the success of the Angel Flight 44 and *Partners Helping Partners* operations was the fact that those who were in critical positions of responsibility were also given the full authority to execute their mission.

Too often, well-meaning organizations only create bureaucracies when they send people into a disaster area, and then refuse to trust them to make decisions.

Responsibility given to a person must also be accompanied by an equal amount of authority delegated to that same person. Anything else is actually a failure to give that responsibility at all. Such a dilemma creates extreme frustration for the one who is told he is shouldering the load (responsibility) when he does not also have the strength (authority) to carry it.

Responsibility and authority are two sides of the same coin; both sides have to be given if there is to be any actual value transferred. At that point, the only thing required is ensuring that the person is carrying out his tasks reliably.

Kenneth Copeland knows how important this is. He fully delegates the authority necessary for his executive team to carry out the tasks he had assigned to them. Having also previously served his country in the U.S. Army, Kenneth understands the proper protocols of delegation. Moreover, his revelation of the love of God and mountain-moving faith allows him to trust his Heavenly Father to work through those who are delegated such authority. This leadership ensured that things could be done smoothly, quickly, and *effectively* during the humanitarian aid effort.

"I knew that any decision I made there would be fully supported—that Kenneth Copeland had authorized me to go out there and make those decisions," Chris comments. "But like a good soldier, I was going to represent him like I was supposed to, and I wasn't going to do anything foolish. But it was great to know that Pastor Larry Roques could come up to me and say, 'I've got to have this, this, and that,' and I could just make the decision to do what was necessary and would not be second-guessed by my commander.

"I praise God that Kenneth said, 'You guys do whatever needs to be done.' He trusted us to do that. I was always aware of the fact that I was representing the Copelands [both Kenneth and Gloria], and I wanted to make sure I did everything that they wanted done. Of course, we would update Brother Copeland regularly. He would be down at the hangar when the plane would come in, and we would see him on many occasions.

"I also knew that Glen and the entire KCM support team would back up any commitments we made one hundred percent. If we said, 'This plane will be back here with what you need tomorrow,' then I had the assurance of knowing it would be there *tomorrow*.

"Kenneth and Gloria obviously heard from God in moving and directing things the way that they did. It really blessed me as an executive at KCM to see their faith in us. I mean, I walked out of that experience with a new understanding of what my job was at KCM—and what it means to be a leader who represents those who entrust you to get a job done. And I want to tell you, working for folks like that…that trust you to do your job, that trust you to hear from God, that trust you to represent them, that trust you to make decisions—*even* life and death decisions—was so encouraging. It took a lot of faith on their part and on ours—but the burden was never heavy. The grace was there to do it all.

"Consequently, even though the things I did *logistically* during this time were not in my natural skill sets, I was still able to accomplish them anyway—because I just totally trusted in Jesus. I wanted to make sure that I did not do anything that was going to hinder what God wanted me to do. Quite frankly, this experience was one of the highlights of my life."

CHAPTER
28

Working Together

From the very beginning of the Katrina relief effort when Kenneth and Gloria Copeland first called Bill Horan, up to operations happening in that region even today—there has been a covenant partnership functioning between Kenneth Copeland Ministries and Operation Blessing. Consequently, it was only "natural" for KCM's appointed ground logistics man to connect with his OBI counterpart in Slidell.

As Chris Clem shares, "On one of the first few missions I flew out there, Glen said to me, 'Look, you really need to hook up with Ron Oates [of Operation Blessing].' On top of that, Brother Copeland had already told me to make sure that I hook up with Operation Blessing. Well, the problem was that we had no way of getting into contact with these people out there. The cell phone towers were so messed up by the storm that you could only get a call through very intermittently. Consequently, I was having some trouble at first making arrangements with him so that we could hook up.

"So, we flew over and landed that night in the DC-3 in a nighttime landing operation. The Marines immediately came over and were helping us unload everything. I was standing out there on the tarmac, in the middle of Slidell, at about 8:00 at night, and I said, 'Lord, I've got to meet this Ron Oates guy.'

"Then this van pulls up, and the guy in the van rolls down his window and says, 'Hey, can I help you?'

"So I told him who we were, and he said, 'Oh, really? Well, I'm Ron Oates. Did you know I was coming?'

"I said, 'I had no idea you were coming!' He was just there! That was one of those divine connections. In fact, that was typical. That is an example of a typical day for us. God just moved and performed miracles, one right after another."

Chris continues, "I had talked to Bill Horan over the phone. Glen and Kenneth had given me his number, so I had been in touch with him already. Bill and I stayed in touch, but he told me to get with Ron whenever I got out there. So I think I had spoken with Ron on the phone, but communications were completely intermittent. Sometimes the cell phones would work, and sometimes they would not. So you really had to make all your communications in person. Unless we had the sat-phone with us or something, it was very intermittent.

"So when we got down there and saw Ron that night, we were able to talk to him and let him know we were going to be coming in and out of there and to get us a list of things he needed for Operation Blessing."

About Pastor Larry...

Concerning Pastor Larry, Glen Hyde comments, "Here's a guy who just put his faith to work. He meditated in the Word, stayed in the spirit, stayed grounded and rooted, stayed established, stayed anchored, stayed focused—and carried out God's instructions."

Chris Clem adds, "There were days that Pastor Larry would call me, and we'd talk for thirty or forty-five minutes. I knew that talking for those few minutes was allowing him to 'get away' from where he was for a short while. This was so important because of the massive responsibility he was carrying on his shoulders down there. The needs were enormous! At one point, we even got a call from his wife, Leslie, that Larry had collapsed from exhaustion and was in the hospital down there. So, we did whatever we could do to help him out in any way—even if it just meant talking on the phone a while to help him 'escape' the situation for a little while. We did whatever we could.

"For instance, he called me one day and said, 'Chris, the transmission in my minivan died. I do not even know who *could* fix it because none of the mechanic shops or parts stores down here are even open yet. So we do not have a way to deliver this food. There are elderly and handicapped people who are shut in. They cannot get out of their homes to get in line for food—and I just lost my transportation. What are we going to do?' We went down to an auction the next day, bought him a Suburban, and drove it down there to Lafayette.

"I met with Kenneth. I believe it was the next day. He called me in to debrief him about the Katrina operation. He was getting ready for the TV program when I walked in, and he was asking me a bunch of questions. I was answering them the best I could from what I remembered.

"Then he said, 'Tell me about Pastor Larry.' And I did.

"He looked at me with those penetrating Brother Copeland eyes and said, 'Chris, you take care of that man. Give him whatever he needs.'

"I knew what that meant! So I said, 'Yes, sir.'

"In fact, before we got back on the airplane, Brother Copeland handed me a Bible for Pastor Larry. He had put a personal note in it for him. He said to me, 'You make sure he gets this.'

"I'm telling you, that ministry is all about partners. KCM has helped a number of churches and tons of partners—sent money to them and everything else. Pastor Larry just happened to be in the center of it. He was the one we were actually able to get in touch with to be our local 'general' on the ground."

Salvation Army

The Body of Christ came together and interfaced "part to part" to form the complete whole. KCM connected with Operation Blessing, Joy Fellowship Church, and many other ministries. They even connected with major corporations like McKesson Pharmaceutical, Air BP, Sysco Foods, and others. Networking the Body of Christ together while further connecting them with the business sector, created an unstoppable army of humanitarian aid that far exceeded the response-time capabilities of even the federal government of the United States.

Again, when the faith-based community came together with "what each joint supplieth" (Ephesians 4:16, KJV), and connected with the business sector too, powerful things began to happen. Case in point, consider for a moment the following connection between Kenneth Copeland Ministries, Joy Fellowship Church, and the Salvation Army—all via Angel Flight 44.

As Chris continues, "I want to tell you about one of the first missions I went on. In fact, it was the same night I ran into Ron Oates. We left the airport and rode over to Pastor Larry's church with Ron. The airplane was sitting on the tarmac and we only had about an hour or so before we had to fly out of there. So we had to get over to the church and get back pretty quickly.

"When we got there, we discovered that the Salvation Army had come in and set up camp over there. Pastor Larry was giving us a tour of his church; and I want to tell you, it really was not a church at that point—it was a *warehouse*. He was saying, 'Here's the diapers in this section, and these four pews are full of such and such…' I mean the whole church had been converted into a warehouse to support the food efforts. They were sleeping in there on floors, and the whole nine yards.

"So as he was giving me this tour, he introduced me to a couple of the Salvation Army guys. I asked them, 'What do *you* guys need?

"At first they were like, 'Well, we could use a couple of this and that.' However, pretty soon we had about four or five Salvation Army guys crowded around us. They all started pitching in things to add to the list. By the end of that conversation, we had a *few pages* full of notes. We got a semi-truck loaded back at KCM because we could not get everything on the airplane. We loaded up the semi, and within twenty-four hours, it was headed out there with everything on their list that they needed. Primarily, their main need was actually food.

"The Salvation Army could not get the food in there! They had their emergency response team there cooking in their mobile kitchens, but the situation there was so 'fluid' that some of them did not have enough food to serve...or would run out of certain things. So we supplied their portable kitchens with food to cook for a while."

Joy Fellowship Church provided the location and relief-supply distribution, the Salvation Army had the portable kitchens, and Kenneth Copeland Ministries kept them stocked with food to cook and serve to the people. As was shared earlier, the cars would drive in through the horseshoe-shaped parking lot. They would receive a box of food, hygiene supplies, baby supplies (if needed), a hot meal—and the Word of God through the church's staff and volunteers, and the ministry materials and Bibles sent there by KCM.

Here was an excellent example of how the Body of Christ is designed to work together. God was constantly "connecting the dots" between various people and organizations, and then they all teamed up to make things happen. With all the miracles that took place, it is obvious that diligent and fervent prayer was being offered up to the Creator of all things. In the following chapter, we will discuss the vital role that prayer played during the course of the relief missions, and how faith and works melded together to bring about optimum results.

CHAPTER 29

The Spiritual and Very Practical

Kenneth Copeland Ministries had to have a variety of spiritual, intellectual, and practical elements working simultaneously to see the outstanding results they achieved. We already discussed a considerable number of their intellectual elements within the preceding chapters, as we delved into their logistical efforts. Now we will turn our focus toward a few more of the spiritual and practical issues.

Prayer Power

"From the time that the first hurricane, Katrina, was in the news, we had all of our prayer people praying over it," Chris shares. "During all of the Katrina and Rita operations, the prayer staff was diligently keeping everything bathed in a constant covering of prayer. Of course, Pastors George and Terri had their own staff praying over everything…and the entire church was praying. From Day One, we all knew that this entire relief effort had to be first and foremost a prayer effort to keep things working smoothly."

Glen Hyde adds, "Denny and I prayed on that airplane all the time. When I left that first meeting with Kenneth, Chris, George, and Terri, one of them asked me what I needed. I said, 'Just pray. The power of prayer needs to be loaded on top of that airplane. Pray for that airplane. This mission is not easy. It is all about fighting Satan. I cannot afford to pop a motor, especially over those swamps at night. There is Satanism down there right now, and we are going to go down there and fight it. And I do not need any problems with this airplane.' And I knew that the airplane would make it if the power of prayer was there.

"Kenneth later told me, 'Glen, in forty years of Gospel ministry…I have *never* seen the Hand of God move so often, and so quickly. In years past, sometimes we would go months before seeing another miracle—and a few times it was actually a year or two. But throughout this entire relief effort, it has been miracle after miracle—and many times only minutes apart! I have never seen anything like this! This entire operation was the Hand of God at work.' And he was right.

"It seemed like everything we needed was already in place when we got there, or it showed up immediately after. I know that God's Hand was in this thing from the day He told me to get that Super DC-3 ready, all the way through to the last relief mission flight. There were twenty flight missions in all—seventeen with Katrina and three we flew after Rita hit. Through it all, it was like walking from one miracle to the next. And I am here to tell you, the prayer support of God's people was what made it all happen so smooth."

"Pass the Ammunition"

Regardless of your denominational persuasion, it is likely that you probably share the same desire for safety that we all do. Glen Hyde, Denny Ghiringhelli, Chris Clem, Dennis O'Brien, (and anyone else that went into the disaster area) are no exceptions to this fact.

Security conditions in the disaster areas were deplorable. Law enforcement agencies many times were immobilized by the catastrophe. Citizens turned into scavengers as they hunted around for what they needed to survive. Worse yet, *criminal elements* roamed the streets—often in gangs—looting and taking advantage of the helpless. Most of the mayhem was outside of the Slidell area (to the credit of their wonderful police department), but the nightly news was still full of stories of hijackings and looting in many areas.

Security, therefore, was primarily the responsibility of those who dared to venture into this chaotic situation. Thus, through faith in God's protection—and a few practical measures as well—the Angel Flight 44 team members were able to complete their missions without anyone suffering harm.

Chris shares, "The first couple of days when we landed, I was thinking, 'Here we are landing an airplane, and there are people down here that don't have anything, and there are all kinds of looting going on…' Then I was thinking, 'I'm going to be driving a truck loaded with stuff!'

"I think Glen read my mind. He said, 'There's a "45" [.45 caliber semi-automatic pistol] back there behind the seat. If you leave the property, carry it with you."

Glen adds, "Yeah. We gave everybody handguns. We had to. There were too many cutthroats roaming the streets to take any chances—especially in New Orleans. In fact, just having a handgun with you was enough to keep the wrong people away. They would rather go harass someone who did not seem so able to take care of himself.

"Everywhere you went, you would see people carrying handguns or some other form of protection—especially if they were guarding their home, or some business somewhere. The guys we first encountered at the Slidell airport were all well-armed in case the wrong people tried to show up and cause trouble."

One delivery driver we interviewed for this book also expressed the same:

"Yeah, I carried a pistol every time I drove into those areas. In fact, once I drove into an area to make a delivery of supplies. I was stopped at a checkpoint. The policeman, who checked my I.D. to find out who I was, also asked me, 'Do you have any firearms?'

"At first, I couldn't tell if he was trying to get me to expose myself, or was concerned for my safety. Then he made it real plain to me that he felt it was necessary for me to carry a pistol or something—especially since I was driving a delivery van (even though it was unmarked). It really impressed me that *even the police* in that situation realized that people had to be armed to take care of themselves. There were just too many hijackings and lootings going on, and somebody unarmed risked getting killed."

The Scriptures clearly indicate that it was common practice to carry contemporary weaponry when traveling. Even the disciples kept a few swords on hand:

> "Then said he unto them, But now, he that hath a purse, let him take it, and likewise his scrip: and he that hath no sword, let him sell his garment, and buy one....And they said, Lord, behold, here are two swords. And he said unto them, It is enough."
>
> (Luke 22:36, 38, KJV)

Various Bible teachers prefer to spiritualize Scriptures like these and say, "He's talking about the Bible—the Sword of the Spirit." However, there is generally a practical and spiritual application to almost any Scripture.

Since most translations have Jesus simply saying, "It is enough," it would also seem that He is indicating *sufficiency*, and not reproving them for misunderstanding his directive. In other words, he was telling them that they did not have to be heavily armed and look like "Rambo" as they traveled—just have something with them to deter the "bad guys" from thinking they were helpless.

Moreover, I think it is interesting to point out that Jesus certainly already knew they were carrying swords. Yet, He did not seem to take exception to it at any point in Scripture. If He had, then Peter would not have been armed in the Garden of Gethsemane—where Jesus said to him, "Put your sword away." The Lord did not tell his disciple, "Get rid of your sword!" He simply told Peter to sheath it.

Divine protection—God's power and ability to keep us safe—is a promise of Scripture. Psalm 91 is a tremendous example. However, we must consider that psalm in the light of the man who wrote it. King David is often considered its author. This man had a terrific reputation of being one with whom you did not want to face off in hand-to-hand combat. People had a habit of getting killed that way.

God often puts His "super" on your "natural" in order to give you the supernatural results you want. Of course, if you find yourself caught off guard without any other form of protection, we have a Biblical right to expect His protection to be more than sufficient to keep us safe—King Hezekiah proved that. (See 2 Chronicles, Chapter 32 for the whole story.)

Nevertheless, consider what young David did after he said to Goliath, "All those gathered here will know that it is not by sword or spear that the LORD saves; for the battle is the LORD's, and he will give all of you into our hands." He immediately went out and fought Goliath with his sling; and cut off his head with Goliath's own sword (1 Samuel 17:47, NIV). The Lord surely gave him the miraculous victory over the giant—but David did participate a little. Moreover, he used weapons to do it.

Even the Christian men who wrote our U.S. Constitution over two hundred years ago knew that the Bible was replete with references to carrying arms for personal protection and civil defense. Subsequently, they altered the Constitution to convey the "right to bear arms" in the Second Amendment. And given that even under "normal" conditions the police cannot always prevent a criminal act, it is not hard to understand why our founders wanted us to have the ability to protect our own lives, homes, and property—especially in times of disaster. Recent history has proven that the founders were very wise in their decision.

Chris Clem comments further, "The security issue was one of those things that really stuck out in my mind. It made the seriousness of the situation very real. Of course, we were also talking to Marines, and they were providing security—which was important. God worked that out for us, for sure. However, there were times we were not around the Marines. But when we were…it was a huge blessing that the Marines were there to help us with whatever we needed."

Regardless of the method, it was obvious that God had provided safeguards for His servants: supernaturally, militarily…and practically, through the wisdom of carrying firearms for personal protection.

CHAPTER
30

Endurance

The relief operations for Hurricanes Katrina and Rita were enormous—and nearly non-stop. Consequently, even the stoutest individuals began to wear down from the strain, but they did not quit. Dennis O'Brien comments, "The entire team was exhausted. All experienced fatigue, but they just kept on going because there was a job to be done."

Chris adds, "After a while, I just started to get tired. Eventually, you are just worn out physically, emotionally, and spiritually when you are doing something like that day and night. Of course, what I experienced was not anything like what Glen and Denny were going through. They motivated me because I knew that if they do not get tired, I could not get tired.

"Of course, it wasn't all about Katrina. Twenty-nine days later, bam! Rita hit. Now we were flying missions down to south Texas. We were still sending semi-trucks, and Glen was still flying the DC-3 out to the Katrina area, while Rita relief was now going on. It was a continual thing.

"I remember just about every day I would come down there to the hangar and there would be Glen and Denny. Nobody had shaved and everybody was worn out and red-eyed."

For his part, Glen Hyde adds, "I kept going over that one verse in my mind, 'I can do all things through Christ which strengthens me.' [Philippians 4:13]

"As long as Denny and I got to the restaurant in Lafayette before 11:00 p.m., we would be able to eat. We were going to be able to shower and clean up. We each had our own bedrooms and bathrooms in a beautiful home. We would go into the restaurant, and I would think, 'Well, what am I going to have? I think I'll have a steak. Well, on second thought, I had that last night. I think I'll have seafood.' It was kind of a bittersweet meal because you are thinking about all those people who could not get any food, and here we are feasting like kings.

"Of course, we were very tired too. We were going to get up at 5:30 a.m. the next morning. We would have to leave the house then at six because we had to be at the airport at seven, airborne by eight—and back at Kenneth Copeland's by 10:30 a.m. We were going to be downloaded and uploaded, and airborne again by 1:00 p.m., and so on."

Volunteers

Picking up from there, Chris Clem comments, "It would be cool too, to come down at 11:30 at night, and there would be all the volunteers standing out there if necessary. They would work all night on the airplane. There would be the mechanics—Melvin, and some of our guys—working on it. Then there would be EMIC and KCM volunteers and staff washing the airplane down, asking, 'What can we do?'

"I cannot tell you how many people Dennis and I talked to who said, 'What can I do to get on that airplane? I want to go help!' We even had guys, staff here that volunteered their time to go out to the disaster areas to drop off fifty-three-foot trailers loaded with food and supplies using our semi-trucks."

Dennis O'Brien adds, "We would also have vendors coming out to KCM and dropping off semi-truck loads of food, medical supplies, and whatever the needs were. We had volunteers from the ministry staff who would come out here a number of nights working all kinds of hours.

"Our ground crews here were run like a military operation. The plane would land, and the crews would go to work. Then the DC-3 would fly away, return, land—and then get worked on, fueled, and washed all over again. It would be flying away again the next morning."

Glen Hyde is also very impressed by the diligence of the KCM/EMIC staff and volunteers. He observes, "We had at least three all-nighters that I can think of when the airplane landed, and we had to work on it all night to have it ready the next morning. The KCM/EMIC team just jumped all over it—whatever needed to be done."

The volunteers were certainly a key to the success of Angel Flight 44 and all the KCM/EMIC humanitarian relief efforts. As Glen also comments, "The blessings of the prayers and support of the volunteers will remain in my heart forever. The volunteers made things happen."

CHAPTER 31

What is in Your Hand?

Revelation. That is what anyone truly needs if he or she is to move forward into his or her divine destiny. Everyone needs to hear from God and have revelation from His Word. Then and only then does he have the foundation he needs to engage the enemy with victory assured. Moses did not need an army to deliver the Jews from Egypt, just a revelation:

> "And the Lord said to him, 'What is that in your hand?' And he said, 'A rod.'...'And you shall take this rod in your hand with which you shall work the signs [that prove I sent you].'"
>
> (Exodus 4:2, 17, AMP)

> "But take this staff in your hand so you can perform miraculous signs with it."
>
> (Verse 17, NIV)

"What Kenneth and Gloria and Pastors George and Terri have taught us is that you do not prepare for war while you are in one," Chris Clem explains. "You prepare for war now, and then when the war comes, you are ready for it. That is why there was no hesitation. There was no, 'Gee, what do we do? Let's come up with a plan.' Rather, there was faith that the Lord is going to meet us—and we are going to be able to accomplish this mission.

"That is why it went off the way it did. We did not really have the opportunity to mess it up. It was complete faith and trust in God. There was no logistical system set up. There was no operational handbook. Of course, I am not saying those things are wrong—they are not. In fact, my wife Tricia wrote an operational handbook for disaster relief based on our experiences with these disasters. There is a logistical system at KCM now. But what I am saying is that we just were not at that spot to begin with.

"What Kenneth Copeland Ministries and Eagle Mountain International Church have always taught us is that you step out on faith in His Word and you trust God. You have just got to do this thing. Like when the Lord asked Moses what was in his hand, you look at what is in *your* hand. So the Lord was saying to us, 'What have you got in your hand?'

Our answer was, "Well, Lord…we've got a DC-3. And we've got guys that fly it, and we've got a lot of people and a lot of faith.' Just like Moses had to use that 'rod,' we had to use our faith.

"God moved on people's hearts. He had people willing to do what He wanted them to do. All of this was God's will. We just got to be a part of it, and were honored to be a part of it."

All He Ever Asks...

The Lord does not ask you for just anything…He demands it all. Service on behalf of the Savior is the duty of any and every Christian believer. He gave His all to buy us back from the hand of our enemy (Satan), and He expects us to give Him our all in return. Is that not reasonable?

> "And he died for all, that those who live should no longer live for themselves but for him who died for them and was raised again."
> (2 Corinthians 5:15, NIV)

> "I beseech you therefore, brethren, by the mercies of God, that ye present your bodies a living sacrifice, holy, acceptable unto God, which is your reasonable service."
> (Romans 12:1, KJV)

When believers give their entire lives—spirit, soul, body, finances, possessions, family, etc.—to the service of Jesus; then they can expect the very provision of God to be theirs to accomplish the task. Regardless of the need, the Lord will always provide for us in abundance.

> "And my God will liberally supply (fill to the full) your

every need according to His riches in glory in Christ
Jesus."

(Philippians 4:19, AMP)

"Now if we are children, then we are heirs—heirs of
God and co-heirs with Christ, if indeed we share in
his sufferings in order that we may also share in his
glory."

(Romans 8:17, NIV)

This fact has been a reoccurring theme throughout the Angel Flight 44 story.
Whether they needed fuel for the airplane, food for the hungry, water for the
thirsty, chainsaws, generators—even just needing to meet Ron Oats, like Chris
did on the tarmac in Slidell—God was always right on time with His provision.
As Kenneth Copeland said to Glen, "In forty years of ministry, I have never seen
the Hand of God move like it has in this thing."

Even when the Angel Flight 44 team just needed airspace, the Lord
provided…

Clear Skies

Chris Clem explains, "It was the favor of God that Glen was able to get those
'Angel Flight' designations for the mission aircraft, and that we were able to get
flown in so efficiently. Every time we hopped up in that airplane and got off the
runway at Copeland Field or out of Grand Prairie and called, 'Angel Flight 44'
over the radio, the skyways opened up."

"They really did," Glen adds. "They flew us right across DFW Airport—even
in the middle of congested air traffic—rather than route us around the Metroplex,
which would have taken up precious time and burned extra fuel.

"I filed my flight plans and told them it was a mission relief effort. And
Denny had made a phone call before to a friend of his at the ATC [Air Traffic
Control] and told him, 'When you hear "Angel Flight 44," or any of the other
Angel Flight call signs, open up the doors. Make things happen for those guys.
They've got a lot of high-dollar, emergency medical supplies that need to get
down there into that disaster area.'"

Taking off from Copeland Field, as soon as Glen or Denny would call in to
Air Traffic Control at the DFW Airport, they would get priority clearance for a
direct flight straight through toward Slidell. All other traffic was diverted while
the big Super DC-3 came barreling through with a load of medical supplies or
humanitarian aid.

Even the Cessna 210 and other smaller aircraft used at times during the
relief efforts had their own individual "Angel Flight" call designators. Glen had

secured them previously, and they were on record with the Federal Aviation Administration for relief aid use.

"It seemed like most times we ran into a need, it was already filled before we even realized it existed. Then there were times when we realized we had a need, and then we would pray and—bang! There it was. Sometimes we did not even have to pray! It just showed up about the time we realized we needed it. Every time, right after each miraculous door would open, we would know that the Hand of the Lord had moved on our behalf once again.

"There's a saying I picked up from church when attending EMIC one Sunday, 'If God brings you to it, He will bring you through it.'

"Then in another service, I wrote something else down on a piece of paper, which I carry with me to meditate on: 'Happy moments? Praise God. Difficult moments? Seek God. Quiet moments? Worship God. Painful moments? Trust God. Every moment...thank God.' I lived by that throughout the entire mission... and it got me through it all—one miraculous moment after another."

PART VI

Spiritual
Commentary

by Kenneth Copeland

"Throughout the relief efforts, the Body of Christ worked together to make things happen."

–Kenneth Copeland

Pictured above: Kenneth Copeland visits with Glen Hyde after Angel Flight 44 lands at Copeland Field during the Katrina relief effort. Photo provided courtesy KCM

CHAPTER 32

Praying Over Katrina

by Kenneth Copeland

*Rich's Note: One person mentioned throughout "Angel Flight 44" is Kenneth Copeland. Therefore, it behooved us to invite Brother Copeland to contribute his thoughts for this book—and he graciously accepted. Subsequently, Glen Hyde and I sat down with him one afternoon to get his perspective on the hurricane, the relief efforts, and the future of Angel Flight 44. Thus, the next four chapters contain the thoughts of **Kenneth Copeland—in his voice**—with occasional notes within the text (as this one), and supporting Scripture added as sidebars.*

Gloria and I were in Eastern Europe when this disaster began. There is not a whole lot of television available where we were, but we were able to get CNN. Katrina was on their news all the time.

We immediately started praying about the situation. We were in services a couple times a day; and between the meetings, and when we came back to the hotel at night, we immediately prayed and continued praying for all of our partners and friends. Of course, Jesse and Cathy Duplantis live in New Orleans. Charles and Barbara Green and their family live in New Orleans. And there are other churches in that area in which we have preached. We prayed for everyone we could think of that might be affected by the storm. However, we spent most of our time speaking to the storm itself in the Name of Jesus. That is what Jesus did in the face of the storms He stopped with the power of faith.

The Weather's Response to Prayer

Weather, if it is just a weather phenomenon, will respond to prayer almost instantaneously most of the time. You can see it in the New Testament: Jesus spoke to the wind and the sea, and the thing calmed. That is not in the Scripture just because He is the Son of God. God's Word says that we have dominion over "the curse." All those weather phenomena started after the curse came on the earth through the fall of Adam. There was no disastrous weather until after sin came into the earth and then death by sin. The Law of Sin and Death brought this earth through a process of things—including Noah's flood—that changed the atmosphere over a period of centuries.

The atmosphere that we have now is totally different from how it was when God created it. It was not created to destroy—but it does now. Well, the Scripture just simply says, "Christ redeemed us from the curse of the law, being made a curse for us, that the blessing of Abraham might come on the Gentiles through Jesus." [Galatians 3:13-14] Contained within that blessing is command authority over certain forms of the weather.

Then, on the other hand, there are disastrous things that come on the earth that have greater spiritual elements in them. In these cases, it is a form of judgment where certain things get into motion that are hard to stop, or hard to change, or hard to move.

Concerning Hurricane Katrina, I realized after a short while that we were really up against something strong spiritually. We really "hit the wall" in praying over this thing. I did not know at that time what to think about it because in all my thirty-nine years of ministry, I had never run up against anything quite like it.

The Groaning and Travailing of the Earth

Gloria and I both were praying over this disaster—and with the feedback we received from our prayer staff back home, we knew that we were, sure enough, up

> "In the beginning God created the heavens and the earth.... God saw all that he had made, and it was very good."
>
> (Genesis 1:1, 31a, NIV)

against a spiritual bear. Later, we learned that it was a form of judgment. When something like that comes, there is more to it than just the weather conditions. I will explain why that is, in more detail, shortly. However, for now, suffice it to say that you can find that type of thing throughout the Bible—and there is even more of it happening today. The tsunami of 2004 was one of them. Instead of being in the category of weather phenomenon, they come under what is called the "groaning and travailing" of the earth in Romans 8:22.

You see this earth was not created to have sin and death. And when there is a "sin spot"—a place of concentrated sin that just goes against the spiritual and natural laws of God so hard and for so long—it will eventually break something.

Jesse Duplantis and his ministry are based in the New Orleans area. He has been praying against hurricanes for years. Yet, he said to me, "You know, I was praying against this thing, but then I realized that I was up against something I did not know anything about." He saw, like we did, that he could not stop it. So, he stood on God's Word for divine protection over his home and ministry. It looked like a war zone two miles to the east of Jesse's house, church, and ministry. Miraculously, however, they did not even have any tree damage on their own property. Nevertheless, you could see that, unlike other hurricanes, there was no stopping Katrina.

So I began to receive this understanding from the Lord. It was a while before I eventually learned what I know now about that storm. What I did need to know then, and what the Lord began pressing in on me about was: "There's going to be a lot of trouble there, so start getting things together." That is the time to begin praying for the wisdom of God. Wisdom for the how, when, where, and with what; and, of course, to pray for the people!

Out of all of this, we have all learned many things. The Lord has taught us things from His Word, things about spiritual laws that govern these kinds of disasters...and things that I could have and should have been praying about already, that I did not even know about before this event. It changed my prayer life. I will now pray in some areas in different ways than I have before.

Pre-Katrina Provision and Preparation

by Kenneth Copeland

Not too long before Katrina hit, our ministry experienced a major upsurge in finances. Miraculously, we had money to put into relief efforts immediately upon landfall of that storm. The Lord had already provided much of the extra capital we needed *in advance* to begin helping people down there.

Because of the timing of the financial increase, it was obvious where much of the overflow was to be directed. This was a move of God. This pre-storm provision happened within hours of the need's manifestion. As we were praying for the people and praying against that storm, I knew that the Lord had already moved for us. We took that upsurge of finances and poured it into purchasing water, food and everything else we could think of that people would need.

> *"...for your Father knows what you need before you ask him."*
>
> (Matthew 6:8, NIV)

A few days later, we went on the Internet, and a lot of our partners began responding. Thanks to our partners' obedience to the Holy Spirit in this matter of giving, we were able to not only start off on the right foot, but we were also able to continue the efforts for as long as was needed.

God-Directed Preparation

It is one thing to find out about a disastrous situation and then, out of desperation, try to respond to it—which is like trying to build a house in the middle of a flood. It is another thing entirely to hear and obey God-directed "unctions" in advance so that, when the situation comes, the preparations have already been made for immediate action. Thank God, Glen Hyde was sensitive to the Holy Spirit's promptings to do something at a certain time, without even knowing why he was doing it.

The day after Katrina struck, I called Glen and said, "Where's that '3'?" You see, Glen and I had talked about this many times over many years. From time to time, we asked the Lord, "What are we supposed to do with that Super 3?"

The Lord would say, "I'll let you know."

We would ask, "Well, are we supposed to sell it?"

The Lord's response was, "I'll let you know."

More than anything else, it was that inward witness saying, "Don't do anything with it yet."

However, he and I would get to talking about it. We would start throwing ideas back and forth: "Well, what about this? And, what about that?"

We had some really dynamite ideas—but all of them were wrong. However, when Glen was praying just six weeks before the storm hit, the Word of the Lord came to him saying, "You get that 3 going now!" I mean, he went to work on that thing. I could not find him half the time. He was "knee-deep" in that airplane getting all the inspections done and preparing it for whatever the Lord had in mind; and when it was ready to fly, that storm hit.

> *"Nation will rise against nation, and kingdom against kingdom. There will be famines and earthquakes in various places. All these are the beginning of birth pains."*
>
> (Matthew 24:7-8, NIV)

And out of this, a new and different form of ministry has been born: Angel Flight 44. It is growing right now. It is still a baby, but it is growing. Right now, it is in its infancy, but we will never again get caught partially prepared for such a disaster. Angel Flight 44 is a ministry that is here to stay, and I will tell you why…

Katrina is not the last catastrophe that will occur. We are going to see more of those kinds of things. There are other places around the world where sin has become so heavy that the atmosphere will not be able to withstand it. And when that happens, it will explode. In those instances, the earth just breaks. It groans and travails and buckles under the pressure that sin has put upon it. In those times, you cannot fix things with a few prayers and some half-hearted hallelujahs.

Certainly, there are ways to pray effectively in times like these, and I am learning more and more about it; but being prepared for it is just as important as praying after it has happened. We must have certain arrangements already set in place. Some preparations are based on experience from previous incidents, and some are simply Holy Spirit-directed instructions that may seem strange, but are actually critical steps that will make perfect sense later on—either when you see the catastrophe coming, or just after it has happened.

We are not going to be caught like that again, having to scramble to meet people's needs and learning how to meet those needs in the process. We found out in Katrina, and later in Rita, what people needed. So, we are preparing. Angel Flight 44 is alive and growing rapidly.

CHAPTER 34

The Responsibility of the Church
by Kenneth Copeland

We also learned from this experience that the government could not handle it. I am not saying that in order to criticize the government. The truth of the matter is that they are not *supposed* to handle stuff like this. It is not their job. The government can help, but it is actually the job of churches all over this country to help meet the needs of people. The proper order of things would be for the government to help the church help the people—which is why the church is there.

Throughout the relief efforts, the Body of Christ worked together to make things happen. And I have noticed we are all *still* working together to meet the needs of people. We have noticed it locally, around our local area. There are now over thirty different churches working with our church in helping to feed this county and the county right north of us. We make food deliveries to them and they distribute. There are Presbyterian churches, Baptist churches, and all kinds of churches. They all come together because people need help.

We all love the Lord Jesus; and after all, He is the key issue of this whole thing. Our denominational differences are not worth arguing about. Jesus is the key. And if you are going to follow Him, you must realize that He is a "people" Man. People are more important than anything—more important than cars, airplanes, houses, and all our possessions. People are what are important to Him.

Katrina turned us all towards people. It is easy to get busy with things.

Things are important. You cannot do without them. However, they are not the most important part. Again, the people are what are important. We use "things" to bless and help people.

People in the Body of Christ are just now learning how to rise up and do what they are supposed to do to help people in such disasters. I have been in this ministry for almost forty years, and we are just now learning how to serve people on the scale to which God called us. We are not here just to go to church. We are here to make a difference in this world.

Jesus said that if you are going to be His disciple, you must be a servant of all. Well, there is more to it than just being a welfare organization or just feeding people. Feeding people is part of it, but you certainly have to minister to the whole man—the spirit, the soul, and the body.

If you just feed a person's body, you have only provided temporary help. But if you can feed his spirit-man, Jesus becomes Lord of his life. In a short period of time, He will be helping you feed the others. He then becomes an asset instead of a liability.

And in that process, ministries are born. Television ministries are born in that process. Youth ministries are born in that process. Prison ministries are born in that process. Church ministries are always at the heart of it all. The local church is the axis around which the wheel turns. The prison ministries and the TV ministries, and all these other wonderful things that serve people come out of the centerpiece—which is the local church. It is not just a place where people come on Sunday and sing a few songs; it has to do with the welfare of the earth.

The Ongoing Mission of Angel Flight 44

The government is a welfare organization, whereas the church has a heart of love for people. And when Katrina hit, the churches went into action. All the churches needed were some supplies—and that is where we came in. We felt that was our job—to help supply those churches who in turn supply the people in need. Therein was born the ministry of Angel Flight 44.

That is our mission in the future: we will help churches help people. And from this time on, we are still building, we are still gathering, and we are still preparing as if there is a storm on the way—because there is. We just do not know where it is going to hit, but the storm is coming. Jesus said so in His Word.

So, we are preparing for it. We are preparing equipment. We have plans for more airplanes as the Lord provides funds for them—and He will. Great big things that fly into places, and little bitty things that fly into other places. We need airplanes that haul a lot of stuff, and airplanes that haul a little stuff. We need airplanes that land on the ground, and airplanes that land on the water. We are also believing for helicopters. Now, I have not seen any use for a balloon yet, but

I am not ruling that out!

We have plans for acquiring other types of equipment. We have hangars on the drawing board right now in order to be equipped in all areas of flight.

So, that is where we are now. A ministry has been born, and we are going to nurse it and build it and grow it and do our part.

Yes, there is a new baby in town, and her name is Angel Flight 44. And she is coming on strong because...*the storm is coming*. I do not know whether it is a hurricane or a bunch more tornadoes, or what. But we are going to be ready next time.

Impossibilities Become Realities

We were praying about the details of our part in the relief efforts, and then were just following what the Lord said to do. I woke up the morning after Katrina hit wanting to talk to Bill Horan. Later that morning, Gloria and I were watching the 700 Club, and Bill came on the broadcast. I said, "That's it. I've got to call him."

He and I talked for an hour, I guess. As soon as I hung up, I contacted Glen and gave him Bill's number. He called Bill, they got together, and the show was on the road. It came together just that quickly. It was a constant flow of supply meeting demand and demand meeting supply. Pray and obey!

It was like that, day after day, hour by hour. Of course, Glen was "boots on the ground" and "wings in the air." He was involved in it on a *personal* basis. God was answering prayers and doing miracles right in front of him. I mean, *every minute*, right in front of him. People would come running up to the airplane saying, "We've got to have hospital supplies," and, "We have to have this, and this, and this."

I am not talking about a case here or there. I am talking about a constant flow of impossibilities being turned into realities. Without the power of God, the whole thing would have just caved in.

For instance, Glen connected with the pharmaceutical reps from McKesson. They loaded all that medicine on the airplane, then flew it to Slidell, and got it down there by dark. Everyone else was telling those people that it was going to be at least a month before anyone could get to them. As many as a thousand people didn't die over the next twenty-four hours because of that load—*that one load*.

It was one miracle right after another. It was walking out the Scripture that says, "The feet of a righteous man are ordered of the Lord," [Psalm 37:23] and "His Word is a light to my pathway" [Psalm 119:105]. It happened in every step. When there was no water, we got water. We were hauling airplane loads of water when they said there was not any water. We had fuel for the airplanes when they said there was not any fuel. We had a place to land when they said there was no place to land. And on and on, following Jesus, step by step.

All of this taught us and trained us. You know, God does miracles, but He does not plan on your trying to live your life depending on them. A miracle is a divine intervention on the normal course of nature to get you back on His track. You are then, however, supposed to stay on track by living on the power of His Word. We are supposed to live by the Word, not just by miracles.

Now, in this situation we had to have the miracles because "the bridge was out," so to speak. Something had to happen to get us from one place to the other, and He did the miracles that we needed. The next time something like this happens, we will be way ahead. Even though we will still have the miracles, we will also get better at helping the people. Moreover, the whole Church will get better at it. That is the way it ought to be.

The same thing was happening with other ministries, too, such as Operation Blessing and our close friend and partner, Buddy Shipp of American Samaritan. Those guys, thank God, were ahead of us because they had been in that ministry for a long time. They had a lot of things prepared that we didn't. But they didn't have any wings. The idea of there not being any highways available was never much of an issue before Katrina.

Let's say, for instance, there was an earthquake someplace and the highways were wiped out. Your ability to get in and out would be lost. I was thinking about certain parts of the country where they have gotten away from their ferryboats; they have gotten away from any public transportation except for the highway-type. Even with the trains, in most cities if you ask somebody, "What would you do if you had to ride a train?" They wouldn't even know where one was. They would not know how to get on the thing.

If an earthquake were to tear the highways up, what would you do? That is when we need to have airplanes flying in. But what if it also tears up all the runways? That is when you must have helicopters—or flying boats. You are not going to get rid of the ocean! It will be there no matter what. That is the way God has us praying and thinking now. He had to bring us up to a higher level in our mentalities—He jerked us up there through Hurricane Katrina.

CHAPTER 35

Understanding Judgment

by Kenneth Copeland

In December of 2003, I had a visitation of the Lord. I was praying over my New Year's Eve service for January of 2004. In that visitation of the Lord, He said to me, "2004 will be known as the Year of Fullness; 2005 will be known as the Year of Overflow…and *how much* overflow depends on how much *seed* you sow towards it in 2004."

I prayed over that for a year to receive more understanding about the overflow. Out of that, about halfway through the year, the Lord began to talk to me about how that 2005 was also the Year of Judgment. He said, "The kind of judgment that I am referring to is overflow."

There is an absolute law of reaping what you sow [Galatians 6:7]. This whole planet is governed by seedtime and harvest. You cannot get away from it. Everything on this planet begins with a seed. Everything here started with a seed; and after some time, it is harvested, or is born. Then the Lord said, "One man's blessing, one man's overflow, is another man's *judgment*. If you just continue to sow the same seeds, one of these days, you are going to get an overflow. That overflow is judgment on one side or blessing on the other." It is not a matter of judgment where God rises up one day and judges a place. It is not like that. It is not time yet for that kind of judgment. Rather, He said, "This kind of judgment is something that has already been judged. If you just keep sowing the same bad seed—you are going to eventually hit the wall. Harvest, or judgment, will come."

And that is what happened in New Orleans. On the spiritual side of it, voodoo and witchcraft have been practiced seriously in New Orleans for over three hundred years. It is the *only* place in the North American continent where that is true. There is witchcraft practiced in other places in North America, but not to that extent.

Judgment is directly tied to the practice of black arts. And the places where they practice those things seriously are always extremely poverty-stricken. With a six percent poverty average around the United States, there was over thirty-three percent in New Orleans. Well now, you can see something going on there…witchcraft, along with every other vice for which that city is infamous, is the chief cause.

Now, I am not judging those people. They have already been judged. And God did not send that storm on those folks. Storms are not heaven-sent. That is not what God does. But when it comes to the place where even the city government and the police department are known for their corruption—that city was corrupt from one end to the other—and they keep sowing bad seed and do not pay any attention to Jesus or His people, something is going to happen.

There are churches in that city that have been preaching God's Word and prophesying to those people for years. They have been warning them over and over and over again—and it has finally come to pass. Their harvest finally came. The seed just did what it always does. Well, one does not have to be a prophet to know that there are other places like that where trouble is coming.

You can find places where they are burning churches and killing Christians. Go check out the background of the tsunami of 2004. The earth cracked right in the heart of an area where there was more persecution, more burning of churches, and killing and murdering of Christians—on purpose—than almost any other place on the earth. That is where the earth broke. Well, everything but the churches washed away. God protected His people. And after it happened, do you know who came to the rescue? The churches! Those pastors there fed the very people that were trying to kill them and their families, and burn their churches. They fed those very same people. That is what we are supposed to do.

It is also amazing after that tremendous tsunami; they got in there and cleaned that place up in no time, compared to New Orleans. Most all that territory around that tsunami is all cleaned up—I mean you can hardly tell it was there. But in New Orleans, it is still a mud hole (and I will explain more about that in a moment).

So you can look around the country and see different spots—whether it is now or it is later—where "reaping" is coming.

Abraham Knew Ahead of Time

There are a lot of things going over and over again in my spirit. Out of this, we are going to learn how to use faith in God to divert these disasters. God went to Abraham before the destruction of Sodom and Gomorrah—and Abraham talked Him out of it, if God could find ten people there that were righteous. God said, "No, I will not destroy them for ten." Unfortunately, there were not ten righteous people there. God did, however, deliver Abraham's family.

What I am seeing in this is that, spiritually, we have been asleep at the switch. We *let* this storm blow in on us. Previously, we were not seeking God's face on these disasters until *after* they took place—but we are seeking Him *beforehand* about these events from now on.

I am spiritually wise enough, with what little I have learned, to recognize certain places that are earmarked for this kind of thing. I mean, my goodness, you do not have to be a spiritual "rocket scientist" to figure out that there are certain places that, in the natural, are set up for disasters.

> "Surely the Lord God will do nothing without revealing His secret to His servants the prophets."
>
> (Amos 3:7, NIV)

There are whole cities built on huge faults. There are whole cities built in the shadow of volcanoes, and that kind of thing. Well, we need to be spending more time praying and listening to God concerning these things because God went to Abraham before Sodom and Gomorrah were destroyed. That fact let me know that it is God's will to reveal to His people where these things are going to happen, and to direct us to get into prayer and change what we can. Then when one does actually happen…we *fix* what we can after it takes place.

So we are learning. Big things have been born out of Hurricane Katrina. We will never be that 'dumb' again.

The Glory of God

The Lord said during that same word to us in 2003, "2006 is the Year of the Glory."

It is an amazing thing. When something like Katrina happens, God will move by His Spirit. Of course, that kind of thing brings about repentance. People start repenting, and God begins turning things around for them—and that is what brings on the Glory of God.

Church historians point to Azusa Street in Los Angeles, in April of 1906. There were some of the greatest outpourings of the Glory of God in the history of the church—*the* greatest up until that time, other than the Day of Pentecost.

At the same time, April of 1906 is also when San Francisco burned down. What a mess that was. What a government rip-off that was. When that earthquake hit in San Francisco, they had the most crooked government that they had ever had in their history. They had a bunch of shysters in there that even lied about how many people got killed.

In fact, nobody knew until afterwards in the 1970's when a librarian looked into it—not because she questioned the number (the government had said it was 485 or so), but because she wanted a list of the ones killed. In the process of her nearly thirty years or so of making this list, she found the names of about 3,000 of those who had been killed.

The reason the officials had lied about it was they wanted the eastern people to come invest in San Francisco. But they were stealing the city blind before the earthquake hit and, therefore, the municipalities did not funtion properly afterwards. *Nothing* worked, because they had been stealing from it.

Therefore, in two separate cities you had manifestations of judgment and glory in the same month of the same year. There was the Glory of God just down the road a little ways in Los Angeles on Azusa Street—located *on the same fault* that San Francisco was sitting on. The Glory manifested down there, and people ran into it from all over the world. That revival was the seed outpouring of the Holy Spirit that has produced six hundred million Holy Ghost believers that we know about. I mean, there are six hundred million of us alive on the earth right now that can be traced back to that outpouring. So there was the Glory of God being manifest in the one area, and a judgment seed being harvested right down the road from there in San Francisco. Both were the result of seed sown.

Of course, now we are in the middle of the most outstanding move of the Spirit of God that has ever been on Earth. Consequently, we are also right in the middle of more activity that is demonic, because Satan operates and functions in the same earthen envelope that God does regarding this creation. The devil does his best to screw it all up. However, all he really does whenever he makes a mess is bring people to repentance.

There are always a few people that hold out until they end up dead—but most are not like that. They are tenderhearted, and things like this call attention to what is real and what is true—and that is life and death. Basketball tickets did not mean a thing in the world the day after Katrina hit. In such circumstances, those kinds of things lose all of their importance, so people turn to God. And I am glad they do. That is why we are here. We need to be on hand when they *do* turn. We need to be there to help them, to feed them, to clothe them, to put some shelter over their heads, to pray for them, and to give them hope. But most importantly, we need to introduce them to Jesus and His Word.

Signs in the Heavens

Rich's Note: During the Summer of 2004, Oral Roberts experienced a sudden visitation of the Lord while walking into his kitchen to join his wife, Evelyn, for a meal. The vision he saw regarded a coming sign from God to New York City. This vision was subsequently dubbed "The Wake-Up Call" and was then described in an interview with his son, Richard Roberts, and Kenneth Copeland.

That broadcast aired from September 27th-October 1st of that same year on KCM's Believer's Voice of Victory (BVOV) broadcast and Richard Roberts' program. The subsequent week, Kenneth was joined on the BVOV broadcast by his wife, Gloria, and Billye Brim, to discuss the significance of the vision in greater detail. These broadcasts are still available on-demand from the KCM.org website in streaming video and MP3 audio downloads.

In visiting with Oral Roberts over the visitation of the Lord he had about New York City, what he saw happening there was more of a manifestation of the Hand of the Lord. Although it is spiritually in the same department, the thing about Katrina was that it was not a manifestation of the Hand of the Lord. It was a catastrophic eruption of natural forces, beyond the power of natural force. Spiritual force was involved, but not the Hand of the Lord.

This other thing, from what little insight I receive from it in listening to his heart, started out probably as some sort of catastrophic thing. Then the Hand of the Lord stopped it and held it in place, right *over* New York City. He then moved it and took it elsewhere—and really stirred the city in the process. But the thing that was so outstanding about it was the *sustaining* of the manifestation.

In that vision, the Hand of the Lord stopped the disaster and it hung there for a long time. And everybody in the whole area knew that if that thing hits the city, *we have had it*. In the vision, they also knew that it was God that had stopped it. Now, this kind of thing has happened before.

The day that Jesus was crucified, darkness came on the whole area. It was so dark that you could not see anything. And everyone knew, "If this darkness stays, we're all going to die."

During the Passover, darkness came on the earth so thick that all of Egypt knew that if it stayed on them they were all going to die. God lifted it. But then, in just a short time, death came on every firstborn male, every firstborn animal—every firstborn in Egypt.

This disaster that Oral Roberts saw in that vision is in that kind of category. It is one of those things where God is personally involved. That "something" he saw is coming…and in the vision of it, God stopped it, moved it a safe distance away, and then turned it loose. Moreover, in the vision everybody in New York knows, "Oh, my goodness. If He hadn't have moved that, we'd all be dead today."

That vision that Oral Roberts saw is coming to pass—it is a manifestation of the Hand of God. Hurricane Katrina, on the other hand, was simply a reaping of three hundred years of wicked seed sown. Consequently, it had a supernatural element to it—but again, it was not the Hand of God Himself.

Katrina Versus 9-11

Spiritually, there was a major difference between the Katrina disaster and the 9-11 terrorist attack back in 2001. There are some churches in New York City that had been declaring the authority of God over that city; and the city responded to the Spirit as a result. However, the same type of preaching was going on in the city of New Orleans, and the city did *not* respond to it.

Today, the police department in New York City is the best it has ever been. It is no longer a crooked police department. They have a few crooked cops there as everybody else does, but it is not a crooked police force as a whole.

Do you remember "Hell's Kitchen" and Bedford-Stuyvesant in Brooklyn that were just so mean that people could not safely go in there? They are good neighborhoods now. What has turned that around? It was the preaching of the Gospel. I mean, great revivals of God occurred in Bedford-Stuyvesant and places like that. It is no longer "Hell's Kitchen." There are some bad neighborhoods still in New York, but not like there used to be.

Now, if the pastors and preachers in New York had not been standing on the Word of God as they were, 9-11 would have been a different thing. There were supposed to have been 100,000 or more people killed in that disaster. There should have been 90,000 casualties just in the train station—because at any given time between 7:00 and 10:00 in the morning in the World Trade Center, from 90,000-100,000 people travelled through there. And to lose only 3,000 people! We are not discounting that loss, but any way you look at it, that is a miracle in itself—a big miracle.

And if it had not been for the faith-filled pastors that God had pre-positioned all over that city, who had been teaching the Word of God Almighty, and faith, and doing all these things—there would have been a significantly different outcome. Some of these ministers have been in there for forty years now; I mean, they have been preaching in that city for all this time. And that pays off! Moreover, it will pay off big time when this other thing comes that Oral Roberts saw.

People have declared for years that New York City was the worst city in the world. No, it is not. Right now, it is the *safest* city. There is less crime rate now per capita than just about any other city. It is not because of the great police department. It is because of the power of God *on* the police department; and it is because there is a whole spiritual army of believers who are all over that city in different places. The city is responding to the Gospel.

A number of the ministries I have known for years. I know what they preach, and I know where they stand. They would go down into those sorry neighborhoods and risk their lives to preach, teach, and set people free from drugs. Now there are some good neighborhoods there that used to be horrible.

Well, when you bring God in on the scene, it makes no difference how big the city is. New York City is not all that big to God. In fact, when you compare it to the City of New Jerusalem in Heaven—1,400 miles square—it's pretty small [Revelation 21:15-16].

New Orleans was not in the same category as New York City. They had a chance to be because of people like Jesse Duplantis and Charles Green. The first time I went to Charles Green's church was in 1968, and it was a thriving, gospel-preaching church then. He even stood right up in the governor's face—more than once—and that same governor would not listen, and finally went to prison.

Charles told him. But that governor just said, "Yes, sir, Brother Green. I know what you're saying is true," but he ignored it. Eventually, people called the police on him. He just kept on doing what God told him not to do—and it caught up with him.

In fact, the whole city of New Orleans has been doing that for 300 years. That city has been ruled by that same voodoo spirit for all that time. But just because that foul spirit has been in charge down there for so long, does not make it alright. All these years, God has had men and women preaching the uncompromised Word of God to them—and they have not listened.

Well, New York City listened—and God spared them when disaster struck. On the other hand, New Orleans did not—and God could not help them any more than He did to stop that storm because they were *used* to not listening to Him. If people will not listen to God in their everyday lives, and reject His counsel just to keep their sin, then they will not be able to hear Him when He tries to warn them of pending disaster. Really, that is why He tells them not to sin in the first place…it brings disaster.

But thank God, He had a whole bunch of us willing to go down there when it was all over. He knew full well those people's hearts would finally be open to receive His Word…and many of them have repented and turned to God since then as a result. One Word from God can change your life forever.

All of this was because His Church would listen to Him, get ready when He said to—and then work together to help those people when they were in need.

PART VII

The Vision of the Future for Angel Flight 44

by Glen Hyde

"We know from the Bible that more of these storms, earthquakes, and tsunamis are coming—and we want to be ready to help provide the aviation relief necessary for those efforts."

–Glen Hyde

Pictured above: Flight instructor Glen Hyde in the cockpit of the Super Gooney during a post-Katrina training flight. Photo by Rich Vermillion

CHAPTER 36

The Mission of Angel Flight 44

by Glen Hyde

*Rich's Note: What lies ahead for Glen Hyde and his vision for the continued mission of Angel Flight 44? In the preceding chapters, Kenneth Copeland mentioned his involvement in the future of Angel Flight 44 in partnership with Glen Hyde. Now we will allow the "commandant" himself to share his thoughts. The following subsections are in **the voice of Glen Hyde**.*

Angel Flight 44 (AF-44) has been integrated into the service and support of KCM operations worldwide. Accordingly, AF-44 adopts and readily supports Kenneth and Gloria's aviation ministry mission as well.

The purpose for the ministry of AF-44 is to provide additional aviation support to Kenneth Copeland Ministries, Christian humanitarian organizations, pastors, and missionaries—both domestically and internationally.

As the Katrina and Rita hurricanes illustrated, sometimes a need arises that requires airborne assets in order to accomplish the mission. This not only applies to disasters, but also to a myriad of other faith-based missions. I will discuss the disaster relief component first, and then cover the other support functions after that.

Disaster Relief

A real key to our ongoing mission is to support disaster relief efforts in partnership with Kenneth Copeland Ministries and other ministries, such as Operation Blessing. We know from the Bible that more of these storms, earthquakes, and tsunamis are coming—and we want to be ready to help provide the aviation relief necessary for those efforts. To do this, of course, we will need to acquire the appropriate aircraft, crews, and support logistics.

All aircraft are mission-specific. For instance, it would have been tremendous if we had possessed some air-sea rescue capability during Katrina. For example, if we had a big seaplane such as the Grumman HU-16 Albatross, we could have done some air-sea rescue work along the Gulf Coast. There were numerous people swept out into the Gulf by the receding storm surge. We would have been able to rescue many of them if we had possessed the right air assets.

In addition, if we had managed to have at least one Bell Huey 205 helicopter operational, we could have rescued those people who were stranded on the I-90 Bridge outside of New Orleans. We would have had them all off in a few hours— maybe in about ten hours or so. For a mother and child to be stranded with many other people on the bridge for two and a half days with little food or water— while a team of government-contracted aircraft (paid for by the taxpayers) is flying back and forth right over them and will not stop to pick them up—is totally unacceptable.

You see, the Body of Christ does not have those limits. We would not be prevented by some FEMA contract from rescuing people. That is the difference between Angel Flight 44 and the secular aviation contractors who sell their services to the government by signing a piece of paper.

However, the Body of Christ did not *prepare*. If we had been ready, we could have rescued those people from that bridge. In fact, there would have been nothing the government could have done to stop us. We do not work for the government—we work for God. We certainly have more flexibility in the Body of Christ than anyone else, but we have to *invest*—sow seed into those assets so that we can draw on those assets to take care of humanitarian needs when the call arises.

That is where we fell short in the Katrina disaster. It is not going to happen again. If this book sends out a message at all, it is "Let's get ready. Let's stay prepared. Let's invest into an Angel Flight 44. People will soon need them again. Help us to help those in need when disaster strikes."

Pastor/Minister Support

Sometimes a church or ministry needs to set up an aviation department to facilitate their Gospel mission. I have forty years of experience in aviation, so I am in a position to help with that. I also have friends and other resources with significant aviation expertise. Therefore, Angel Flight 44 can help them choose the right aircraft and walk them through the complexities of developing an aviation department. In many instances, we can assist them in training their flight crews. This is an important aspect of the Angel Flight 44 mission: supporting both pastors and other types of ministries in their various aviation projects.

Serving the Body

Angel Flight 44 works for the Body of Christ. We work for *you*. My message is, "What can we do for you, pastors? What can we do for you, missionaries? How can we be of service to you with the assets from the Body of Christ? Angel Flight 44 is a funnel. We are channeling aviation assets where they need to go. Tell us what you need, and we will try to partner with you to serve your mission, as aviation assets become available."

Again, this is also for the humanitarian aid efforts. We want to be ready to do disaster relief the next time something happens. We could have a disaster in Dallas/Fort Worth. We could have a hurricane on the East Coast. We could have an earthquake in California. We could have a tsunami off the coast of Maine. We could have one *wherever*. Therefore, if we can launch wars on the other side of the globe—and put billions of dollars per month into those efforts—we certainly can put a few million dollars into rescuing people.

We want to eventually support the Body of Christ anywhere on the globe it needs us. Disasters have already been hitting places all over the earth, and we need to position ourselves to help our brothers and sisters whenever they happen again. Of course, this means we will have to acquire the appropriate aircraft; hire pilots, mechanics, and other personnel; and build the appropriate hangar space to accommodate all of these.

Training Squadron

Our vision for the future also includes having a small training squadron. In order to keep aircraft flying to help ministries and relief efforts worldwide, there needs to be a growing new generation of pilots filling our ranks; and the pilots of the future, who are going to be a part of Angel Flight 44, are going to come from the faith-based ministries. We intend to train young Christian men and women to pilot these aircraft—believers with hearts to help others—and have them ready to perform when the need arises.

We will also be seeking experienced flight instructors to accomplish this training. Christian men and women have already begun to be drawn to AF-44 by the Spirit—and these folks will help train the next generation of pilots.

Ready Reserve

Plans are being developed for a ready reserve of Christian pilots worldwide who already have flight training, and many of these will have their own aircraft. Through our new website and developing command-and-control capabilities, we will activate them in their regions when crisis happens or a ministry need arises. In some cases, we might have to connect an experienced pilot with someone else who owns a suitable aircraft.

Maintaining an inventoried aviation database of all the available aviation assets (aircraft, pilots, mechanics, etc.), we will be able to develop a solid reserve force, available for rapid activation when needed. We can then connect the right pilots to the right aircraft (if they are not already), augment them with a team of mechanics and fuel resources, then connect them with the mission coordinators, and perform the rescue and relief operations. This will allow Angel Flight 44 to expand its capabilities well beyond our core aviation assets, and enlarge emergency relief efforts rapidly in a time of disaster.

Summary

I welcome and encourage all those who want to support an aviation ministry with a mission like ours. I sincerely believe that there are more corporations like Air BP, McKesson Pharmaceutical, Sysco Foods, and others, that will be willing to partner with us to help people in distress.

That is the heart and mission of Angel Flight 44. It is our primary mission to integrate into Kenneth and Gloria Copeland's aviation ministry, and adopt their mission statement. You can find out how you can become a partner with Angel Flight 44 by going to:

ANGEL FLIGHT

Spirit Born • Spirit Fed • Spirit Driven • Spirit Led

www.angelflight44.com

The Most Important Decision

As you have been reading this book, have you begun to realize that you do not know the Savior personally? The Lord Jesus Christ came to the earth to "seek and save those who are lost" (Luke 19:10). By "lost," the Bible is referring to those who have not yet been reconciled to God through the forgiveness of their sins committed against Him. Every lie, every theft, every wrong thought or evil deed ever committed by any human being is a crime in the eyes of the Holy God Who created us—all of which is defined as "sin." However, Jesus came to reconcile us all back to God by paying the eternal price for our sins on our behalf. In short, He bore the punishment for our crimes against God.

Born of a virgin by the Holy Spirit of God (Isaiah 7:14; Matthew 1:23), Jesus walked this earth about 2,000 years ago as the sinless Son of God. However, at the age of thirty-three, He became the "Lamb of God slain before the foundation of the world" (Revelation 13:8) and allowed Himself to be crucified on a cross as a criminal. Thereon, He shed His precious blood for your sins and mine, and died a painful death as a sacrifice on our behalf (Daniel 9:26; Romans 4:25). Nevertheless, since it was our sins and not His that sent Him to that cross, after three days and nights, God raised Him again from the dead (Mark 8:31; Acts 10:39-41).

Over a period of forty days, Jesus was seen by His disciples and over 500 people at different times (1 Corinthians 15:6). These men and women sacrificed their own lives to preach and proclaim the good news that Jesus had been raised from the dead and ascended to the right Hand of God in Heaven—and will soon return in the same manner in which He left (Acts 1:10-11; Revelation 22:7-20). Many historical documents from that period in history also attest to these same facts. Moreover, the martyrdom of many Christian believers for their faith and confession of His lordship is a magnificent testimony to the truth of these words. After all, if this truth were not a reality in their souls, then why would they have willingly died for such testimony?

If you do not know the Savior personally...if you have not embraced this good news of your paid-for salvation by accepting Him as your personal Lord and Savior…then this is an excellent time to do so. Salvation is certainly yours for it is for "whosoever will." If you will accept it from Him, you can have it right now. However, if you will not receive His free gift for yourself, His sacrifice for you personally will have been to no avail. Jesus Himself expressed it this way:

> "For God so loved the world that he gave his one and only Son, that whoever believes in him shall not perish but have eternal life. For God did not send his Son into the world to condemn the world, but to save the world through him. Whoever believes in him is not condemned, but whoever does not believe stands condemned already because he has not believed in the name of God's one and only Son."
>
> (John 3:16-18, NIV)

What does this mean? If you accept God's pardon (forgiveness of sins) by receiving His free gift of salvation through His Son, you will experience eternal life and joy. If you reject the pardon given only through His Son Jesus, the penalty for your crimes against God will remain yours. Consequently, if you die without first accepting God's pardon, then the punishment will have to be forever. Thus, the choice is yours…but Jesus died to give you the choice of eternal life.

You have read within the pages of this book about the love of God manifested in His work to save the lives of those torn by Hurricanes Katrina and Rita. Now, this is the best time ever to embrace that love by asking the Savior Himself to take over your life and change it for His glory. You can experience the kind of love and fellowship with God that you have seen within the pages of this book in the lives of the Christian men and women who lived this *Angel Flight 44* adventure. Tremendous peace and forgiveness for your sins is available to you through God's Son, Jesus. Just believe it and receive it…and you will experience it today.

Pray the following prayer out loud, with sincerity of purpose, and He will work another miracle right there within you. If you are Jewish, feel free to substitute the Savior's Hebrew Name, Yeshua, as you now embrace your Messiah:

Heavenly Father, I come to You in the Name of Jesus. Your Word says, "Whosoever shall call on the name of the Lord shall be saved" (Acts 2:21). Therefore, I am calling on You right now. I pray and declare that I hereby make Jesus Lord over my life according to Romans Chapter 10, verses 9 and 10. "If thou shalt confess with thy mouth the Lord Jesus, and shalt believe in thine heart that God hath raised him from the dead, thou shalt be saved." I do that now. I confess that Jesus is Lord, and

THE MOST IMPORTANT DECISION

I believe in my heart that God raised Him from the dead. Take over my life, Lord Jesus. I now belong to You. Therefore, according to Your Word, I am now saved from my sins, and I have a new start on life. With Your help, I will now live for You forever. Amen.

If you prayed the prayer above, then the folks at Kenneth Copeland Ministries want to know about it and to help you begin your new life in Jesus Christ. Visit **www.kcm.org** to find helpful teaching resources and to request your free Salvation Package of support materials.

In the United States, you can also call 1-800-600-7395 to speak to a prayer counselor. If you live outside of the U.S., you can find the listing of international offices on the contact page of the KCM website, including phone numbers to call to request prayer at the KCM office nearest you. When calling, be sure to tell the person you talk with that you prayed the salvation prayer found in *Angel Flight 44*, and request your free Salvation Package materials.

God bless you...and welcome to the family!

-Rich Vermillion

Angel Flight 44
Special Recognitions

Kenneth Copeland

Kenneth Copeland is, without a doubt, the most experienced aviation-oriented minister in ministry today. He understands aviation as it relates to doing the Lord's work.

It was after Kenneth called me for use of the Super DC-3 that I realized why the Lord had me working on it six weeks before Katrina hit. Words cannot express how I felt when I informed Kenneth, "It's ready," just forty-eight hours after Katrina hit the Gulf Coast. It was a divine calling.

Without Kenneth and Gloria's financial support on the Super DC-3, all flight operations would have been seriously degraded. From the use of Copeland Airport, his entire hangar facility, his staff, and the gift of his loving counsel, he gave generously in the effort to help his partners. His spirit of "whatever it takes" to locate his partners in Louisiana, rescue them, restore them, render faith, hope, and love—for however long it takes—has made a lifelong impression in my heart. He is a true man of God.

Kenneth, I cannot thank you enough for the "call to duty," a divine opportunity to honor God by serving his people. Your partners will always respect you as a true loving prophet and servant of the Lord.

Denny Ghiringhelli

What a great guy to work with! Denny was the glue that kept the Angel Flight 44 missions airborne. He was always positive, upbeat, funny, and a worker. The 100-degree Texas heat and ninety percent Louisiana humidity did not slow him down. He was the Energizer Bunny®* working at "full throttle." Loading, unloading, turning wrenches, flying—he did it all. He just kept working long after my energy had expired. Just trying to keep up with Denny kept me moving!

I could not have been blessed with a more competent, experienced pilot in the entire United States. He also shared my heart and spirit in serving the victims of Katrina and Rita. Without his professional efforts, flight operations would have been seriously compromised. He is, without a doubt, another one of the true heroes in this story. There are just not enough words to express my sincere gratitude for all his efforts.

President John F. Kennedy once said, "Ask not what your country can do for you...ask what you can do for your country." This is Denny Ghiringhelli. When I first told Denny I needed his help, he did not hesitate. He simply asked, "What do you need? How can I help?" His heart is truly American and his blessed talents benefited thousands of Katrina and Rita victims. I cannot recall in my forty-year aviation career, a single pilot that has blessed my aviation efforts on the "front line" as much as Captain Denny Ghiringhelli.

You, Denny, were—and always will be—a true blessing to aviation and your country.

David Orozco (and Dr. John Barnett)

David is a guy who worked with us and flew with us for over two weeks. He helped change carburetors and did other necessary maintenance. He worked ten- to twelve-hour days in the 100-degree Texas heat and humidity, and yet never complained. He just wanted to help...and help he did—from turning wrenches to even flying one mission as the copilot on the Super DC-3 to relieve Denny. His positive and upbeat attitude greatly enhanced the Angel Flight 44 missions and was greatly admired by all.

David volunteered his time and took off from work. When he returned to his regular job, he was informed by his employer, Dr. John Barnett, that he was never off the payroll. Dr. Barnett insisted on paying him in appreciation for David's efforts beyond the call of duty. This is just another example of how "kindness in heart" was contagious throughout the whole relief effort.

Thank you for your benevolence, Dr. Barnett.

What's more, David Orozco, a Mexican citizen and American resident, did all this as a non-citizen wanting to help Americans in distress. How often do we see that? As of this writing, he has now gained his American citizenship, and his dream is to serve his new country as a pilot for the U.S. Border Patrol. Without a doubt, Mr. Orozco will be a valued citizen of the United States of America. He is what America represents.

David, I sincerely thank you for all your generous support.

Pastors George and Terri Pearsons

Pastors George and Terri are my pastors at Eagle Mountain International Church. Learning who I am in Jesus Christ from their teachings is what equipped me to hear the Spirit of God that early morning, six weeks prior to Katrina. More importantly, their teachings enabled me to follow His orders in preparing the Super DC-3, without knowing why I was doing so.

Pastor George, I would have never been blessed with the opportunity to do God's work if it were not for your spirit-filled teachings, and those of Pastor Terri, over the last several years. Thank you both so very much.

T.W. Wheelock

My dad once said, "Glen, you will always count your best friends and allies on one hand." T.W. Wheelock is definitely one of them.

When I started working on the Super DC-3, six weeks prior to Katrina, T.W., a 74-year old man and a licensed A&P mechanic, worked from 5:30 a.m. to noon relentlessly in the Texas heat until the inspection was completed, and the Super DC-3 was once again airborne. Not knowing when or how he was getting paid, he just pressed on through the lengthy inspection process. I cannot say enough good things about this man as a friend and ally. The Super DC-3 would never have flown without his professional efforts. Before, during, and after Katrina, the Super DC-3 flies primarily due to T.W.'s efforts.

T.W., I cannot thank you enough. Your efforts are a blessing beyond measure.

Mike Delk – Air BP, President and CEO

When I contacted Ken Moline, my Air BP Distributor, to ask for fuel for the Katrina relief, he contacted Mike Delk. Mr. Delk approved the request in less than one hour. This was certainly a blessing well beyond the call of duty. Mike Delk is a living example of what corporate America should strive to be. Air BP's generous fuel contribution kept Angel Flight in the air—which directly and positively impacted thousands of lives in the disaster area.

Mr. Delk, you are a living example of "We live to give," and proof that corporate America has a "heart" for its fellow Americans in time of need.

Participating Pilots

Once again we would like to sincerely thank all the pilots who contributed to Angel Flight missions:

1. Captain Denny Ghiringhelli
2. Captain Chuck Weese
3. Bill McNeese – FAA pilot/examiner
4. Captain Ron Hyde
5. Tom Westberry

Continued...

6. John Coon
7. David Orozco
8. Captain Lee Whatley
9. Carol Walker

You all really made a difference in the lives of others by helping to ensure the success of the Angel Flight 44 relief operations. May God bless you one-hundredfold.

Corporate Acknowledgments

First, I would like to also express my additional sincere appreciation for all the individuals and companies, if not already acknowledged within this book, that contributed to the success of the original Angel Flight 44 missions. One by one, they are:

- Mr. Damon Ward: President, Business Air, Denton, Texas
- Mr. Andy Johnson: President, Aviation International Supply, Denton, Texas
- Mr. Mike Sutphin: Vice-President, Aviation International Supply, Denton, Texas
- Mr. Ralph Stahl: CEO, Stahl Air Instruments, Northwest Regional Airport, Roanoke, Texas
- Mr. Chester Roberts: Roberts Aircraft Supply, Collinsville, Texas
- Mr. Russell Roberts: Roberts Aircraft Supply, Collinsville, Texas
- Mr. Carl Byam: President, Byam Propeller Service, Fort Worth, Texas
- Mr. Shawn Young: Byam Propeller Service, Fort Worth, Texas
- Mr. David Mills: Co-owner, Fieldtech Avionics, Fort Worth, Texas
- Mr. Kevin Nelms: Co-owner, Fieldtech Avionics, Fort Worth, Texas
- Mr. J.B. Todd: CEO, Southwest Coolers, Dallas, Texas

Finally, I would like to thank Dan Stratton for introducing me to Rich Vermillion. Rich is a wonderful writer, and now a very close friend. Thank you, Pastor Dan. I believe that you were certainly hearing from the Holy Spirit on that day. May God continue to bless your vision for ProVision in the "year of the open door" and beyond.

*Energizer Bunny® is a registered trademark of Energizer Holdings, Inc.

Seed Publishers ™

To learn more about this publishing imprint, or our other outstanding authors and books, please visit us on the Internet at:

www.pspublishers.com

Be sure to join our free email list for periodic announcements and timely updates.